THE GOLD MEDAL STANDARD
Exploring The Power of Music
And
The Legacy of The Vocal Majority Chorus

By Bob Arnold
Founder and First Marketing Director
Of The Vocal Majority Chorus
(Dallas Metropolitan Chapter of the Barbershop Harmony Society)

Printed by CreateSpace, An *Amazon.com* Company

Who Would Benefit The Most From Reading This Book?

If you've always loved music, but you wondered *WHY* you always loved music, this book can give you some answers. The research I've done into what makes music such a dominant and powerful part of most people's lives will make you a better, more informed listener of music, and a much better performer – if that's what you're driven to do. You'll find that music has actually been around *longer than spoken language*. And you'll discover the many benefits of music for people who have mental and physical illnesses, and also how music can make *YOU* a healthier human being.

I hope you'll also re-discover some memories about what first turned you on to the music you love, and who some of the performers were that made you a fan of their music for life.

If you've never heard of The Vocal Majority Chorus and its smaller vocal ensembles, I think you'll find it fascinating to learn why this organization of both amateur and professional singers has captured the admiration of millions of fans throughout the world. You'll learn what this organization did in its first twenty years that set into motion their well-earned reputation as the most prolific popular recording and performing choral group in the world?

I also think the *lessons learned* during my 45 years of being associated with this organization can be of benefit to anyone who wants their own group to be the best they can be. It's a virtual *how-to* history of what it takes to become the **Gold Medal Standard** for community choral organizations.

Please travel along with me on the journey. I think you'll really enjoy the ride!

Bob Arnold, Dallas, TX
2017

v

About The Author

Bob Arnold is recognized as a Founder, first President, and the first Marketing Director for The Vocal Majority (VM) Chorus during its first quarter-century. He was also the organization's weekly/bi-weekly bulletin editor during that time, and has earned ten Gold Medals in International competitions as a Lead Singer in the chorus. He has also been a member of the Barbershop Harmony Society for 50+ years, and was on the faculty of the Society's Chapter Officer Training School (COTS) for almost two decades, teaching chapter Program Vice Presidents how to create exciting and meaningful activities that could grow their membership and provide community and media exposure for their chapters.

Bob also conducted personal weekend workshops for both Barbershop Society and Sweet Adeline chapters throughout the continental U.S. and Hawaii teaching chapter leaders how to market and "brand" their chapters. Chapters who hosted Bob for workshops included Columbus (OH), Houston (TX), Manhattan (NY), Denver (CO), Foothill Cities (CA), New Orleans (LA), Tampa (FL), St. Charles (MO), Aloha (HI), Minneapolis (MN), Northbrook (IL), and Tulsa (OK) among many others.

Bob received his BFA Degree from Ohio University in Radio-TV and Speech, and an MA Degree from Baylor University in Oral Communication. In his professional life, Bob spent 10-years in broadcasting as an announcer and TV sports anchor, and has worked in a variety of other industry segments as an advertising and marketing professional. He began to use his advanced college degree as an adjunct community college instructor starting in 1966, and today is a part-time Lecturer at the University of Texas at Dallas and an Adjunct Faculty Member at Richland College as an instructor in Speech, Public Speaking and Human Communication. He can be reached by email at barnold@tx.rr.com.

Former VM singer David Anderson, posting to this book's Facebook page, said recently: *"I do not think very many people realize that you, individually, changed the face of the Barbershop Harmony Society for the better, Bob. It was your efforts and vision that created everything about The Vocal Majority except for the sound (that one goes to Jim Clancy and Don Clause)."*

Table of Contents

Part I

Part II
The Legacy of The Vocal Majority Chorus

Introduction by Jim Clancy
Founding Member and Currently
Executive Music Director for The Vocal Majority Chorus

Bob Arnold was one of the first people to tell me about the concept of a new Barbershop chapter in the Dallas area back in 1971 – a chorus that would have challenging goals and be unlimited in the kinds of arrangements it would sing – as long as they were interesting and appealing to its members and audiences. As a professional studio singer, I found this concept most intriguing, and I knew this was something in which I wanted to participate.

In this book, Bob describes the magical vocal sounds of the first rehearsals and how we rose to prominence in such a short period of time.

Bob was instrumental in developing the image and marketing success of The Vocal Majority from the very beginning. You will read some things that may surprise you. For instance, Bob explains why the Silver Medal we won in 1978 was perhaps even more valuable than any of the Gold Medals that followed. He continues writing about the amazing journey we enjoyed through the years, and the thrilling experiences that none of us could have imagined when we began.

Whether you're a Vocal Majority fan, an avid Barbershopper, or just someone who has always loved music and never really known why, I believe you will find this book entertaining and educational. *I hope you enjoy reading it as much as I have!*

Introduction by Greg Clancy
Chorus Director for The Vocal Majority Chorus

The power of music is unlimited. It affects us all in different ways. Music inspires and heals, and it can quickly transport us to 'lifetime landmarks' from our past, as we associate music with events that shaped our lives. Bob Arnold has done a beautiful job explaining the 'phenomenon' of music . . . where it came from, how it touches us, and what it means to the world. Bob understands the value that music brings to humanity.

I first met Bob when I was a ten-year-old boy. He was incredibly enthusiastic in creating his vision . . . a men's chorus that was excellent in every measure. Bob was a brash young man back then, who knew how to inspire others to chase the same dream. I will always be grateful to Bob for 'dreaming up' The Vocal Majority. I can never repay the gifts I have been given by associating with this great organization. *Thank you, Mr. Arnold!*

FOREWORD

"Absorb everything. Love every style. Love every musical thing. No matter its place of origin, you will find yourself in that style. You will become part of everything. And everything will become part of you."

Willie Nelson from his book, *"It's A Long Story"*

"When you give back, you get back—and along the way, you find that the return from giving of yourself to others is the greatest gift of all. Giving back is one of the best things that anyone can do."

Tony Bennett from his book, *"Life Is A Gift"*

I like to think of myself as a perpetual student of the world, of history, and of creative people from all walks of life. I'm also a music junkie. So, this is a book about reflections on a lifetime filled with musical experiences and research that I think any reader – no matter if you're a fan of music or not – might find interesting and useful. At one time or another in my life, I've played the guitar, bass guitar, violin, banjo, saxophone, and autoharp – none of them very well. And I've sung solo gigs and participated in small and large ensemble performances. I've received a lot of joy and satisfaction from those experiences, as have others I've managed to entertain and harmonize with. Because of sharing my involvement in music, I've also been fortunate to have acquired many lifelong friends and colleagues, many whose names you'll find inside the pages of this book.

I've had the idea for this book for about 20 years. At first, it was solely a desire, strongly encouraged by my wife Susan, to capture an early history of **The Vocal Majority Chorus** that I'd been associated with since its creation in 1971. But after five decades of researching and exploring the effects of *all kinds* of music on college students in my classrooms and fellow human beings elsewhere, I decided to expand the scope of this book. I have included an historical overview of music, touched on some very exciting new research on how music is positively affecting various mental and emotional illnesses, and what music has come to mean in the lives of you and me. I'll also take a stab at how our experiences with music might change in the decades ahead.

3

I have been called the "founder" of the 100+ voice male chorus based in North Texas known as *The Vocal Majority*. However, truth be told, there were three of us – Bill Thornton, Charlie Lyman, and me – who did most of the ground work to bring about the formation of what has become one of the most revered and popular male choruses in the world. The VM concept was mine from the beginning. I just happened to be named the organization's first president, and spent the next 25 years as its marketing director, and then another 20 years as a chorus member in the Lead Section. I also conceived and wrote the group's newsletter called *The Vocalizer*. With Susan's help, I have collected a file of all original copies of *Vocalizers* – around a thousand in all – since the 1971 editions through about 1994. This vast collection of chorus history has provided me with a unique opportunity to recall facts about the development and early successes of this internationally acclaimed chorus that even the most senior members and past-members may have forgotten.

But even if you're not particularly interested in those historical mementos, I think you'll find the first part of this book both interesting and surprising. After doing research about music for the past several decades, I feel fairly confident in discussing its history, and what it means to all of us humans from a social, psychological, emotional, and economic standpoint.

First of all, full disclosure dictates that I admit I'm not a trained professional musician. I have performed as a semi-professional soloist and participant in various vocal groups for over 60 years, and I've been an ardent fan of folk, country, pop and vocal ensemble music. I've spent the past 50+ years working a day job as a radio disk jockey, TV sports anchor, and as a marketing/advertising professional in a variety of industry segments. Throughout that time, I've enjoyed part-time work as an adjunct community college professor of Speech/Human Communication and Public Speaking, and as a university lecturer in the same disciplines.

One of the experiments I began several years ago was to survey my students at the beginning of classes about their favorite music selections and performing artists. Almost every one of my classes now begins with a *YouTube* version of some student's favorite song/artist, followed by a discussion about *why* that song/artist is so important in that student's life. Many of their reasons are rather mundane and temporary. But often students' favorite songs reflect a close historical relationship with a friend or

4

relative who introduced them to an artist or song from a previous generation. These are personal examples of how music from an earlier time in a person's life can stay with them forever.

There are many other examples from my research where this musical phenomenon strongly and amazingly affects people with Alzheimer's or other neurological and emotional afflictions. (I'll discuss the positive effects that music can have on our lives and those we care about in Chapters 1 and 4.)

Like many other musicians and singers, my own musicality was strongly influenced by my parents. My dad was a German immigrant who came to the U.S. when he was in his early 20s just prior to the rise of the Nazi Party in his homeland. He met and married my mother, also of German heritage, in Cleveland, Ohio. With just an 8th grade education, he became a U.S. citizen, somehow learned English well enough to become a public speaker, and worked his way up to an administrative position with a northern Ohio manufacturing company.

Throughout my childhood, my dad filled our house with recordings of famous symphonies and operas. I have no idea where he obtained his list of favorite recordings, but he yearned to know more about the underlying meanings of those compositions. I remember him saying, "I know what I like, but I don't know what is going on in those selections that make them so interesting to me." Perhaps you had a parent or close friend or relative who had a similar fascination with a certain type of music but couldn't explain their reasons?

One of his favorite American composers was Stephen Foster, whom Wikipedia calls, "the father of American music". Foster was born on July 4, 1826, which makes him a *REAL Yankee Doodle Dandy*. My dad's favorite Stephen Foster songs were those that reminded him of his Old Country *lieder* (German for romantic songs). Songs like *"Old Folks at Home"*, *"My Old Kentucky Home"*, *"Jeanie with the Light Brown Hair"*, and *"Beautiful Dreamer"*. (Check out *YouTube* for some nostalgic versions of these old Southern songs.)

5

I was born on April 11, 1938, which also happens to be the <u>exact</u> <u>birthday</u> of the *Barbershop Harmony Society*. The earliest recollection of my own musical exploration was on the stairs leading down to our base-

Teenage Bob Arnold – Elvis Imitator

ment in rural Ohio. I gathered together a couple of my friends from grade school to see if we could harmonize on a couple of the popular songs of those late 1940s. (You could say this was when I formed my first choral music organization—*smile*.) Shortly after that I was provided with a ukulele, which I found I could play with the help of a ukulele chord book my mom obtained for me at a music store. I soon graduated to a *Les Paul* electric guitar and amplifier in high school, and became a fairly competent "Elvis imitator". (That's pop singer Elvis Presley if you're too young to remember.) I astonished my parents with my ability to change to the appropriate chords on the guitar whenever a song's melody called for it. Everyone agreed that *I had a musical ear and a pretty decent solo voice!*

Just prior to my teenage years, my parents must have thought I had some musical talent because they invested in an inexpensive violin and two years' worth of violin lessons. Unfortunately, by that time I was so used to learning songs and singing them with a guitar *by ear* that my violin teacher threw up his hands and told my parents that he couldn't seem to teach me to read music. I'd completely fluster him by playing all my favorite songs on the violin without any sheet music. From then on, I had a knack for playing just about any musical instrument for the rest of my life without the need for lessons or written music. Unfortunately, it was both a talent and a curse if you ever wanted to play as a professional musician.

When it came time to choose a career path for college, I was really in a quandary. I would have loved a career in show business if I could only guarantee myself a weekly paycheck. So, the closest I could come to that dream was to study radio-TV as an academic subject. While in college at Ohio University, I continued my folk singing and Elvis imitation activities, along with choir and campus musicals. *(I even managed to get the Sky Masterson/Frank Sinatra role in the campus Broadway musical "Guys and Dolls", where I met my first wife, Marsha.)*

After graduating with a BFA (Bachelor of Fine Arts) in the early 1960s, I got my first radio announcing job in Washington, DC. The radio station that hired me right out of college was WQMR-FM/WGAY-AM. *(True story:* The station's owner was a local businessman named Connie B. Gay. The word "gay" obviously had a much different connotation in those days than it does today.)

While the job didn't pay all that great for a rookie announcer just coming out of college, it did have its perks. When I wasn't on the air pushing buttons and giving weather reports, I was responsible for programming the music on WQMR (Washington's Quality Music Radio). That meant listening to dozens of the free vinyl LPs that were mailed to the station each week by worldwide record companies and choosing album cuts that fit with the rather restrictive music format dictated by the station's management (quality music). One day I asked the station manager, "What should I do with the albums that don't fit our format?" He said he didn't really care; I could take them home with me if I wanted. Consequently, today I have some of the most popular and classic folk, pop and rock-n-roll vinyl LPs from the 1960s – all in mint condition.

For the two years while I was in the Washington-Maryland-Virginia area, I also performed solo folksinger gigs in several coffee houses. The Washington radio job began a 10-year sojourn in broadcasting that led to a TV sportscaster job in Waco, Texas, and then a *big-time* job in Dallas at WFAA Radio in the mid-1960s. There I continued singing folk songs at various Dallas clubs. The radio job also allowed me to tape some interviews with recording stars that were passing through Dallas – people like **Sonny & Cher, Raquel Welch** and **Robert Goulet.**

7

Then, one day while working in sales at WFAA, a co-worker invited me to be the *Master of Ceremonies* at his Dallas Barbershop chapter's annual show. I not only got to do my folk singing act in front of a large audience and tell jokes as the MC, but I got *PAID* for it too! *Show business at last!!!*

That first exposure to the Dallas Town North Chapter of the *Society for the Preservation and Encouragement of Barber Shop Quartet Singing in America* (the precursor to the *Barbershop Harmony Society*) had a tremendous impact on my life. It set in motion a 50+ year avocation and hobby (some jokingly call it a "cult") that would ultimately involve me in the formation of the world's most successful and famous men's chorus, *The Vocal Majority,* in Dallas several years later.

But I'm getting ahead of myself here. Before telling the Vocal Majority story in Part II of this book, I want to first explore how music came to possess so much influence over most of the world's population, and how that population went from being a music-*playing* society in past centuries to a mostly music-*consuming* population today. It's a fascinating tale, and I will attempt to show you how The Vocal Majority success story is an essential part of it. So please stay with me. You might even discover what **Wolfgang Amadeus Mozart** and The Vocal Majority's **James Norwood Clancy** have in common.

PART I

Chapter 1
WHY MUSIC AFFECTS US SO STRONGLY

"The world is inherently musical. Cutting across all ages, sexes, races, religions, and nationalities, music is a language with universal components. Its adherents outnumber the speakers of Mandarin, English, Hindi, Spanish, Russian, and all other tongues combined. Music rises above all income levels, social classes, educational achievements. Music speaks to everyone – and to every species. Birds make it, snakes are charmed by it, and whales and dolphins serenade one another with it."

From *"The Mozart Effect"* by Don Campbell

The ***Mozart Effect*** is a book that has had an influence on scientists, musicians, neurologists and an entire cadre of the medical community worldwide. In his introductory chapter, Don Campbell explains, "The word music derives from the Greek root *muse*. Mythology tells us that the nine muses, celestial sisters presiding over song, poetry, and the arts and sciences, were born to Zeus, the King of the Gods, and Mnemosyne, the Goddess of Memory. Thus, music is a child of divine love whose grace, beauty, and mysterious healing powers are intimately connected to heavenly order and the memory of our origin and destiny."

The United States used to be called a "melting pot" where cultures and nationalities from throughout the world could come together and pursue the American dream. New immigrants were expected to assimilate quickly into American culture and language. All our country asked in return was that these immigrants – my own father included – pledge allegiance to our flag and to the principles upon which our country was founded. However, it wasn't always easy for these new citizens to "melt" or be welcomed into our

American culture. Especially during World War II in the early part of the 1940s, American citizens had strong prejudices against immigrants from Germany and Japan. Those countries were our enemies at the time. I remember going with my father to *internment camps* in northern Ohio set up by our government to house German-Americans and taking food and clothing to these unfortunate individuals.

It appears that the *melting pot* image of the 1900s, when new citizens were expected to lose their native cultures and languages and assimilate quickly into the American culture, has given way these days to that of a "salad". That image more accurately portrays the many nationalities and cultures being "tossed together" much like a *salad* that lives and works together under the Stars and Stripes while still maintaining their individual cultures, languages and unique characteristics.

In my Human Communication and Public Speaking classes at **Richland College** and the **University of Texas at Dallas**, I have the honor of teaching an extremely diverse student population. It's almost like a cultural "laboratory" as students from around 80 different countries attend our campuses, and you'll hear over 120 different languages and dialects spoken. We get into some interesting and challenging discussions in class about the differences in the cultures we deal with on campus, and how we are expected and encouraged to cooperate with people from other cultures, religions, and beliefs when we become involved in the workforce and as a contributing member of our civil society. When we begin our classes by playing some student's favorite song and/or artist, you can imagine what a diversity of musical tastes emerges. And yet I find that most of my *international* students have very American tastes in the music they request. Except for maybe a Bollywood tune or some Salsa music, most students' favorite artists are either American or world music icons.

As Don Campbell notes in his *Mozart Effect* book, "Music is rapidly becoming the common tongue of the modern world. People today spend more money, time, and energy on music than on books, movies, and sports. The most popular cultural icons of our era are not statesmen or saints, but singers and vocalists. Beyond our addiction to rock concerts and CDs, stereos, and MTV, our daily communication and commerce is largely based on a musical model."

10

Campbell goes on to explain what he means. "We use the word *sound*— a synonym for health and *sound* advice, *sound* investments, and *sound* business procedures. When things are going smoothly, we are *in tune* and *in harmony* with others and the world around us. When things are stuck, we are *out of tune* and *out of sync*. In romance or relationships of any kind, we hope to set the *right tone*, strike a sympathetic *chord*, or communicate on the same *wavelength*. When the unexpected happens, we decide to *play it by ear*. We admire the executive who can *orchestrate* a deal and cheer the team that can administer the opposition a sound *beating*. We commonly crave or shun an audience— from the root *audio*, to hear. Bombarded from morning until evening with modern advertising, we put up with the pitches of salespeople and commercials that are aimed (all too successfully) at drumming images and rhythmic *jingles* into our psyches."

[**Author's Comment**: It's interesting to note that among the original group of singers who were instrumental in forming The Vocal Majority Chorus, we were privileged to have at least six professional "jingle singers". These were men who made their living recording those rhythmic radio station and commercial jingles that have become ubiquitous since broadcasting stations started accepting commercial messages. It is also a fact that these professional singers and musicians provided us "amateurs" with valuable music lessons each and every week at chorus and section rehearsals.]

Studies by Scottish musicologist Laurence O'Donnell III have shown that Mozart's music and baroque music in general, with a 60-beats-per-minute pattern, activate the left and right brain. The simultaneous left and right brain action maximizes learning and retention of information. The information being studied activates the left brain while the music activates the right brain. Also, activities which engage *both* sides of the brain at the same time, such as playing an instrument or singing, causes the brain to be more capable of processing information.

According to *The Center for New Discoveries in Learning*, learning potential can be increased a minimum of five times by using this 60-beats-per-minute music. (For example, the ancient Greeks sang their dramas because they understood how music could help them remember more easily.) A renowned Bulgarian psychologist, Dr. George Lozanov, designed a way to teach foreign languages in a fraction of the normal learning time. Using his system, students could learn up to one half of the vocabulary and phrases for the whole school term (which amounts to almost 1,000 words or phrases) in one day. Along with this, the average retention rate of his students was 92%. Dr. Lozanov's system involved using certain classical music pieces from the baroque period which have around a 60-beats-per-minute pattern.

Another book I found to be very inciteful regarding how forcefully music plays into our lives is *"The Music Instinct: How Music Works And Why We Can't Do Without It"* by **Philip Ball**. It seems that the beliefs about music being a healing force for man-kind go all the way back to the ancient Egyptians and Greeks. Ball notes that, "The ancient Egyptians regarded music as 'physic for the soul', and the Hebrews used it to treat physical and mental disturbance – an early form of music therapy. The Greek philosopher Thales is said to have used music to cure a 'plague' of anxiety suffered by the Spartans. According to Plutarch, Thales' songs dispelled the affliction with concord and harmony, in an echo of the magical healing powers attributed to the music Orpheus sang while playing his lyre."

Even in the Middle Ages, music was thought to have as much of a *moral* purpose as an aesthetic one. Rather than being performed for enjoyment, it was performed to guide the soul. According to Ball, "For Plato and Aristotle, this made music a tool that could either promote social harmony or, if improperly used, discord. (It's no coincidence that those are both musical terms.)"

Ball believes music should be indispensable for a well-rounded education. He says, "For one thing, we will see that it is a gymnasium for the mind. No other activity seems to use so many parts of the brain at once, nor to promote their integration." I'll have more to say about the effects of music on our minds and emotional faculties in Chapter 4.

MUSIC IS HUMAN EMOTION

I read somewhere long ago that, historically, music and musical instruments may actually be older than human speech. Recently, in re-search for this book, I came across a publication by Barbara J. Crowe called *"Music and Soulmaking"*. Her research would seem to agree with what I had heard as she wrote in her book: "Music, performed as chant, likely preceded speech as human communication. There is anthropological evidence that music came before speech . . . Early human skeletal remains reveal signs that the use of the voice to produce speech goes back only eighty thousand years, while also suggesting that chanting (early forms of music) began perhaps half a million years earlier."

She continues, "Why did we put certain sound combinations together and then remember them for future use? Why did we begin to beat on hollow logs and stretched animal hides in repetitive rhythmic patterns? Why did we make holes in bamboo stalks to make a flute? Why music? Humans from the beginning of history have asked this simple question. Music's various roles in past cultures give us some idea of how they answered the question."

I go into much more detail about the fascinating history of how music – as we know it today in Western cultures – came into existence in *Chapter 2*.

Since I teach a curriculum in "human communication" in my college subject area, I've always known that – whether we realize it or not – music is an inescapable part of our lives. *Music is the ESSENCE of human communication.* Think about how ubiquitous both instrumental and vocal music is in our electronic world: Radio, TV and Internet music and singing commercial "jingles"; dramatic and whimsical theme music surrounding TV shows and movies; cellphone ring tones; "elevator" music; obnoxious music played while you wait on the phone for a "help desk" human being. I may have missed a few, but you get the idea.

In his fascinating book, *"This Is Your Brain On Music"*, Daniel J. Levitin provides some ancient historical perspectives about the origins of music: "No known human culture now or anytime in the recorded past lacked music. Some of the oldest physical artifacts found in human and prehuman excavation sites are musical instruments: bone flutes and animal skins stretched over tree stumps to make drums. Whenever humans come together for any reason, music is there: weddings, funerals, graduation from college, men marching off to war, stadium sporting events, a night on the town, prayer, a romantic dinner, mothers rocking their infants to sleep, and college students studying with music as a background. . . . Only relatively recently in our own culture, five hundred years or so ago, did a distinction arise that cut society in two, forming separate classes of music *performers* and music *listeners*. Throughout most of the world and for most of human history, music making was as natural an activity as breathing and walking, and *everyone* participated. Concert halls, dedicated to the performance of music, arose only in the last several centuries."

Levitin shows us in the following image from his book that music affects different areas of the brain, but we're really unable in the scope of this book to fully explore how all this happens – and you may not even want to get into that much detail in the first place.

In a *New York Times* article on February 8, 2016, writer Natalie Angier comes up with a surprising statistic: Americans listen to music nearly *four hours a day*. She notes that, in international surveys, people consistently rank music as one of life's supreme sources of pleasure and emotional power. In the past, scientists didn't have the technology to peer into the domains of the human mind to find out how music affects that four-pound mass inside our skulls. But now, according to the *Times* article, researchers at the Massachusetts Institute of Technology have devised a radical new approach to brain imaging that reveals what past studies had missed.

Angier writes, "By mathematically analyzing scans of the auditory cortex and grouping clusters of brain cells with similar activation patterns, the scientists have identified neural pathways that react almost exclusively to the sound of music – any music. It may be Bach, bluegrass, hip-hop, big band, sitar or Julie Andrews. A listener may relish the sampled genre or revile it. No matter. When a musical passage is played, a distinct set of neurons tucked inside a furrow of a listener's auditory cortex will fire in response. Other sounds, by contrast – a dog barking, a car skidding, a toilet flushing – leave the musical circuits unmoved."

Three neuroscientists at M.I.T. – Nancy Kanwisher, Josh McDermott, and Sam Norman-Haignere – reported these new results in the journal *Neuron* with an article titled. ***"Why do we have music?"*** Dr. Kanwisher said in an interview. "Why do we enjoy it so much and want to dance when we hear it? How early in development can we see this sensitivity to music, and is it tunable with experience? These are the really cool first-order questions we can begin to address."

The *Times* article stressed that the M.I.T. team demonstrated that speech and music circuits are in *different* parts of the brain's sprawling auditory cortex, where all sound signals are interpreted, and that each is largely deaf to the other's sonic cues, although there is some overlap when it comes to responding to songs with lyrics. In fact, Josef Rauschecker, director of the **Laboratory of Integrative Neuroscience and Cognition** at Georgetown University, in commenting on the M.I.T. research, said,

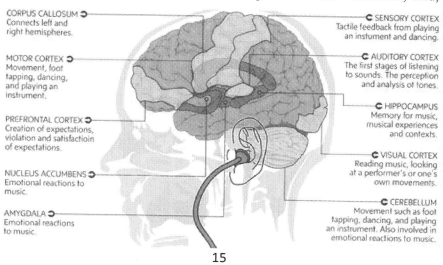

CORPUS CALLOSUM
Connects left and right hemispheres.

MOTOR CORTEX
Movement, foot tapping, dancing, and playing an instrument.

PREFRONTAL CORTEX
Creation of expectations, violation and satisfaction of expectations.

NUCLEUS ACCUMBENS
Emotional reactions to music.

AMYGDALA
Emotional reactions to music.

SENSORY CORTEX
Tactile feedback from playing an instument and dancing.

AUDITORY CORTEX
The first stages of listening to sounds. The perception and analysis of tones.

HIPPOCAMPUS
Memory for music, musical experiences and contexts.

VISUAL CORTEX
Reading music, looking at a performer's or one's own movements.

CEREBELLUM
Movement such as foot tapping, dancing and playing an instrument. Also involved in emotional reactions to music.

15

"Music sensitivity may be *more* fundamental to the human brain than is speech perception. There are theories that music is older than speech or language," he said. "Some even argue that speech evolved from music." (The Georgetown University group provided the preceding diagram.)

MUSIC AS "MEDICINE FOR THE MIND"

A 2016 study released by Johns Hopkins School of Medicine essentially said that if you want to make your body healthy you should trot on down to the fitness center. But if you want to exercise your brain, you should listen to music. "There are few things that stimulate the brain the way music does," says one Johns Hopkins otolaryngologist. "If you want to keep your brain engaged throughout the aging process, listening to or playing music is a great tool. It provides a total brain workout." The same research shows that listening to music can reduce anxiety, blood pressure, and pain as well as improve sleep quality, mood, mental alertness, and memory.

Johns Hopkins researchers have had dozens of jazz performers and rappers improvise music while lying down inside an fMRI (functional magnetic resonance imaging) machine to watch and see which areas of their brains light up. "Music is structural, mathematical and architectural. It's based on relationships between one note and the next. You may not be aware of it, but your brain has to do a lot of computing to make sense of it," notes one otolaryngologist.

Professor Aniruddh D. Patel, Ph. D of Tufts University, actually has a series of online seminars he'll sell you for a few bucks with titles like: *"Music, Language, and Emotional Expression"; "Brain Sources of Music's Emotional Power"; "Nature, Nurture, and Musical Brains"; Cognitive Benefits of Musical Training"; "Neurological Effects of Making Music"; "Music: A Neuroscientific Perspective".*

The writer I quoted earlier, Laurence O'Donnell III, likes to call himself a "musicist", and he writes extensively about the power that playing music must positively affect some of history's greatest icons. When Thomas Jefferson was creating the Declaration of Independence and couldn't seem to find the right words, he played his violin to help him get the words from his brain onto the paper, according to O'Donnell. And he's quoted as describing how the parents of the world's most famous genius, Albert Einstein, were told by his grade school teachers that he was "too stupid to learn" and they should consider taking him out of school and learning manual labor skills. His parents didn't believe them and bought young Albert a violin. He became good at the instrument, and Ein-

stein himself says the reason he became so smart was because he played the violin. A friend is quoted as saying that the way Einstein figured out his problems and equations was by improvising on the violin. [**Author's Note**: I obviously didn't respond to my violin lessons in quite the same impressive way as Dr. Einstein.]

SING YOURSELF HAPPY AND FIT!

That's the heading in a series of articles on the **Barbershop Harmony Society**'s web site (www.barbershop.org). Obviously, an organization that promotes singing as a way of life might have some persuasive arguments in favor of taking up choral and ensemble music activities, right? The BHS contends that the health benefits of singing are well documented:

- Singing improves your mood. It releases the same feel-good brain chemicals as sex and chocolate!
- It is very effective as a stress reliever and improves sleep;
- Singing releases pain-relieving endorphins, helping you to forget that painful tooth/knee/whatever;
- People who sing are healthier than people who don't;
- Your posture improves;
- Lung capacity increases;
- Singing clears sinuses and respiratory tubes;
- Your mental alertness improves;
- Singing tones your facial and stomach muscles;
- It boosts your immune system, helping to fight disease and prolonging life expectancy;
- Your confidence increases.

17

According to **Professor Graham Welch**, Director for Advanced Music Education at London's Roehampton Institute, singing can prolong your life in many ways. He states, "Singing exercises the vocal cords and keeps them youthful, even in old age. The less age-battered your voice sounds, the more you will feel, and seem, younger." He goes on to say that when you break into song, your chest expands and your back and shoulders straighten, thus improving your posture. Singing lifts moods and clears the "blues" by taking your mind off the stresses of the day, as well as releasing pain-relieving endorphins. As you sing along, the professor adds, your circulation is improved, which in turn oxygenates the cells and boosts the body's immune system to ward off minor infections.

Professor Welch concludes by saying, "Given that every human being is, in principle, capable of developing sufficient vocal skills to participate in a chorale for a lifetime, active group singing may be a risk-free, economic, easily accessible, and yet powerful road to enhanced physiological and psychological well-being."

And of course, the social benefits of group singing are important too. Singing widens your circle of friends. And some of us go on to the pub or pizza parlor afterward to continue to enjoy our friends after rehearsals.

According to **Dr. John Lennon** (*No, not the former Beatle!*), Emeritus Professor of Vocal Performance at Emporia State University, singing starts in infancy. "I contend that singing is an inborn response in those moments of absolute emotional tranquility. Babies sing to themselves. The fact that we recognize no identifiable melody sequence does not mean that it is not singing. Such spontaneous oral response has sustained emission, rhythm, pitch variation and emotional expression. Like the infant, we sing because we feel good and singing makes us feel even better. When we sing to ourselves we are, in effect, communicating with the inner-self . . . it may well be counterproductive to one's wellbeing NOT to sing."

Preschool and kindergarten teachers have known for a long time that children learn best through songs. They remember the material easier and it is easier to keep them engaged in the activity. [**Author's Note**: Several of the students in one of my university Speech Communication classes recently told me that they could still remember the formula to a

18

complex mathematics rule because they were taught to SING it when they first were introduced to it.]

You can't really deny the power of music. Studies have shown that high school students who study music have higher grade point averages than those who don't. These students also develop faster physically. Student listening skills are also improved through music education. **Laurance O'Donnel**, in his writings on music, says, "The top engineers from Silicon Valley are all musicians. **Napoleon** even understood the enormous power of music by observing: 'Give me control over he who shapes the music of a nation, and I care not who makes the laws'"

I recently opened one of my 2017 issues of ***AARP THE MAGAZINE*** and saw an interesting headline that caught my eye, ***"Your pipes lose muscle tone with age"***. "The result:", it says, "a growly, less-clear voice. The change typically starts in your mid-50s, when vocal cords loosen and stop closing completely (sort of like old rubber bands). Extra air escapes, causing a weaker, breathier voice. Some men compensate by speaking in a higher pitch; others reflexively go to a lower pitch." The brief article then goes on to advise readers to try going hmmmmmm. "Home exercises to strengthen the vocal cords – lip trills, humming through a straw and more – really work", says Joel Portnoy, an otolaryngologist and assistant professor at the Hofstra School of Medicine in New York.

I would venture to say that going back in the history of America in the 1800s and early 1900s, there were many rural families that passed the time (before radio and TV) by making music together, and realizing that singing had healing qualities.

Remember the words to the chorus of that old Gospel/country song?:

Daddy sang bass, momma sang tenor
Me and little brother would join right in there
Singin' seems to help our troubled soul
One of these days, and it won't be long
I'll rejoin them in a song
I'm gonna join the family circle at the throne

What was American music like in those early Colonial and Pioneer days? Well, I'll get into that at the end of the next chapter which explains how music evolved since the dawn of mankind.

Chapter 2
THE STORY OF MUSIC

Another fascinating book on the history of how music came into existence and accompanied virtually all aspects of early human activity is *"The Story of Music, From Babylon to the Beatles: How Music Has Shaped Civilization"* by **Howard Goodall**. Mr. Goodall is a British historian and musician, so you will notice some of his words have a slightly different spelling then our Americanized versions. On the next several pages, I'm going to take extensive quotes from his book *verbatim* and edit them down, and at times insert my own comments along the way. I think you'll find those pages of history to be extremely interesting.

"Perhaps your favourite music was written by Monteverdi in 1600, Bach in 1700, Beethoven in 1800, Elgar in 1900, or Coldplay in

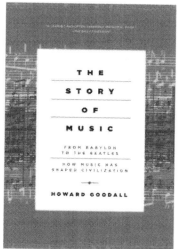

2000. Whichever it is, it is a sobering fact that everything that had to be discovered to produce that music – its chords, melodies, and rhythms – had already been discovered by around 1450. . . . And in order for me to sit at a piano and play . . . masterworks in the comfort of my own home – instantly and just as the composer intended – someone had to work out a way of writing the notes down, alongside performance instructions.

"Indeed, it is easy to overlook how utterly spoiled for musical choice we are in the twenty-first century. We can listen to almost anything we want at the press of a button (or computer mouse). But as recently as the late nineteenth century, even the most devoted music lover might hear his or her favorite piece just three or four times in his or her whole life. Unless you happened to be a virtuoso musician with access to both sheet music and instruments, it was almost impossible to bring large-scale forms of music into your own home. Not until the dawn of recording and radio technology did our ancestors have any great choice as to what they listened to and when. If you like, it is only since recorded music has been available to buy that music has become democratic.

"What we call 'Western' music – the medium in which nearly all music on earth is now conceived, recorded and performed, and which has in the past hundred years or so absorbed into its fold most of the 'other' music cultures of the world – started out as merely one localised branch of a global musical map. European-Mediterranean tribes had their particular brand of music much as African, Asian, American and Antipodean tribes did (and still do). What became the generic category 'Western music' was an amalgam of, among others, Egyptian, Persian, Greek, Celtic, Norse and Roman strands of music. It started, though, just like all the world's traditional music cultures: improvised, shared, spontaneous and transient."

THE AGE OF DISCOVERY

"You may think that music is a luxury, a plug-in to make human life more enjoyable. That would be a fair supposition in the twenty-first century, but our hunter-gatherer ancestors wouldn't have agreed. To them, music was much more than entertainment.

"The famous rock paintings in Chauvet, France, made by cave-dwelling people of the Upper Paleolithic period, or European Ice Age, are 32,000 years old. They are among the oldest surviving examples of human art ever found anywhere in the world. . . . It is thought that the paintings were created and venerated as part of a ritual, and we now know that music of some kind played an important part in these rituals, since whistles and flutes made from bone have been found in many Paleolithic caves (similar to those shown to the left).

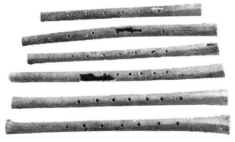

"A particularly ancient find was a flute made of bear bone, discovered in a Slovenian cave in 1995, which was dated at roughly 41,000 BC.

"Although these deceptively simple ancient flutes are almost all that survives of Paleolithic music, acoustic scientists have recently made an extraordinary discovery about the lifesaving importance of music to cave-dwellers of this period. In 2008, researchers from the University of

Paris ascertained that the Chauvet paintings – which lie within huge, inaccessible, pitch-black networks of tunnels – are located at the points of greatest resonance in the cave network. From these special points, then, human voices would carry, echoing and ricocheting, throughout the whole subterranean system. It has been suggested that people would sing not just as an adjunct to communal ritual, but more crucially as a bat-like form of sonar to provide location bearings in the vast labyrinth of the cave – rather like a *musical SatNav* (navigation system).

"Our own day-to-day survival may no longer depend on our ability to sing, but our ancient ancestors were on to something that applies to modern lives, too. Study after study around the world has shown that singing enables infants to train their brains and memories, to recognise pitch differentiation as a preparation for the full development of spatial awareness. In the Paleolithic Age, this was an absolutely crucial skill, if survival depended on knowing from which direction a wild animal's cry was coming, what size it was and what mood it might be in. But even now, singing and the mastery of pitch play a large part in a child's development of language. For an infant in China, for example, pitch recognition is an essential building block of language – but in all languages, it is certain that sound modulations enable us to enhance the sophistication, tone and meaning of our words.

MUSICAL CONTRIBUTIONS BY THE EGYPTIANS

"The considerable body of art left to posterity by the Ancient Egyptians . . . shows us that by their time (3100-670 BC), the playing of

music was closely associated with the exercise of power and homage, with religious and secular rituals, and with state ceremony, dancing, love and death. These pieces of art depict a variety of instruments, from the simple *sistrum* or *sekhem* – a hand-held U-shaped shaken percussion instrument – to harps, ceremonial horns, flutes and wind instruments whose sound is made by blowing across strips of reed, the same technique that produces the sound of the modern oboe, bassoon and clarinet families.

23

"They also depict expert performers of high status, including members of royal dynasties and deities. The prevalence of music in Ancient Egyptian life is demonstrated by the fact that over a quarter of all tombs at the necropolis found at the site of the city of Thebes are decorated with iconography of music-making of one sort or another.

"The Egyptians were not alone in their preference for the power of music. Psalms sung by the priests of King David, who united the kingdoms of Israel and Judaea in 1003 BC, are riven through with references to instruments and to singing. (The Greek word 'psalm' itself, strictly speaking, refers to a religious song with accompaniment by a plucked stringed instrument.)

"And yet we have absolutely no idea what this music sounded like. Nor do we know what the music of the earlier Sumerian civilisation sounded like (4500 – 1940 BC); nor that of the Egyptians, nor – save for a few tiny fragments of tunes – that of the (more recent) Ancient Greeks.

"No civilisation, except perhaps for our own, has valued, venerated and taken pleasure in music more than the Ancient Greeks, whose culture dominated south-eastern Europe and the Near East for nearly seven hundred years in the first millennium BC, before it was absorbed into the Roman Empire. Even the word 'music' comes from the Greek *mousike*, referring to the fruits of the nine muses in literature, science and the arts. . . . The Greeks believed that studying music would produce better, more tolerant and nobler human beings. Plato declared in *The Republic* that 'musical training is a more potent instrument than any other, because rhythm and harmony find their way into the inward places of the soul, on which they mightily fasten, imparting grace, and making the soul of him who is rightly educated graceful'. Young students were accordingly expected to learn an instrument and perform music daily, alongside gymnastics.

"Greek philosophies on the beneficial behavioral qualities of music find striking parallels with Confucius-influenced writings of the second and third centuries BC in China. Chinese belief in the potential of music *(yue)* to improve and refine the human condition was so pronounced that in the Zhou and early Han dynasties the control of music activity was enshrined in a specific government department. Like their contemporaries in Greece, the Han Chinese saw virtue in the relationship between musical pitch in music – the relative distance between notes – and the arrangement of the stars and planets they observed above them. Thousands of pages of theory and instruction survive, detailing how it might be possible through careful calculation, through manipulation of the calendar, through codifying the elements of music and through study of the cosmos, to formulate good governance, based on the correct alignment of these associated forces.

"The Ancient Greeks reserved their greatest excitement in relation to music, though, for competitions, of which they had a large number. Everyone knows that the Ancient Greeks invented the Olympic Games; for the

Greeks, though, it wasn't just running, nude wrestling and hurling the javelin that were important. The earliest Olympic Games were religious, as well as athletic, festivals, and as such would have included some music-making. But a distinct tradition of singing competitions grew up separately, and attracted participants from all over the Greek-dominated eastern Mediterranean. Singer-songwriters would gather for festivals and sing their homespun songs for the benefit of a panel of judges and a live audience." [**Author's note:** *Sounds like today's format used in the Barbershop Harmony Society and Sweet Adeline competitions may actually be three thousand years old!*]

"There were also choral competitions, with a festival atmosphere and plenty of group choreography – ancient versions, if you like, of the present-day carnivals in Rio de Janeiro, Trinidad, and Notting Hill. The significance of these competitions is that they prompted the emergence of a new class of elite musicians – individuals and groups striving for musical excellence who could earn money and prizes for their endeavours. The Greeks began a process that became unusually pronounced in Western music: emphasis on a VIP class of performers whose brilliance was intended to strike awe and enchantment into the hearts of the ordinary listener.

"The third thing you need to know about the Greeks and music is that, by inventing European drama, they in effect invented the musical,

25

since their dramas were all accompanied by music and choral singing, declaiming (close to the modern notion of rapping) or chanting. Their surviving amphitheaters, dotted around the eastern Mediterranean, are among the most vivid reminders to us of the artistic sophistication of their civilisation."

HOW VOCAL HARMONY BEGAN

If you want to explore one whimsical version of how harmony began, check out The Vocal Majority's recording of *"Harmony"* from their 198 album, *"The Music Never Ends"*, which includes the following verse:

Now when the Lord invented the chord
It sounded and then he listened again
Then He cried right out with delight
I'm so elated I just created Harmony
Harmony, thank you Lord for Harmony
It brightens up the day and carries us away
Harmony just carries us away, carries us away!

Words & Music by David Wright
Arrangement for The Vocal Majority

I must admit that Mr. Goodall's fascinating *"The Story of Music"*, made me appreciate how music was, at first, an indispensable tool our prehistoric ancestors used to stay alive and flourish, and then became ingrained into the social, political, recreational and religious lives of all people who came after them. But since my ultimate goal in this book is to bring you, dear reader, into the world of exquisite vocal harmony exemplified by *The Vocal Majority Chorus*, I'd like to borrow some more history from Mr. Goodall's book regarding how *HE* describes musical chords and the method by which they came to be discovered.

"The incredible thing is that, for the first few hundred years of the first millennium AD, before a universal notation system emerged, all of the chants that monks and nuns sang was memorised. It was passed on aurally, monk by monk, nun by nun, painstakingly for century after century. This chant, also called plainchant or plainsong, has by default often

26

been described as 'Gregorian' chant, after Gregory the Great, who was Pope at the end of the sixth century.

"Indeed, plainsong developed gradually and separately all over Christian Europe according to local tastes and traditions. But what all this chant had in common was that it was just one memorised, meandering tune with no accompaniment and no harmonising, the Greek term for which is *monophonic*: one voice. Plainchant is our only audible link with the musicians of the first thousand years AD. Its survival into the modern era we owe to two gigantic musical discoveries that began to make their presence felt in the two centuries before AD 1000. To grasp the significance of these two discoveries, we need to transport ourselves back to the sound world of that period, one thousand five hundred years ago.

"It is a Sunday morning service in an abbey or cathedral. Some monks are singing a section of  plainchant, together, in *unison*. After a couple of lifetimes, someone thinks it would be a good idea to add some young lads to the choir, to feed and clothe them and keep them out of mischief, and to begin the long, slow process of teaching them from memory the entire plainsong repertoire for the Church year.

"The musical effect of adding the boys is that there are now two parallel lines of music, not just one, since the boys' voices are higher than those of the men. The higher version the boys sing is made up of identical notes to the men's, but at a higher register; so there is a fixed, natural distance between the two identical lines of music. This fixed distance between a note and its higher self is something that occurs in nature – we humans didn't invent it, we just found it to be lurking behind all musical sounds.

"(But) what if we had two notes together that *weren't* an octave apart? Believe it or not, this possibility didn't occur to medieval musicians for *centuries*. It was as if they had discovered black and white, and maybe brown, but never thought to look for further colours. . . . This was a really major breakthrough: layering two lines of voices singing at the same time, but singing slightly different notes. And yet, when the musical monks finally started doing it, their caution was staggering.

"Medieval church musicians called the technique of running two notes in parallel – which they improvised on the spot – '*organum*', because to their ears it sounded like an organ. Which it does. The Greek term for more than one voice line singing together is *polyphonic*: many voices.

"As time went on, more adventurous musicians, such as ninth-century Byzantine (female) composer Kassia of Constantinople, began mixing the parallel organum style with the drone style. Kassia's haunting music has recently been recorded for the first time in a thousand years, and it rather gracefully refutes the assumption that the development of early music is exclusively the handiwork of men.

"These new layered sound effects, built on plainsong tunes, were edging very close to what today we would call 'harmony' – that is, the existence and exploitation of simultaneous clusters of notes. This was the first giant step our medieval ancestors took as the year 1000 loomed.

"The other (step) was to alter the course of music history dramatically. It was the invention of a reliable, universally adopted musical notation. It took an Italian monk, immortalised as Guido of Arezzo, to crack the code in around AD 1000 and gave Western music its unique system of notation, still in use today.

"His job at the cathedral in Arezzo was to train the young choristers, and he calculated that teaching them the whole of the Church's plainsong repertoire by ear, parrot-fashion, would take over ten years. What he desperately needed was a method of notation that you could read and turn into singing *at sight*, and he set about developing this miraculous time-saving device. His methods were simple and clear. First he gave the plainsongs a standardised, easy-to-read form. Each note had its own identifiable blob, a mark on the page, and they were placed in the order, from left to right, in which they were meant to sing."

God   save   our   grac-   ious   Queen

God   save   our   grac- ious   Queen

"He then drew four straight lines on to which the notes would be placed, so that it was instantly possible to see the relative positions of every note:"

(All above notations and graphics are taken from "The Story of Music" by Howard Goodall)

"These days we call the collection of lines a *stave* or *staff.* . . . The position of each note represented its pitch position, that is, whether it was  an A, a B, or any other note. If the tune went up, the notes went up. If it went down, the notes went down, step by step. This method has been refined over the years, for example, by altering the blob shapes to indicate the duration of a note, or to group notes together in clusters to pick out a rhythm, and in time his four lines became five, but it is essentially the same system for notating music as is used universally in the twenty-first century.

"The revolutions in both notation and harmony during this period had been hundreds of years in the making, but once they were in place the pace of innovation accelerated rapidly. The development of layered voices and notation ushered in a period of great experimentation and adventure – particularly with regard to harmony – and because of them, Western music by 1100 was already utterly distinct from every other musical culture that had ever existed.

29

". . . a group of younger composers working at Notre-Dame in Paris had become known for their radical approach to harmony. The trailblazer of this group was called Leonin, and by the standards of the early twelfth century he was both prolific and admired, regularly combining plainsong chant melodies with a second voice, a technique now known as *organum duplum*. His greatest legacy to music, though, is the inspiration he provided for his young colleague, and possibly pupil, Perotin.

"What Perotin did was ask a very simple question: what would happen if you had *more* than two voice lines singing at the same time? What would it sound like to hear three or even four notes simultaneously? Such a cluster of notes, known to us as a *chord*, did not even have a name at this time, so novel was its concept. . . . He was truly the first musical radical, referred to in a contemporary record as *'Perotin the Master'*. Harmony made from chords came alive in his four-part vocal music, even if some of his note combinations sound accidental rather than intentional."

WHAT WAS EARLY AMERICAN MUSIC LIKE?

Now let's move from a European focus in our history of music to America's first music innovations. We always say that we're a nation of  immigrants. In America's colonial times, the same apparently held true for its music. According to *The Colonial Music Institute*, based in Maryland, music before the Revolution wasn't so much music that was created here but music that was *brought* here by early settlers. Their music included ballads, dance tunes, folk songs and parodies, comic opera arias, drum signals, psalms, minuets, and sonatas. This music came mostly from England, Scotland, Ireland, Germany, Italy, France, and Africa, and it was played on whatever instruments were handy.

Most instruments that we have today were around by the time of the Revolution when pianos became popular. After pianos in popularity were the violin and flute. The grandmother of our modern guitar was around also, but not as popular; it was a small version of what we know as a classical guitar with gut strings, frets of gut tied around the neck, and strung as a modern 12-string *without* the bass E strings. So, it was actually a 10-stringed instrument using materials that could be found on American soil at that time – wood and animal guts.

Drums and trumpets, trombones and French horns, cellos, violas da gamba, clarinets, oboes and bassoons, hammered dulcimers, organs – all these appeared, in varying numbers, within the colonies.

In his book, *"The Complete Idiot's Guide to Musical History"* (*the perfect research source for yours truly*), by **Michael Miller**, he states that, "The first music of the early American colonists was religious music,

in the form of traditional English hymns brought across the ocean. The Plymouth pilgrims originally sang directly from the **Ainsworth Psalter**, a book of psalms set to music, published in Amsterdam in 1612. They used this book until a local hymn book, the Bay Psalm Book, was published in 1640. This book became the standard used by New England churches for many years. These traditional psalms were eventually supplemented by newly composed hymns.

"One of the foremost musical figures of the Colonial era was **William Billings** (1746-1800), a Boston-area composer with no formal musical training. Billings, a friend of **Samuel Adams** and **Paul Revere**, wrote hundreds of hymns and secular songs, including *"When Jesus Wept,"* *"David's Lamentation,"* and *"Chester"* (the unofficial national hymn of the American Revolution).

"In 1770, he published the first book of *American* music, **The New-England Psalm-Singer**. His hymns were all written for four-part *a cappella* chorus, reflecting that period's objection to playing instruments in churches. Their chief innovation was doubling the male and female voices in an octave and then filling out the harmony with close-position chords; this texture was unknown in the European choral tradition.

"Church music wasn't the only music heard in the colonies. Many private citizens owned and played their own instruments—fifes, fiddles, violins, and flutes were common. The people used these instruments to play folk tunes and ballads, typically derived from British, Irish, and Scottish forms. Folksingers of the day performed both traditional and newly composed songs; often the new songs were merely new lyrics over traditional folk tunes. Once the Revolution got underway, newly written songs such as *"The Battle of the Kegs"* and *"Hail Columbia"* expressed the patriotism of the day.

"So, the colonists were singing folk tunes that originally came from Europe. But where did those European folk tunes come from? Indirectly, most Western European folk music evolved from the troubadours of the Middle Ages. The troubadours originated in southern France around the eleventh century; they were roving minstrels who sang their secular songs for lords and ladies of the upper classes."

THE STORY OF "YANKEE DOODLE"

According to **Michael Miller**, "Perhaps the most famous folk song from the Revolutionary War era is *"Yankee Doodle."* You know how it goes, but do you know how the song came about? Perhaps, as legendary radio newscaster Paul Harvey would say, "it's time to learn the rest of the story". The song "Yankee Doodle" actually originated as a tune sung by British military officers *prior* to the Revolutionary War. The lyrics mocked the disheveled and disorganized colonial "Yankees" with whom they served in the French and Indian War (1754-1763). At the time, the word 'doodle' was a derogatory term for 'fool.'

"But," he continued, "the Yanks had the last laugh. During the Revolutionary War, the colonists embraced the song and made it their own. They made up new lyrics and used them to mock the Brits who had mocked them previously; the British army learned to hate the song. By the way, the version sung by schoolchildren today, with the verse about sticking a feather in his hat and calling it macaroni, was apparently a British variant, not the American version. At the time, a "macaroni" was a dandyish young man who affected upper-class mannerisms; it was a joke that a

Yank could stick a feather in his hat and think that was enough to make him fashionable." Now you know the rest of the story.

APPALACHIAN FOLK MUSIC

Continuing with **Michael Miller**'s extensive history of the post-Civil War era: "The folk music from the colonial era seemed to find a permanent home in the Appalachian Mountains of the central states. This area was settled from 1775 to 1850 or so, primarily by poor Europeans of Irish and Scottish descent. It's no surprise, then, that Appalachian music resembled native Irish and Scottish folk music. Listen to Appalachian music of the day (or of today, for that matter – the music hasn't changed much), and you hear echoes of Celtic folk tunes, Scottish harps and bagpipes, and British broadside ballads. Melodic lines followed simple traditional harmonies, often with a distinctive "slide" between notes of the vocal line. It continues to this day in the form of what some call "old time" music. It is also a big influence on modern bluegrass and country music. Singers were typically accompanied by guitar(s), banjo, fiddle, harp, and other easy-to-play and easy-to-make instruments."

AFRICAN AMERICAN WORK SONGS AND SPIRITUALS

African slavery is a blight on the history of the United States, but it's a part of our history that can't be ignored. It was also a source of some uniquely American music, in the form of work songs and spirituals, as **Michael Miller** describes to us in his *"Complete Idiot's Guide"* book.

"The first slaves were delivered to the colonies from West Africa as early as 1619. These slaves brought with them music from their native countries, including religious music and work songs—music sung as they toiled in the fields. Many slave owners encouraged their slaves to sing as they worked, believing that it improved morale. Thus, the typical work song consisted of one or more unaccompanied vocal lines, often with a noticeable beat that matched the rhythm of the work being done. The most notable characteristic of this music was its call-and-response vocal style, where one or more singers would echo or answer the vocal line of another.

"African music also differed from traditional western music in its use of rhythm. Whereas the sacred and folk music of the time employed relatively simple rhythms, African folk styles were much more rhythmically complex. This rhythmic complexity would find its way into the African-influenced music of later generations, especially jazz and rock and roll. Negro spirituals applied African vocal styles and rhythms to the traditional American colonial hymns. Many of these songs, such as *"Swing Low, Sweet Chariot"* and *"Go Down Moses,"* directly or indirectly used religious imagery to symbolize their own plight. The Negro spiritual was both an expression of religious devotion and a (somewhat veiled) yearning for freedom from bondage."

EARLY POPULAR SONG

The purpose of this book is not to cover the entire range of early American music. Obviously, a significant portion of our early settlers and those from Colonial times were sophisticated enough to appreciate the more classical and symphonic forms of music that were brought with them from their countries of origin. My father's taste in symphonic music has carried over to my own affection for similar genres, and you can probably find my car's radio mostly tuned to the classical music station in Dallas when I'm driving by myself. But, as you can probably tell from my introductory remarks on the first few pages, I fell in love with *POPULAR* music from the time I was old enough to carry a tune and listen to the radio. And, by "popular" I personally include **easy listening, rock, jazz, country, folk, Barbershop, Broadway, inspirational**, etc. Those are the types of music I hoped I could sing when I first put together the organization now known as **The Vocal Majority**, and those are the types of music I intend to explore in this section of the book.

The music we've discussed so far is alternately referred to as "classical," "serious," or even "art" music. This is distinct from "popular" music, or the music of the masses. In his book on musical history that I quoted earlier, **Michael Miller** states something that we all should understand: "While it's true that the music of Bach and Beethoven was enjoyed by the masses of their times, it's also true that *this music was made by and for the elite*—it wasn't what the common man was playing or singing in his home.

"Popular music, then, is music that is accessible to the general public, as opposed to that music which is created for an elite class. This is

34

typically simpler music, more easily grasped and more easily played or sung. It's also typically the music of *song*, rather than of longer, more complex musical works. While many snooty music historians tend to focus solely on classical music, popular music is just as important—especially in recent times, when printed music, recorded music, and musical instruments are readily accessible to all levels of the citizenry. It's not like it was back in Bach's day, when only the well-heeled could afford a harpsichord or a concert ticket; today, even those with relatively low incomes can buy a guitar, obtain sheet music, or listen to music on the radio. This has led to a *musical democratization*, enhancing the importance of popular music."

According to **Wikipedia**, the patriotic songs of the American Revolution constituted the first kind of mainstream American popular music. These included *"The Liberty Tree"* by Thomas Paine. Cheaply printed as broadsheets, early patriotic songs spread across the colonies and were performed at home and at public meetings. Fife (or flute) songs were especially celebrated and were performed on fields of battle during the American Revolution. The longest lasting of these fife songs is *"Yankee Doodle"*, which we've already discussed.

Patriotic songs were based mostly on English melodies, with new lyrics added to denounce British colonialism. The song *"Hail Columbia"* was a major work that remained an unofficial national anthem until the adoption of *"The Star Spangled Banner"*. The lyrics to that anthem come from **"Defense of Fort McHenry"**, a text written on September 14, 1814, by the 35-year-old lawyer and am-

ateur poet **Francis Scott Key** after witnessing the bombardment of Fort McHenry by British warships in Baltimore Harbor during the War of 1812. *"The Star Spangled Banner"* was made the national anthem of the United States by a Congressional resolution on March 3, 1931, which was signed by President Herbert Hoover.

During the Civil War, when soldiers from across the country comingled, the various strands of American music began to cross-fertilize each other, a process that was aided by the burgeoning railroad industry and other technological developments that made travel and communication easier. Army units included individuals from across the country, and they rapidly traded tunes, instruments, and techniques. The war was an impetus for the creation of distinctly *American* songs that became and remained wildly popular. The most popular songs of the Civil War era included *"Dixie"*. The song, originally titled *"Dixie's Land"*, was made for the closing of a minstrel show; it spread to New Orleans first, where it was published and became one of the great song successes of the pre-Civil War period.

In addition to popular patriotic songs, the Civil War era also produced a great body of brass band pieces. The composer **John Phillip Sousa** is closely associated with the most popular trend in American popular music just before the start of the 20th century. Formerly the bandmaster of the United States Marine Band, Sousa wrote military marches like *"The Stars and Stripes Forever"* that reflected his nostalgia for his home and country. (Did you know that this band march also has *words*? Check out both **The Vocal Majority**'s and our quartet, **Acoustix**, recordings of this stirring – and rather difficult – a cappella vocal arrangement.)

Following the Civil War, **minstrel shows** became the first distinctively American form of musical expression. The minstrel show was an indigenous form of American entertainment consisting of comic skits, variety acts, dancing, and music, usually performed by white people in blackface. Minstrel shows produced the first well-remembered popular songwriters in American music history: **Thomas D. Rice, Daniel Decatur Emmett**, and, most famously, **Stephen Foster** (whose picture is to the left). If you read my introduction to this book, you'll remember that Stephen Foster was my dad's favorite composer of early American popular songs.

Foster was born near Pittsburgh, Pennsylvania, according to *"The Complete Idiot's Guide To Musical History"*, the youngest of 10 children. He had no formal music training, but nevertheless published his first song, *"Open Thy Lattice Love"* (1844), when he was just 18. When he was 20, Foster moved to Cincinnati, where he penned his first hit, *"Oh! Susanna"* (1848); this song would become the unofficial anthem of the following year's California Gold Rush. He returned to Pennsylvania in 1850 and signed a contract to provide music to the **Christy Minstrels**. He wrote some of his most famous songs during this period, including *"De Camptown Races"* (1850), *"Old Folks at Home"* (1851; also known as *"Swanee River"*), *"My Old Kentucky Home"* (1853), and *"Hard Times Come Again No More"* (1854). Later in his career, Foster turned to writing sentimental ballads, most famously *"Jeannie with the Light Brown Hair"* (1854) and the posthumously published *"Beautiful Dreamer"* (1864).

"Foster was notable for being one of America's first professional songwriters— that is, a composer who made his living from writing and publishing songs, rather than from performing live. That said, the copyright laws were primitive in those days, and Foster saw very little of the profits that his songs generated for the sheet music publishers. For example, Foster was paid a flat $100 for the rights to *"Oh! Susanna"*—a fraction of what the song actually earned. And Foster's name didn't even appear on some printings of his music. As a result, Foster died virtually penniless, at the age of 37, in a Bowery hotel in New York City."

In the same book, Michael Miller notes that "Not all American songwriters of that era were white men. **Scott Joplin** (1867- 1917) was a black man born in east Texas who later moved to New York City. At the height of his popularity, Joplin worked in Tin Pan Alley alongside composers like **Irving Berlin** and **George Gershwin**. Joplin was a formally trained musician who first heard Sousa's brass band music at the 1893 World's Fair in Chicago. His first compositions were marches and minstrel songs; he was even part of a minstrel troupe himself for a short period in the early 1890s. He sold his first songs in 1895, and had turned to the ragtime genre by 1898.

"Joplin's ragtime work was a big hit, propelling him to the front of that era's professional songwriting ranks. His *"Maple Leaf Rag"* (1899) was the first instrumental sheet music publication to sell over a million copies and became the classic model both for Joplin's later works and for rags by other prominent composers. He was a master creator of memorable melodies, from the bouncing *"The Entertainer"* (1902) to the lyrical *"Wall Street Rag"* (1908). *"The Entertainer"* returned to international prominence as part of the ragtime revival in the 1970s, when it was used as the theme music for the 1973 Oscar-winning film **The Sting**."

In the early 20th century, American musical theater, headquartered in New York City's Broadway theaters, was a major source for popular songs, many of which influenced blues, jazz, country, and other styles of popular music. Theatrical composers and lyricists like the brothers George and Ira Gershwin created a uniquely American theatrical style that used American vernacular speech and music. Musicals featured popular songs and fast-paced plots that often revolved around love and romance.

THE BIRTH OF THE RECORDING INDUSTRY

Howard Goodall in his *"The Story of Music"* book has done a mountain of research about, among other things, the beginnings of music recording technology. It seems that a humble strip of waxed paper in 1860 with the voice of a woman singing is the oldest surviving recording technology. I've always heard that Thomas Edison was the inventor of music recordings, but his tinfoil phonograph of "Mary had a little lamb" didn't premier until seventeen years later. The inventor of that 1860 recording technique went unknown until 2008 when a group of American audio historians and engineers digitally scanned the waxed paper – which the French inventor called a *phonautograph* -- and converted it into sound.

Goodall goes on to explain what resulted in 1877 after Thomas Edison invented a machine that could play recordings back. He writes, "A new breed of musician-researcher popped up, traveling around remote rural areas recording and preserving the folk songs that doubtless bemused locals were persuaded to perform. It is thought that the oldest surviving field recordings are those made in 1889 among the Passamaquoddy Indians in Maine by American Anthropologist Jesse Walter Fewkes. From the 1890s onwards, Edison's wax-cylinder recording devices were being used all over the world, capturing forever the oral and musical culture of communities now long disappeared."

From that point on, the music "industry" was born, intent on making money selling recordings of popular singers and musicians of the day. The first million-seller was a record of Italian tenor **Enrico Caruso** singing *"Vesti la giubba"* from Leoncavallo's opera *I Pagliacci* in 1907. And then when radio broadcasts of recorded music began around 1920, people started to collect their own records and the music recording industry took off from there.

Goodall concludes this section of his book by saying, "Certainly, for popular music, recording was an unqualified blessing. It empowered and spread forms of music that had developed without notation, making available to a mass audience folk and ethnic music that had up to then been confined to local communities. For these communities, music was not just an entertainment. It was a refuge. But the music they had nurtured and were now able to share with the wider world was to have a profound revolutionising impact on the twentieth century's musical story."

Let's leave Howard Goodall's amazing history lesson at this point and move on to a more recent historical perspective about the way music and performers have developed since the recording industry invaded virtually all aspects of our collective lives.

Chapter 3
THE MUSIC WE GREW UP WITH

"A long, long time ago
I can still remember
How that music used to make me smile
Do you believe in rock n' roll
Can music save your mortal soul?"
Don McLean – *American Pie*

I've toiled in the fields of marketing, advertising and broadcast media for most of my working life. Audience demographics and I have been friends for a long time. So, when I started writing this book I tried to envision the demographic who would be reading it and have an interest in its contents. So, I presumed that my readers would be both men and women between the ages of 20 and 80, and who would have at least a passing interest in Western forms of music. I hope I was right.

If my analysis is correct, we're talking about a range of music genre dating back to almost the  "swing era" of the big bands and bandstand crooners to present-day hip-hop and rap. You may find it hard to believe but some of my younger college students have never even heard of the term "rock n' roll". Sometimes it challenges an old speech professor to relate to his students when it comes to music.

Unfortunately, the recollections of my early childhood are spotty at best. Since I was born in 1938 and spent my early years during World War II, my most memorable recollection was when that war ended and I heard a newspaper boy yelling outside our small house in northern Ohio, *"Extra! Extra! Read all about it! The war has ended!"* I'll bet you thought that only happened in the movies?

These days when my college classroom discussions get into early broadcast technologies, I have to reveal to them that television didn't really exist in our household until my teenage years. Radio was our only means of listening to the popular singers and comic performers of the day. Names like Bing Crosby, Perry Como, and Frank Sinatra had their own radio programs and sold millions of records and sheet music folios. When we'd have a quarter to spare, we could go to the movies – black-and-white only – and see singing cowboys like Roy Rogers and Gene Autry. Vocal groups were also popular, and almost all the musical radio programs featured at one time or another The Andrews Sisters, the Mills Brothers, Les Paul & Mary Ford. As a matter of fact, Les Paul designed and built one of the first solid-body electric guitars in 1941. He and his wife, Mary Ford, pioneered the use of tape editing and "multi-tracking" to create large 'virtual' ensembles of voices and instruments, constructed entirely from multiple taped recordings of their own voices and instruments.

If you wanted to purchase a recording in those days, you had to buy an inflexible polyvinyl plastic disk that was very prone to scratching and breaking. Then, in 1948, Columbia Records introduced the 33⅓ rpm

LP ("long playing") record, featuring 25 minutes of music per side. And in 1949 RCA Victor introduced the 45-rpm record, featuring 8 minutes of music. I can remember having my little 45-rpm record player in my North Ridgeville, Ohio, home playing my favorite record at the time, Perry Como's inspirational hit of *"Ave Maria"*. I memorized every Latin language word and nuance and tried my best to imitate Como's silky style. (I had a head start on the Latin since I was an altar boy during grade school.) It was so *déjà vu* for me when The Vocal Majority recorded that song *in Latin* on their 1988 album, *"For God, Country & You"*. (I was fortunate because I already knew all the words and how to pronounce them!)

THE ARRIVAL OF ELVIS AND ROCK N' ROLL

While I was learning to play the guitar and participating in Ms. Mitchell's choir program at North Ridgeville High School, a new wave of popular music was making its way onto the radio airwaves in northern Ohio. I can remember sitting in my 1948 Buick outside a favorite ice cream parlor listening to the radio with my best friend, Dick Foley. Out from the radio speakers came the first rock n' roll song we'd ever heard, **Bill Hailey** and the Comets with *"Shake, Rattle and Roll"*. It was awesome to our virgin ears!

Just about that time, 1954, a raw young singer by the name of **Elvis Aaron Presley** started recording songs with producer **Sam Phillips** in his Mem-

phis, TN, studio that would literally shake the music world. RCA Victor eventually acquired his contract in a deal arranged by **Colonel Tom Parker**, who managed the singer for more than two decades. Presley's first RCA single, *"Heartbreak Hotel"*, was released in January 1956, and became a number-one hit in the United States. He was regarded as the leading figure of rock and roll after a series of successful network television appearances and chart-topping records. His energized interpretations of songs and sexually provocative performance style, combined with a singularly potent mix of influences across color lines that coincided with the dawn of the Civil Rights Movement, made him enormously popular—and controversial.

To say that Elvis had a profound influence on me is an understatement. I participated in a trend that is still alive today – *Elvis imitators* – with undoubtedly thousands of would-be heart throbs gyrating, crooning that seductive singing style, and wearing extra-long sideburns and dark clothes. I was even booked for several public appearances through local radio stations in the Cleveland, Ohio, area as I dragged along my **Les Paul** electric guitar, amplifier, and single microphone. I must have been less than impressive because I'm still waiting for my first recording contract.

As I matured a little and moved on to Fenn College (now Cleveland State), I took my guitar with me and began to explore other kinds of music that fit in with my style of singing and musical tastes. One genre that I fell in love with was American folk music. It was certainly around WAY before pop music and rock n' roll, but it hadn't found a mass audience the way it suddenly did as it re-emerged in the 1950s and 1960s.

According to *Wikipedia*, the post–World War II folk revival in America and in Britain started a new genre, contemporary folk music, and brought an additional meaning to the term "folk music": newly composed songs, fixed in form and by known authors, which imitated some form of traditional music. The popularity of "contemporary folk" recordings caused the appearance of the category "Folk" in the **Grammy Awards** of 1959. The term "folk", by the start of the 21st century, could cover singer-songwriters, such as Donovan from Scotland and American Bob Dylan, who emerged in the 1960s and many more. This completed a process to where "folk music" no longer meant only traditional folk songs.

The **Carter Family** was a traditional American folk music group that recorded between 1927 and 1956. Their music had a profound impact on bluegrass, country, Southern Gospel, pop and rock musicians. They were the first vocal group to become country music stars – the beginning of the divergence of country music from traditional folk music. Their recordings of such songs as *"Wabash Cannonball"* (1932), *"Will the Circle Be Unbroken"* (1935), *"Wildwood Flower"* (1928), and *"Keep On the Sunny Side"* (1928) made them country standards.

The individuals and groups in the folk category that first caught my attention were The **Kingston Trio, Harry Belefonte**, and the **Chad**

Mitchell Trio. These recording and performing folk stars, according to *Wikipedia*, are a part of the American Folk Music Revival, including works by **Pete Seeger, Woody Guthrie, The Weavers, Burl Ives**, and others. A more commercially oriented version of folk emerged in the 1960s, and included performers such as **The Limeliters, The Brothers Four, Peter, Paul and Mary** *(my personal favorite)*, **Joan Baez, The Highwaymen, Judy Collins, The New Christy Minstrels**, and **Gordon Lightfoot**, as well as counterculture and folk rock performers like **Bob Dylan, The Byrds, Arlo**

Guthrie, and **Buffy Sainte-Marie**. A little later on you could probably **include John Denver, James Taylor** and **Kenny Rogers**.

When my budding radio-TV career took me to Washington, DC, I auditioned as a solo folk singer in many of the night clubs that were featuring folk acts, and I appeared at several – although I never attracted the attention of anyone offering me a recording or performance contract. *How could they be so blind and deaf!!!* Anyway, I didn't let these snubs slow me down. When I was hired as a morning DJ and program director at a forlorn radio station in Altoona, PA, I produced and promoted several "hootenanny's" that included myself and other folk artists from the local community. Then, when I finally landed in Dallas several years later, I did several gigs at **The Rubyat** and other folk clubs that were active during the 1960s and 1970s.

I recently found an interesting book about the music from that time titled, *"Listen To The Music: The Words You Don't Hear When You Listen To The Music"* by **Steve Richards**. He offers the following comments  about that era: "The music of the 60's and 70's reflects the turbulent events of two decades marked by unprecedented social, political, and economic change. The complex challenges Americans faced in the 60's and 70's are strikingly similar to the times we find ourselves in today. Unlike then, today's pop artists do not speak to the significant issues shaping the world around us, including an unpopular two-front war, an economy in crisis, climate change and divisive social issues. Attracting tabloid and media attention by what an artist is (or is not) wearing or with whom they are seen seems more important to the artist than their music. The MySpace, Twitter, Facebook, Instant Messaging, smartphone generation is looking for entertainment that is *visually* stimulating and immediately accessible. With **YouTube** and streaming videos to your laptop or smartphone, Gen-Y'ers and "Millennials" are more entertained by what they *see* than by what they hear. For those reasons, today's singers and songwriters focus more on style than on substance because that's what sells music and draws young fans to concerts."

Richards talks about growing up and coming of age during this time and never really listening to the lyrics of the music that infatuated him and his generation. "Boomers danced to the music, studied to the music, listened to the music at work, and sometimes even made love to the music. In the 60's we were busy living and exploring life, skipping class or trying to find a date for the next fraternity party. Blame it on youthful exuberance, a short attention span, or other distractions. While we listened to the music, we seldom heard the words to our favorite songs. Many of us are now at a point in our lives where we have the time, the patience, and, most importantly, the perspective to truly appreciate the wit, wisdom, and touch of philosophy within the lyrics of many of our favorite songs."

He confesses to not be sure what he would find when he began his book about the words to songs he and his generation had overlooked during the 60's and 70's. However, he says that he was quite surprised by the number of insightful lyrics in retrospect. "In the end, I learned more than I ever expected about the music that continues to affect my life. The music of singers and songwriters such as **Bob Dylan, Jim Croce, Carole King, Paul Simon, Neil Young** and **John Lennon** had meaning and purpose often protesting injustice or singing of life's trials and tribulations."

I must say that I agree with him to some extent. Maybe it was because I could more fully relate to the singers and songwriters of my 60's through 80's developmental years. Maybe today's music, with its focus on the *visual* aspects of performance that permeates the **YouTube** and the streaming video generation, just doesn't lend itself to meaningful lyrics. Maybe it's simply that the words and emotional overtones don't matter today, only the flash and spectacle of visual performance. Maybe it's me (and possibly you) who are *not listening in the way we formerly did* to the previous generation of songs. I say that because my college students, in at least half the cases when they explain their attraction to certain songs and artists, tell me that the *lyrics* to those songs have a very real meaning to their lives. *Think maybe it's just me who misses the point?*

Chapter 4
TALES OF MUSIC AND THE MIND

"I have seen deeply demented patients weep or shiver as they listen to music they have never heard before, and I think that they can experience the entire range of feelings the rest of us can, and that dementia, at least at these times, is no bar to emotional depth. Once one has seen such responses, one knows that there is still a self to be called upon, even if music, and only music, can do the calling."

From *"Musicophilia"* by Dr. Oliver Sacks

"Musicophilia" is the title of a fascinating book by Dr. Oliver Sacks which I read several years ago. Sacks is the author of several best-selling books, including several collections of case studies of people with

neurological disorders. His 1973 book, ***Awakenings***, was adapted into an Academy Award-nominated film of the same name in 1990 starring **Robin Williams** and **Robert De Niro**.

In the Preface to his Musicophilia book, Dr. Sacks – an impressive jazz pianist himself – talks about this "odd thing" we call music:

"What an odd thing it is to see an entire species – billions of people – playing with, listening to, meaningless tonal patterns, occupied and preoccupied for much of their time by what they call 'music'. This, at least, was one of the things about human beings that puzzled the highly cerebral alien beings, the Overlords, in Arthur, C. Clark's novel *Childhood's End*.

"Curiosity brings them down to the Earth's surface to attend a concert, they listen politely, and at the end, congratulate the composer on his 'great ingenuity' – while still finding the entire business unintelligible. They cannot think what goes on in human beings when they make or listen to music, because nothing goes on with *them*. They themselves, as a species, lack music.

47

"There are rare humans who, like the Overlords, may lack the neural apparatus for appreciating tones or melodies. But for virtually all of us, music has great power, whether or not we seek it out or think of ourselves as particularly 'musical'. This propensity to music shows itself in infancy, is manifest and central in every culture, and probably goes back to the very beginnings of our species. Such 'musicophilia' is a given in human nature. It may be developed or shaped by the cultures we live in, by the circumstances of life, or by the particular gifts or weaknesses we have as individuals – but it lies so deep in human nature that one must think of it as innate."

In his *Musicophilia* book and in other publications, Dr. Sacks provides numerous case histories about the liberating effects of music on his dementia patients – many of whom were elderly and in assisted living environments -- who were stoic and withdrawn until the magic of music brought them back to consciousness.

Dr. Sacks, prior to his recent death, lived for many years in New York City, where he was Professor of Clinical Neurology and Psychiatry at Columbia University. His *Musicophilia* book is filled with personal and other references to the power of music to unlock states of depression in people. In the book's chapter titled, *"Lamentations: Music and Depression"*, he writes:

"Robert Burton, in *The Anatomy of Melancholy*, wrote at length of music's power, and John Stuart Mill (called the most influential English-speaking philosopher of the nineteenth century) found that when he fell into a state of melancholia or anhedonia as a young man, music and nothing else had the power to pierce through this, to give him, at least for a while, a feeling of pleasure and being alive.

"I have had a few similar experiences myself, in which music has 'pierced my heart,' in Styron's words, when nothing else could – especially, perhaps, in bereavement. I was passionately fond of my mother's sister, my Auntie Leri; I often felt she had saved my sanity, if not my life, when I was sent away from home as a child, evacuated from London during the war. Her death left a sudden huge hole in my life, but, for some reason, I had difficulty mourning. I went about my work, my daily life, functioning in a mechanical way, but inside I was in a state of anhedonia, numbly unresponsive to all pleasure – and, equally, sadness. One evening I went to a concert, hoping against hope that the music might revive me, but it did not work; the whole concert bored me – until the last piece was played. It was a piece I had never heard before, by a composer I had never heard of, *The Lamentations of Jeremiah* by Jan Dismus Zelenka (an obscure Czech contemporary of Bach's, I later learned). Suddenly, as I listened, I found my eyes wet with tears. My emotions, frozen for weeks, were flowing once again. Zelenka's *Lamentations* had broken the dam, letting feeling flow where it had been obstructed, immobilized inside me.

"When I got the news of my mother's death, I flew at once to London, to the parental house, where, for a week, we sat shivah for her. But when I returned after this week to my empty and frigid apartment in New York, my feelings 'froze' and I fell into what is inadequately called a depression. For weeks I would get up, dress, drive to work, see my patients, try to present a normal appearance. But inside I was dead, as lifeless as a zombie. Then one day as I was walking down Bronx Park East, I felt a sudden lightening, quickening of mood, a sudden whisper or intimation of life, of joy. Only then did I realize that I was hearing music, though so faintly it might have been no more than an image or a memory. As I continue to walk, the music grew louder until finally I came to its source, a radio pouring Schubert out of an open basement window. The music pierced me, releasing a cascade of images and feelings – memories of childhood, of summer holidays together, and of my mother's fondness for Schubert. I found myself not only smiling for the first time in weeks, but laughing aloud – and alive once again."

MUSIC'S EFFECT ON DEMENTIA/ALZHEIMERS

Oliver Sacks books are filled with stories of how music intervention in the lives of institutionalized people with memory disorders has – at least temporarily – made a significant difference in their lives and those who are caretakers and loving relatives. Again, quoting from *Musicophilia*:

"In particular, the response to music is preserved, even when dementia is very advanced. But the therapeutic role of music in dementia is quite different from what it is in patients with motor or speech disorders. Music that helps patients with parkinsonism, for example, must have a firm rhythmic character, but it need not be familiar or evocative. With aphasics (people with memory problems) it is crucial to have songs with lyrics or intoned phrases, and interaction with a therapist. The aim of music therapy in people with dementia is far broader than this – it seeks to address the emotions, cognitive powers, thoughts, and memories, the surviving 'self' of the patient, to stimulate these and bring them to the fore. It aims to enrich and enlarge existence, to give freedom, stability, organization, and focus.

"This might seem a very tall order – nearly impossible, one would think, seeing patients with advanced dementia, who may sit in a seemingly mindless, vacant torpor or scream agitatedly in incommunicable distress. But music therapy with such patients is possible because musical perception, musical sensibility, musical emotion, and musical memory can survive long after other forms of memory have disappeared. Music of the right kind can serve to orient and anchor a patient when almost nothing else can."

You might think that the power of music is most valuable to people in the early stages of dementia or Alzheimer's. And yet, according to Dr. Sacks, it's just as important to those with advanced diseases as he relates in the following charming story:

"Bessie T., a lady in her eighties, is a former blues singer who used to work at the famous Apollo Club in Harlem. She now lives in a nursing home, though she often thinks she still works in a store ('I work in men's clothing . . . the *better* line'). Her Alzheimer's has left her with an amnesia so severe that she can hold nothing in mind for more than a minute. But learning that there was to be a talent show at the hospital, she (with her music therapist) practiced her songs assiduously, getting better all the time, though retaining no explicit memory of her practice sessions. When the day came, and she was escorted to the microphone and asked if she would sing for the audience, she said, 'Sure, honey –

but why didn't you ask me before?' She then went on to sing beautifully, with great feeling, though a few moments later, she had no memory of having performed."

Dr. Sacks talks about how music is engraved on our brains from an early age. He contends that, "Listening to music is not just auditory and emotional, it is motoric as well: 'We listen to music with our muscles,' as Nietzsche wrote. We keep time to music, involuntarily, even if we are not consciously attending to it, and our faces and postures mirror the 'narrative' of the melody and the thoughts and feelings it provokes."

Then Dr. Sacks moves on to how our knowledge of the healing powers of music can be used to help those very patients he worked with for so many years. "William James referred to our 'susceptibility to music,' and while music can affect all of us – calm us, animate us, comfort us, thrill us, or serve to organize and synchronize us at work or play – it may be especially powerful and have great therapeutic potential for patients with a variety of neurological conditions. Such people may respond powerfully and specifically to music (and, sometimes, to little else). Some of these patients have wide-spread cortical problems, whether from strokes or Alzheimer's or other causes of dementia; others have specific cortical syndromes – loss of language or movement functions, amnesias, or frontal-lobe syndromes. Some are retarded, some autistic; others have subcortical syndromes such as parkinsonism or other movement disorders. All of these conditions and many others can potentially respond to music and music therapy."

I'll close this section on the work of Dr. Oliver Sacks, and preview the next section on how we take advantage of our new-found knowledge of the power of music, with a few final words from Sacks: "There was virtually no neuroscience of music prior to the 1980s. This has all changed in the last few decades with new technologies that allow us to see the living brain as people listen to, imagine, and even compose music. There is now an enormous and rapidly growing body of work on the neural underpinnings of musical perception and imagery, and the complex and often bizarre disorders to which these are prone. These new insights of neuroscience are exciting beyond measure."

51

THERE'S AN ORGANIZATION FOR THAT!

There is a group I came across recently called *Music & Memory*. It was founded in 2010 as a non-profit organization that brings personalized music into the lives of people with cognitive or physical challenges through digital music technology, vastly improving their quality of life. According to its website (www.musicandmemory.org), they currently serve over 3,000 assorted care facilities across the U.S., Canada, and a few other countries. Eleven states have integrated their work into public policy and are funding research based on the group's work.

The organization's web site provides videos and case histories about their outstanding work. Here are a couple of excerpts about their work and philosophy:

"What Music Means To Us: To feel like ourselves, to feel connected to life, to our memories, and to others – music has the ability to do all these things. This is especially valuable to our identity as we age and feel isolated from the rest of the world. Music has a neurological connection for us as well. Music can help us remember how to relax, how to keep going and carries with it happy memories of loved ones and hope. With personalized music, patients can have some of their most powerful nostalgic moments back in their lives with a simple click."

In 2012, a video on *YouTube* went viral for a solid week with the story of **Henry and his iPod** transformation after ten years in a nursing home. It plays like a scene straight out of *"Awakenings"* but as Music & Memory's Executive Director, Dan Cohen, states to surprised viewers, this is real, backed by science and research and sometimes the practical observations by nursing home staff that have quietly gone under the radar before recent discovery by *Gizmodo*, *Gawker*, *Facebook*, and *Twitter* as well as *YouTube*. As an added bonus to their neurological improvement, project staffers find elderly patients become more sociable with each other, like teenagers sharing their favorite music, and the elderly themselves report a lift in mood and richer daily experience at having something precious from their past returned to them.

What got all those social media watchers excited was further exemplified by a story told by music therapist John Abel as he shares a resident's favorite music and memories event: "A patient named Roberta was

silent. Locked in her dementia, seemingly unaware of her surroundings, she would sit and stare at the walls of her nursing home room for hours on end. When John first met Roberta, shortly after he joined the staff of A.G. Rhodes Health & Rehab in Atlanta, he thought music might make a difference. And he was right. When Roberta listened to John play the guitar and lead a group in song, after about 45 minutes, she began to respond with a word or even a phrase. But after a while, she became less and less responsive.

"The music therapy group stopped having an impact," says John. But after an A.G. Rhodes board member saw the documentary film *Alive Inside* at the 2014 Sundance Film Festival, she came back determined to bring MUSIC & MEMORY to the company's three Atlanta facilities. John thought Roberta would be a good candidate for the personalized music program.

"Now, with Music & Memory, I'll put the headphones on her and within two hours she's back at the level she had originally been in music therapy," says John. "The best part, however, is giving her access to her favorite songs. An octogenarian, Roberta still loves **The Grateful Dead!** A staff member who had set up a playlist for Roberta of her favorite songs commented, 'She was the most verbal I'd ever heard, speaking in complete sentences.'"

The ongoing research and evaluation of *Music & Memory's* work in care organizations seem to show consistent results:

- Participants are happier and more social.
- Relationships among staff, participants and family deepen.
- Everyone benefits from a calmer, more supportive social environment.
- Staff regain valuable time previously lost to behavior management issues.
- There is growing evidence that a personalized music program gives professionals one more tool in their effort to reduce reliance on anti-psychotic medications.

Another nonprofit organization affiliated with Music & Memory is the **Alive Inside Foundation** (www.aliveinside.org), also based in New York, taking its name from the award-winning film *Alive Inside*. While it does not provide assistance in nursing homes, it provides the tools to allow schools, teachers and teenage students to do similar work using music with seniors in an at-home environment. **Michael Rossato-Bennett** is the director of the *"Alive Inside"* documentary and has created this new nonprofit to expand the concept of using nostalgic music for elderly patients living *outside* of nursing homes. Rossato-Bennett lays out his foundation's mission in these words: "Seeing how music affects people with dementia changed my life. It showed me how phenomenally alive the emotional systems of people with Alzheimer's are. Music conveys meaning that cannot be expressed in words, and for someone who has dementia, it reignites the pathways of emotions, movement, and memories."

He goes on to explain how America's teenagers could be part of the solution. "We have an empathy deficit in our culture. Young people are being raised through technology and we don't seem to need each other in the way we used to. Yet I've found that when young people connect with the elderly using music, it's a phenomenal teaching moment. It's transformative. I invented headsets that are light, fit on an elder's head, and are wired so two people can listen at the same time. It's my dream to have a million kids give a million elders these headsets. It's cheap and it creates human connection."

THE IMPORTANT FIELD OF MUSIC THERAPY

I must admit that these two organizations have some "gee-whiz" kinds of results to show for their ground-breaking work. But I certainly don't want to overlook the more than 5,000 trained and certified individuals who work in the clinical field of **music therapy.**

According to the **American Music Therapy Association (AMTA)**, the idea of music as a healing influence which could affect health and behavior is as least as old as the writings of Aristotle and Plato. The 20th-century discipline began after World War I and World War II when community musicians of all types, both amateur and professional, went to Veterans hospitals around the country to play for the thousands of veterans suffering both physical and emotional trauma from the wars.

The patients' notable physical and emotional responses to music led the doctors and nurses to request the hiring of musicians by the hospitals. It was soon evident that the hospital musicians needed some prior training before entering the facility, and so the demand grew for a college curriculum. The first music therapy degree program in the world, founded at **Michigan State University** in 1944, celebrated its 70th anniversary in 2014.

The AMTA describes music therapy as "The clinical and evidence-based use of music interventions to accomplish individualized goals within a therapeutic relationship by a credentialed professional who has completed an approved music therapy program. Music therapists assess emotional well-being, physical health, social functioning, communication abilities, and cognitive skills through musical responses; design music sessions for individuals and groups based on client needs using music improvisation, receptive music listening, song writing, lyric discussion, music and imagery, music performance, and learning through music; participate in interdisciplinary treatment planning, ongoing evaluation, and follow up."

Music Therapist-Board Certified (MT-BC) is the credential required to ethically practice as a music therapist. Once coursework and clinical training are completed, potential music therapists are eligible to take the national examination administered by the Certification Board for Music Therapists (CBMT). After successful completion of the examination, graduates are issued the credential necessary for professional practice, (MT-BC). To maintain this credential, music therapists must demonstrate continued competence by completing 100 recertification credits or retaking and passing the CBMT examination within each five-year recertification cycle. There are some universities in the U.S. that even offer a doctorate in music therapy.

THE MOZART EFFECT?

In the fascinating book *"The Mozart Effect"* by Don Campbell that I referenced earlier, he focuses on the effect that the music of Wolfgang Amadeus Mozart has on people. Campbell describes the young composer as follows: "A gifted performer from the age of four, Mozart was one of the most famous child prodigies in history. Like young Jesus, who amazed the elders in the temple, young Wolfgang astonished the royal heads of Europe; and musicians, composers, and audiences everywhere applauded his youthful brilliance and virtuosity. He first composed a minuet and trio for the keyboard when he was six years old, and his last piece came 626 major compositions later. By the time he was twelve, he was writing constantly, creating during his career seventeen operas, forty-one symphonies, twenty-seven piano concertos, dozens of piano sonatas, and music for organ, clarinet, and other instruments. He could imagine one piece as he wrote down another; he seemed to see a whole composition before he committed it to paper.

In a letter to his father, he explained, 'Everything has been composed but not yet written down'." [**Author's Note**: That reminds me of the time **Jim Clancy** told the VM that they had better sing his new arrangement REALLY well because he had *already heard them singing it* while he was arranging it (in his East Texas drawl) *"in mah hayed"* (in my head). *It appears that Jim and Wolfgang could both do those mind games while composing.*]

According to Campbell, a "by-product of this book's worldwide popularity is that much creative and heretofore unknown research supporting the Mozart Effect theory has come to the public's attention. The naïve assumption that music – any music – somehow makes us smarter has been replaced by the more sophisticated understanding and acceptance of music's powerful effect on multiple levels of neurological and physical responses. Classrooms, hospitals, and homes are being utilized as environments in which music can make dynamic changes in emotional, physical, and mental atmospheres. Teachers and health professionals alike are adapting the suggestions in this book for use in their own environments; researchers have been motivated to look at new ways in which the ear can be stimulated and educated."

He continues, "Recently, the Journal of the Royal Society of Medicine in Great Britain published an important paper on the Mozart Effect, which reported that it appears Mozart's music affects the electrical impulses in the brain. Twenty-three out of twenty-nine patients with severe epilepsy showed reduced epileptic activity while listening to Mozart's music. And many other studies in health and education are currently looking at the importance of auditory stimulation and how it affects multiple systems in the body."

HOW MUSIC AFFECTS OUR BRAINS AND EMOTIONS

Many years ago, for my birthday, Susan bought us tickets to a concert performance of *Yanni* (real name Yianna's Chrysalis), the Greek composer, keyboardist, and music producer. Yanni popularized the combination of electronic music synthesizers with a full-scale symphony orchestra. He has employed musicians of various nationalities and has incorporated a variety of exotic instruments to create music that has been called an eclectic fusion of ethnic sounds. We had seen his performances on our Public Television station and wanted to see him live. The concert event was an extremely emotional experience for me. His music was so enriching for me that I had to fight my urge to tear up during certain passages of his music.

"He Stopped Loving Her Today", the 1980 hit song by George Jones still brings tears to my eyes. It's been named in several surveys as the greatest country song of all time. *"He stopped loving her today / They placed a wreath upon his door / And soon they'll carry him away / He stopped loving her today"*. How could you get any more emotion in a brief song verse than that? Many of the arrangements that Jim Clancy has written for The Vocal Majority can also bring a tear to the eye and make the hair on your arms and neck stand up. Try the key modulation in his arrangement of *"You Raise Me Up"* and see if you don't notice a jarring

emotional experience. The same can be said for any number of Jim's ballad arrangements, which sets him apart from almost any other choral arranger in the world. I'll get into that phenomenon and others in the second half of this book when we explore why The Vocal Majority has grown to be considered one of the premier choral groups in the world – primarily on the strength of Clancy's arrangements and commitment to excellence.

Robert Jourdain, in his insightful book ***Music, The Brain, And Ecstasy***, writes, "Many people say that it is beauty alone that draws them to music. But great music brings us even more. By providing the brain

 with an artificial environment, and forcing it through that environment in controlled ways, music imparts the means of experiencing relations far deeper than we encounter in our everyday lives. . . . It's for this reason that music can be transcendent. For a few moments, it makes us larger than we really are, and the world more orderly than it really is. We respond not just to the beauty of the sustained deep relations that are revealed, but also to the fact of our perceiving them. As our brains are thrown into overdrive, we feel our very existence expand and realize that we can be more than we normally are and that the world is more than it seems. That is cause enough for ecstasy."

Jourdain goes on to explain how us humans experience music in our brains. "One reason we hear music when animals don't is that our brains are able to manipulate patterns of sound far more complex than the brain of any other animal can manage. We model patterns upon patterns upon patterns – right up to a movement of a symphony. Successive tones are linked to form melodic fragments, and then whole melodies, and then phrases, and then long passages. Simultaneous tones are integrated into intervals, intervals into chords, and chords into harmonic progressions. Patterns of accentuation are charted as rhythms. Shifts in intensity meld into crescendos and decrescendos. As our brains encode these relations, the sensations of sound arise."

He then says, "Although we say that someone has 'a good ear for music,' credit actually goes to a good *mind* for music – a mind that can hear simultaneous melodies, simultaneous rhythms, even simultaneous harmonies. Only the most basic mechanisms for recognizing individual sounds are 'hard-wired' into our nervous systems. Every other aspect of listening is partly or entirely conditioned by learning. . . . We are all to varying degrees deaf to some genres of music, particularly those of remote cultures."

In his chapter on Melody, Jourdain writes, "It is a curious fact that you can file a copyright on a melody, that you can own a particular pattern of sound. You'd meet with only laughter if you requested a copyright on a rhythmic pattern or a harmonic progression. Such things are considered too basic to warrant copyright protection. But melodies are different. Each is a unique invention in sound, a clever machine that tilts and turns the levers of our minds to produce a quintessential sensation. As is true of so many clever inventions, the workings of a great melody are inexplicably simple yet not at all obvious."

He concludes, "A great melody is magic – magic for its sheer power, and magic because somehow a brain has unearthed it from amidst zillions of possible other melodies. Thousands of new melodies are offered to the listening public every year, yet only a few strike our fancy. When a really good melody emerges, one that digs deep and just won't let go, we celebrate the event by listening to it over and over."

Chapter 5
ALGORITHMS AND DIGITAL MUSIC

"The bounds of algorithms get pushed further each day. They've displaced humans in a growing number of industries, something they often do well. They're faster than us, they're cheaper than us, and, when things work as they should, they make far fewer mistakes than we do. But as algorithms acquire power and independence, there can be unexpected consequences. Perhaps Pandora, the Internet radio outlet that uses algorithms to learn users' musical tastes, is aptly named. According to Greek mythology, Pandora, the first woman on earth, was given a beautiful box that Zeus warned her not to open. She opened it anyway, releasing evil across the planet. Only one thing remained inside: hope."

From the book "Automate This" by Chris Steiner

You may have heard about IBM's attempt to create Beethoven-quality music from scratch using their super computer *Watson*? Well, as you might have read or heard, in 2011 it defeated two human competitors

on "Jeopardy," proving it could out-think people. But can it match humans' creativity?

At the time I was working on this book, I happened to be watching CBS-TV News. My eye caught a report by CBS News correspondent Manuel Bojorquez showing that Watson's next frontier is the universal language of music. It is listening, then writing an original song tailored to a specific mood. "So it listens to this piece and it deconstructs this piece of music, learns from it, and gets inspired by it," explained computer scientist Janani Mukundan, who built the Watson Beat program at IBM's Austin, Texas, campus. "And then it adds on top of it, the layer of emotion that you want it to portray." Musician Richard Daskas is teaching Watson to convey emotions by training it to recognize human patterns. Happy or upbeat songs are more likely to be based on major chords. Sad songs are typically expressed in a minor key.

There are some limitations, and Daskas admits, "To some degree . . . we can only take it so far." But he said the technology is revolutionary. Music has been moving into the digital age for decades. Technology has created more efficient recording methods and spawned an entire genre of computer-generated beats. But Watson's songs are the first digital works based on mood and, according to Watson's chief technology officer, could even outdo humans. Researchers hope anyone will be able to use Watson Beat just by opening an app. "Watson Beat is not constrained by normal human biases, and those biases can actually get in our way," said Rob High, another IBM computer whiz.

But in Austin, the self-proclaimed live music capital of the world, bias is the basis for just about every piece of music you hear. Musicians believe computers cannot replace humans as composers and creators of music. "Nothing's going to replace humans and our human creativity," High said. "But certainly we can be augmented."

Watson is learning to process massive amounts of data – medical compounds, legal briefs, even recipes – faster than the human brain. But its new grasp on human emotions in music could be a breakthrough in the race to perfect artificial intelligence. "The new realm of artificial intelligence is all about teaching computers to be creative", Mukundan said. *"And music is the most creative language that everyone can understand."* (Italics added by the Author.)

COMPUTER COMPOSERS: CHANGING HOW MUSIC IS MADE

I came across an article in doing research for this section of the book that asked the question, *"Could Artificial Intelligence (AI) render human composers obsolete, or will it usher in a new era of creativity in music creation?"* The article was written by **Richard Moss** in a 2015 online newsletter *NEW ATLAS*. Here's a sample of what he discussed.

"You've probably heard music composed by a computer algorithm, though you may not realize it. Artificial intelligence researchers have made huge gains in computational – or algorithmic – creativity over the past decade or two, and now these advances are filtering through to the real world. AI programs have produced albums in multiple genres. They've scored films and advertisements. And they've also generated mood music in games and smartphone apps. But what does computer-authored music sound like? Why do it? And how is it changing music creation?

"Semi-retired University of California Santa Cruz professor David Cope has been exploring the intersection of algorithms and creativity for over half a century, first on paper and then with computers. 'It seemed even in my early teenage years it was perfectly logical to do creative things with algorithms rather than spend all the time writing out each note or paint this or write out this short story or develop this timeline word by word by word,' Cope tells *Gizmag*. [**Author's Note**: *Gizmag* is now called *New Atlas*, and continues to be a magazine that keeps readers up to date with the rise of technology and its impact on our daily lives.]

Moss goes on to say, "Cope came to specialize in what he terms algorithmic composition. He writes sets of instructions that enable computers to automatically generate complete orchestral compositions of any length in a matter of minutes using a kind of formal grammar and lexicon that he's spent decades refining.

"His experiments in musical intelligence began in 1981 as the result of a composer's block in his more traditional music composition efforts, and he has since written around a dozen books and numerous journal articles on the subject. His algorithms have produced classical music ranging from single-instrument arrangements all the way up to full symphonies by modeling the styles of great composers like Bach and Mozart, and they have at times fooled people into believing that the works were written by human composers.

"For Cope, one of the core benefits of AI composition is that it allows composers to experiment far more efficiently. Composers who lived prior to the advent of the personal computer, he says, had certain practicalities that limited them, namely that it might take months of work to turn an idea into a composition. If a piece is not in the composer's usual style, the risk that this composition may be terrible increases, because it

63

will not be built on the techniques that they've used before and know will generally work. 'With algorithms, we can experiment in those ways to produce that piece in 15 minutes and we can know *immediately* whether it's going to work or not,' Cope explains.

"Algorithms that produce creative work have a significant benefit, then, in terms of time, energy, and money, as they reduce the wasted effort on failed ideas.

"Tools such as **Liquid Notes, Quartet Generator, Easy Music Composer**, and **Maestro Genesis** are liberating to open-minded composers. They generate the musical equivalent of sentences and paragraphs with consummate ease, their benefit being that they do the hard part of translating an abstract idea or intention into notes, melodies, and harmonies.

Continuing with the article by Moss, "Those with coding talent have it even better: Algorithms that a programmer can write in minutes could test any hypotheses a composer might have about a particular musical technique and produce virtual instrument sounds in dozens or hundreds of variations that give them a strong idea of how it works in practice. And Cope argues that all of this makes possible 'an arena of creativity that could not have been imagined by someone even 50 years ago.'

"The compositions that computers create don't necessarily need any editing or polishing from humans. Some, such as those found in the album *0music*, are fit to stand alone. *0music* was composed by **Melomics109**, which is one of two music-focused AIs (artificial intelligence programs) created by researchers at the University of Malaga. The other (program), which was introduced in 2010, three years before Melomics109, is **Iamus**. Both use a strategy modeled on biology to learn and evolve ever-better and more complex mechanisms for composing music. They began with very simple compositions and are now moving towards professional-caliber pieces.

"'Before **Iamus**, most of the attempts to create music were oriented to mimic previous composers, by providing the computer with a set of scores/MIDI files,' says lead researcher and Melomics founder **Francisco Javier Vico**. '**Iamus** was new in that it developed its own original style, creating its work from scratch, not mimicking any author.'

64

"It came as quite a shock, **Vico** notes. **Iamus** was alternately hailed as the 21st century's answer to Mozart and the producer of superficial, unmemorable, dry material devoid of soul. For many, though, it was seen as a sign that computers are rapidly catching up to humans in their capacity to write music.

Moss continues his article: "There's no reason to fear this progress, those in the field say. AI-composed music will not put professional composers, songwriters, or musicians out of business. Cope states the situation simply: 'We have composers that are human and we have composers that are not human.' He also notes that there's a human element in the non-human composers – the data being crunched to make the composition possible is chosen by humans if not created by them, and, deep learning aside, algorithms are written by humans.

"Cope finds fears of computational creativity frustrating, as they belie humanity's arrogance. 'We could do amazing things if we'd just give up a little bit of our ego and attempt to not pit us against our own creations – our own computers – but embrace the two of us together and in one way or another continue to grow,' he says.

"Vico makes a similar point. He compares the situation to the democratization of photography that has occurred in the last 15-20 years with the rise of digital cameras, easy-to-use editing software, and sharing over the Internet. 'Computer-composers and browsing/editing tools can make a musician out of anyone with a good ear and sensibility,' he says.

"Perhaps more exciting, though, is the potential of computer-generated, algorithmically-composed music to work in real time. **Impromptu** and various other audio plugins and tools help VJs and other performers to "live code" their performances, while **OMax** learns a musician's style and effectively improvises an accompaniment, always adapting to what's happening in the sound.

"In the world of video games, real-time computer-generated music is a boon because its adaptability suits the unpredictable nature of play. Many games dynamically re-sequence their soundtracks or adjust the tempo and add or remove instrument layers as players come across enemies or move into different parts of the story or environment. A small few – including, most notably, *Spore* from *SimCity* and **The Sims** developer *Maxis* – use algorithmic music techniques to orchestrate players' adventures.

Again, quoting Moss: "The composer Daniel Brown went a step further with this idea in 2012 with the **Mezzo** AI, which composes soundtracks in real time in a neo-Romantic style based on what characters in the game are doing and experiencing.

"Other software applications can benefit from this sort of approach, too. There are apps emerging such as **Melomics' @life** that can compose personalized mood music on the fly. They learn from your behavior, react to your location, or respond to your physiological state.

"'We have tested **Melomics** apps in pain perception with astonishing results,' Vico says. He explains that music tuned to a particular situation can reduce pain, or the probability of feeling pain, by distracting patients. And apps are currently being tested that use computer-generated music to help with sleep disorders and anxiety.

"'I would not try to sleep with Beethoven's 5th symphony (even if I love it), but a piece that captures your attention and slows down as you fall asleep – that works,' Vico says. 'We'll see completely new areas of music when sentient devices (like smartphones) control music delivery.'"

I hope you stayed with me during that long article. I'm certainly no computer geek, but research using a computer and the Internet is a part of my DNA due to my academic teaching discipline in human communication studies. [**Author's Note**: You don't have to be a computer geek these days to do some creative things with recordings. For example, I bought some cheap computer software at **Best Buy** several years ago and edited a collection of live songs performed by my band, the **Folkel Minority**, from very old analog audio cassettes and reel-to-reel monaural tapes and turned them into a double CD with digital surround sound – all crafted on my home computer.] So, when you combine my fascination

66

with research and my love for music, algorithms have recently become one of my favorite topics. I think you'll find them fascinating too as we explore how algorithms are something you need to be aware of if you're a lover of music – especially a *listener* of music.

The fascinating book, *"Automate This: How Algorithms Took Over Our Markets, Our Jobs, and The World"*, by Christopher Steiner is a good introduction to our topic at hand. I'll let him introduce you to the subject from his chapter titled, "Algorithms And Music":

"One of the more unlikely areas for an algorithm invasion is music. To many, music reflects the beating creativity of the human soul. We can have difficulty describing how exactly music affects us, changes our moods, and alters our consciousness. Those who make music can barely explain how inspiration strikes. Creativity is thought of as something so intangible that it can hardly be taught, let alone left for a machine to carry out.

"But there now exist algorithms, including one with a human name – Annie – that can produce music as daring and original as the works of masters like Brahms, Bach, and Mozart, and as popular and catchy as the tunes played inside a big-box store.

"Musician and writer Ben Novak from Aukland, New Zealand, was listening to a short BBC report on technology developed in Spain that, the person being profiled claimed, could predict which songs would turn into pop hits. That was 2004. Once he got home, Novak brought up the Web site belonging to what was then called Polyphonic HMI. For fifty dollars, its algorithm would analyze any music file Novak uploaded. Potential hits earned high scores, duds got low ones.

"Novak had written a song a few years before called *'Turn Your Car Around'* that he believed held significant potential. He uploaded the song and sat at his screen, waiting for a result. Finally, the Web site whirred to life with an answer for Novak. The algorithm behind the site used a number scale to rate songs. Anything more than 6.5 had decent hit potential. Anything past 7 had a "hook" made for the pop charts. Novak's song scored a 7.57 – as high as the algorithm had scored many of the biggest rock hits of all time, such as *'Born To Be Wild'* by Steppenwolf and *'Peaceful Easy Feeling'* by the Eagles.

"Long story short . . . About two weeks after he submitted his song on the Polyphonic Web site, Novak's phone rang. It was a representative for Ash Howes, a music producer in the United Kingdom. Novak quickly agreed to a favorable deal: he would get 50 percent of all royalties when the song was played on the radio, on TV, or in an advertisement. The song debuted at No. 12 on the English pop charts, and in Italy, the song ascended to No. 2.

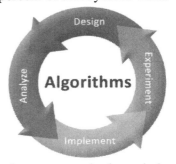

"The algorithms behind Polyphonic work a wondrous dissection on the music they're fed. The particular science behind the company's algorithms is called *advanced spectral deconvolution*. It breaks songs up, isolating tunes' patterns of melody, beat tempo, rhythm, pitch, chord progression, fullness of sound, sonic brilliance, and cadence. The hits tend to be grouped in clusters that reveal their similar underlying structures. The algorithm then compares the song to hits of the past in as objective a way as is possible.

"When he was in Barcelona, Spain, perfecting the algorithm, the head of Polyphonic ran as many to-be-released albums through his algorithm bot as possible. The algorithm rated most of the unreleased CDs as ho-hum. But one, the algorithm said, contained nine likely hits out of fourteen total songs. *Those are Beatles results!* Polyphonic could hardly believe it. Nobody had heard of this artist, which made company executives worry that the bot was wildly wrong. But then the album, *Come Away With Me*, was released and netted its artist, Norah Jones, eight Grammy Awards. Jones had found the clusters.

"In 2005, a competing company to Polyphonic used more algorithms and fewer humans to decide what people should hear, raised a little money, and changed its name to Pandora. By July 2011, the company was trading on the New York Stock Exchange, valued at $3 billion. But there's no denying that the folks at Polyphonic had created something that worked, something that could shape the future of the music industry."

Steiner's book was published in 2012. *Can you imagine how sophisticated those types of algorithms have become since then?*

LISTENING TO MUSIC COULD PUT YOU ON A CLOUD

Over the past several years when I've attended technology-oriented academic conferences, I've started to hear the term "cloud technology" a lot. I've come to learn that the *cloud* they're referring to is a type of Internet-based computing that provides shared computer processing resources and data to computers and other devices on demand. It's like a utility (like the electricity grid) over an electricity network. Nowadays I can envision millions of computer servers located throughout the world where individuals like me – and corporations everywhere – can put their "stuff" so that it doesn't clog up your computer, tablet or smartphone. That's what the cloud means to me.

A 2016 book that covers a LOT of subjects that may be of interest to you is ***"The Inevitable: Understanding the 12 Technological Forces That Will Shape Our Future"*** by **Kevin Kelly**. He speaks at length about how the music industry has been impacted by *cloud computing*, and how you and I are the beneficiaries of all this technology in the following paragraphs.

"The first industry to be steamrolled by the switch to real time and the cloud . . . was music. Perhaps because music itself is so flowing—a stream of notes whose beauty lasts only as long as the stream continues—it was the first to undergo liquidity. As the music industry reluctantly transformed, it revealed a pattern of change that would repeat itself again and again in other media, of books, movies, games, news. Later, the same transformation from fixities to flows began to overturn shopping, transportation, and education. This inevitable shift toward Music has been altered by technology for more than a century.

Kelly goes on to say, "Early gramophone equipment could make recordings that contained no more than four and a half minutes, so musicians abbreviated meandering works to fit the phonograph, and today the standard duration of a pop song is four and a half minutes. Cheap industrial reproduction of gramophone recordings 50 years ago unleashed mind-boggling quantities of inexpensive exact copies—and a sense that music was something one consumed. The grand upset that music is now experiencing—the transformation that pioneers such as **Napster** and **BitTorrent** signaled a decade ago—is the shift from analog copies to digital copies.

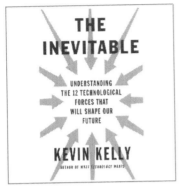

"The industrial age was driven by analog copies—exact and cheap. The information age (today) is driven by digital copies—exact and free. Free is hard to ignore. It propels duplication at a scale that would previously have been unbelievable. The top ten music videos have been watched (for free) over *10 billion times*. Of course, it's not just music that is being copied freely. It is text, pictures, video, games, entire websites, enterprise software, 3-D printer files. In this new online world, anything that can be copied will be copied for free.

"Before liquidity, music was staid. Our choice as music fans 30 years ago was limited. You could listen to the set sequence of songs the DJs chose to play on a handful of radio stations, or you could buy an album and listen to the music in the order the songs were laid on the disk. Or you could purchase a musical instrument and hunt for a favorite piece's sheet music in obscure shops. That was about it. Liquidity offered new powers. Forget the tyranny of the radio DJ. With liquid music, you had the power to reorder the sequence of tunes on an album or among albums. You could shorten a song or draw it out so that it took twice as long to play. You could extract a sample of notes from someone else's song to use yourself. Or you could substitute lyrics in the audio. You could reengineer a piece so that it sounded better on a car woofer (speaker). You could—as someone later did—take two thousand versions of the same song and create a chorus from it.

Author Kelly continues: "At least 30 music streaming services, far more refined than the original **Napster**, now provide listeners a spectrum of ways to play with the unconfined elements of music. My favorite of these is Spotify because it encapsulates many of the possibilities that a fluid service can provide. Spotify is a cloud containing *30 million tracks* *of music.* I can search that ocean of music to locate the most specific, weirdest, most esoteric song possible. While it plays I click a button and find the song's lyrics displayed. It will make a virtual personal radio station for me from a small selection of my favorite music. I can tweak the station's playlist by skipping songs or downvoting ones I don't want to hear again. This degree of interacting with music would have astounded fans a generation ago.

Kelly gives us an interesting example: "What I'd really like to listen to is the cool music my friend Chris listens to because he's much more serious about his music discovery than I am. I'd like to share his playlist, which I can subscribe to—meaning that I am actually listening to the music on his playlist, or even to the songs that Chris is listening to right now, in real time. If I really enjoy a particular song I hear on his list—say, an old Bob Dylan basement tape I never heard before—I can copy it onto my own playlist, which I can then share with my friends.

"Naturally, this streaming service is free. If I don't want to see or hear the visual and audio ads Spotify displays to pay the artists, I can pay a monthly premium. In the paid version, I can download the digital files to my computer and I can start to remix tracks if I want to. Since it is the age of flowing, I can reach my playlists and personal radio stations from any device, including my phone, or direct the stream into my living room or kitchen speakers.

"A bunch of other streaming services, such as **SoundCloud**, operate more like an audio **YouTube**, encouraging its 250 million fans to upload their own music en masse. Compare this splendid liquidity of options with the few fixed choices available to me just decades ago. No wonder the fans stampeded to the "free" despite the music industry's threat to arrest them. Where might this go?

Kelly continues, "In the U.S. at this time, 27 percent of music sales are from the streaming mode, and this mode is equal to the sales of bigger artists because there are still major holdouts, artists like **Taylor Swift**, who are fighting against streaming. But as the head of the largest music label in the world admitted, the streaming takeover 'is inevitable.' With flowing streams, music goes from being a noun to a verb once again. Liquidity brings a new ease in creation. Fungible forms of music encourage amateurs to create their own song and upload it. To invent new formats.

"New tools, available for free, distributed online, allow music fans to remix tracks, sample sounds, study lyrics, lay down beats with synthetic instruments. Nonprofessionals start making music the same way writers craft a book—by rearranging found elements (words for writers, chords for musicians) into their own point of view. The superconductivity of digital bits serves as a lubricant to unleash music's untapped options. Music is flowing at digital frequencies into vast new territories.

"Pre-digital, music occupied a few niches. Music either came on vinyl, it was played on the radio, was heard at concerts, and in a couple hundred films made each year. Post-digital, music is seeping into the rest of our lives, attempting to occupy our entire waking life. Stuffed into the cloud, music rains on us through our earbuds while we exercise, while we are vacationing in Rome, while we wait in line at the DMV.

"The niches for music have exploded. A renaissance of thousands of documentaries per year demands a soundtrack for each one them. Feature films consume vast quantities of original scores, including thousands of pop songs. Even **YouTube** creators understand the emotional uplift gained by a soundtrack for their short spots; while most YouTubers recycle prior art without pay, a growing minority see the value in creating custom music. Then there are the hundreds of hours of music required for each big video game. Tens of thousands of commercials need memorable jingles.

"The latest fashionable media is a podcast, a sort of audible documentary. *At least 27 new podcasts launch every day.* No decent podcast is without a theme song and, more often, musical scoring for its long-form content. Our entire life is getting a musical soundtrack. All these venues are growth markets, expanding as rapidly as the flows of bits. Social media were once the domain of texts. The next generation of social media is conducting video and sound. Apps like **WeChat, WhatsApp, Vine, Meerkat, Periscope**, and many others enable you to share video and audio—in real time—with your network of friends and friends of friends. The tools for quickly making a tune, altering a song, or algorithmically generating music that you share in real time are not far away. Custom music streams, it expands.

Kelly gives us a glimpse into the future: "Here is what a day in the near future looks like. I tap into the cloud to enter the library containing all music, movies, books, VR worlds, and games. I choose music. In addition to songs, I can get parts of the songs as small as a chord. A song's assets are divvied up one channel at a time, which means I can get just the bass or drum track, or just the voices. Or the song with no voices—perfect for karaoke. Tools allow me to stretch or shrink the duration of a song without changing its pitch and melody. Professional tools let me swap instruments in the song I found. One of my favorite musicians releases alternative versions of her songs (for extra cost) and even offers a historical log of every version during its creation.

"The movies, music, books, and games that you access all live on clouds. A cloud is a colony of millions of computers that are braided together seamlessly to act as a single large computer. The bulk of what you do on the web and phone today is done on cloud computing. Though invisible, clouds run our digital lives. A cloud is more powerful than a traditional supercomputer because its core is dynamically distributed. That means that its memory and work is spread across many chips in a massively redundant way.

"Let's say you were streaming a long movie and suddenly an asteroid smashed one tenth of the machines that made up the cloud. You might not notice any interruption in the movie because the movie file did not reside in any particular machine but was distributed in a redundant pattern across many processors in such a way that the cloud can reconfigure itself if any of those units fail. It's almost like organic healing. The web is hyperlinked documents; the cloud is hyperlinked data. Ultimately the chief reason to put things onto the cloud is to share their data deeply. Woven together, the bits are made much smarter and more powerful than they could possibly be alone.

Kelly explains what cloud computing is all about: "There is no single architecture for clouds, so their traits are still rapidly evolving. But in general, they are huge. They are so large that the substrate of one cloud can encompass multiple football field–size warehouses full of computers located in scores of cities thousands of miles apart. Clouds are also elastic, meaning they can be enlarged or shrunk almost in real time by adding or dropping computers to their network. And because of their inherent redundant and distributed nature, clouds are among the most reliable machines in existence. They can provide the famous five nines (99.999 percent) of near perfect service performance.

"A central advantage of a cloud is that the bigger it gets, the smaller and thinner our devices can be. The cloud does all the work, while the device we hold is just the window into the cloud's work. When I look into my phone screen and see a live video stream, I am looking into the cloud. When I flick through book pages on my tablet, I am surfing the cloud. When the face of my smartwatch lights up with a message, it is coming from the cloud. When I flip open my Cloudbook laptop, everything that I work on is actually somewhere else, in a cloud."

Is there any money to be made when, according to Mr. Kelly, almost all music and video is free? Well, I just happened to receive my latest issue of *Forbes Magazine* (June 2017) and a big article in that issue talks about the millions of dollars musical artists and celebrities are making these days on streaming media. In the article by Zach O'Malley Greenburg, he notes that "Five years ago, Spotify was a fledgling music-streaming service only months removed from its U.S. launch and YouTube had just started its push into original programming. Netflix was a year away from doing the same, starting with House of Cards. For members of the Celebrity 100 – our annual accounting of the top-earning entertainers on the planet – meaningful streaming income was a distant dream.

"But sometimes profound change happens quickly. Streaming is now the dominant platform for music consumption and it's growing rapidly – up 76% year-over-year, according to Nielsen.

"'It's not just about music – it's about every form of entertainment,' Nielsen's David Bakula says. 'You don't really have to own anything anymore because for $10 a month you can do this: You can have *everything*.'

"The members of our list have been fattening their pockets accordingly. Income directly related to streaming surged to $387 million from $177 million. For musicians, the going rate of a little less than a penny on-demand stream may not sound like a lot, but it adds up for the 14 performers on our list who topped 1 billion spins over the past year.

A separate article in the same issue had the headline, *"Music Goes Freemium"*. The article had a sub-headline saying, *"Physical album sales and digital downloads are down. But more people are listening to more music than ever."* The article goes on to explain that the pop artist **Abel "The Weekend" Tesfaye** stunned everyone with a live performance of his new single, which premiered on Apple Music and has generated more than 1.5 BILLION spins across all streaming platforms. Again, quoting the article, "Since their Apple appearances, **Drake** (No. 4 on our list at $94 million) and **The Weekend** (No. 6 at $92 million) have clocked a combined *17.5 billion streams.*"

"We live in a world where artists don't really make the money off the music like we did in the Golden Age," says **The Weekend**, who's 27.

Finishing out the Forbes article, "**Chance the Rapper** is a 24-year old who has never sold a physical album or signed a record deal in his life. He has only freely distributed his work via streaming services. He generates enough spins to make several million dollars that way." [**Author's Note**: To prove how inexpensive cloud computing is these days, our Dallas County Community College District now offers each employee a *TERA-BYTE* of space available for them to store their documents and other work-related data. That's awesome to me!]

Finally, I'd like to quote from Mr. Kelly, author of *"The Inevitable"*: *"In Beethoven's day, few people ever heard one of his symphonies more than once. With the advent of cheap audio recordings, a barber in Bombay could listen to them all day long."* To me, that's so cool and democratic in an age where democracy is mostly taken for granted in this country. I'm pretty sure Beethoven would approve.

WHAT MAKES BACH SOUND LIKE BACH?

What if you could teach a computer to write a symphony to mimic the structure and emotion of one that was written by **Johann Sebastian Bach**? A November 2016, article in the University of Washington's newsletter, *UW Today*, says they can now do that.

The article, written by Jennifer Langston, announces a new publicly available dataset from UW researchers called "MusicNet" that labels  each note of 330 classical compositions in ways that can teach machine learning algorithms about the basic structure of music. This collection of classical music recordings has annotated labels that indicate the exact start and stop time of each individual note, what instrument plays the note, and its position in the composition's metrical structure. It includes more than one million individual labels from 34 hours of chamber music performances that can train computer algorithms to deconstruct, understand, predict and reassemble components of classical music.

It seems that Bach left behind an incomplete fugue upon his death, either as an unfinished work or perhaps as a puzzle for future composers to solve. The fact that this classical music dataset released by UW researchers enables algorithms to learn the features of classical music from scratch raises the likelihood that a computer could expertly finish the job.

I'm not sure I want to get into anything more deeply than that about this UW research. But if you do want to dig into this field, you can contact the research team at musicnet@cs.washington.edu. Let me know what you find out – hopefully in language that I might be able to understand.

PART II
The Legacy of
The Vocal Majority Chorus

Chapter 6
THE BIRTH OF CAMELOT IN DALLAS

"Don't let it be forgot
That once there was a spot,
For one brief, shining moment
That was known as Camelot."

From the Broadway Musical "Camelot"

Just after the assassination of **President John F. Kennedy**, it was publicized that the Broadway show recording of *"Camelot"* had been favorite bedtime listening in the White House, and that Kennedy's favorite

lines from that recording were those at the top of this page. In that final number from the show, King Arthur knights a young boy and tells him to pass on the story of Camelot to future generations. In many ways, that's what I'm attempting to do in Part II of this book.

My reason for the Camelot metaphor is that those of us who were present during the first 15-25 years of The Vocal Majority's existence many times discussed the fact that *we have our very own Camelot right here in Dallas, Texas.* We were blessed with so many seemingly serendipitous individual contributors and appearances at so many monumental events that it seemed at times like a performer's magical dream:

77

- Vocal coaches and arrangers who knew how to create a unique, professional sound from over a hundred amateur singers;

- A major media market that gave some excellent exposure to an all-male community choral group during its formative years;

- Collaboration with major show business performers like Jimmy Dean, John Gary, the Four Freshmen, Lee Greenwood, and the world-famous Mormon Tabernacle Choir;

- The opportunity to sing for two United States Presidents on four different occasions;

- Being admired and revered by Barbershop and choral music lovers throughout the world.

It's pretty easy to see why it has fallen to me to be the unofficial – but obvious – historian for this taste of Camelot we've had here in North Texas for the past forty-five years. I was one of the organization's founders, its first incorporated president, and I took on the responsibility for being its marketing director and newsletter publisher during the first twenty-five years. Susan has assisted me in collecting early letters and incorporation papers since we were married 32 years ago, along with newsletters that span most of those years. And it will be my pleasure (a thrill, really!) to re-live those first twenty-five years in the rest of this book.

Any time an author undertakes to write a history of any organization, event or era, you may wonder how much of the author's personal bias goes into the narrative. I must admit that I have inserted quite a LOT of bias into the rest of the book as I lovingly thumb through each newsletter representing several decades of Vocal Majority history. As the historian David Fromkin acknowledged when asked how subjective he was in writing his books, *"Life is a story that each of us tells to his or her self, and it therefore is a tale told by an unreliable narrator."* It might sound smug to say this, but I was surprisingly impressed with the consistently positive, upbeat tone of almost all the *Vocalizers* I unearthed – through both good and bad times in the history of the organization. I hope you can recognize that fact as I summarize the week-in/week-out growth of the VM.

I think this history can also be an instructional tool for those involved in the leadership of any organization that has as its goal to be the best it can possibly be. Not many men or women have the opportunity to be the *best in the world at what they do*. Being a member of The Vocal Majority has given me that opportunity, and I hope it inspires YOU to also explore that goal.

One further warning: You'll notice that a considerable amount of space is devoted to **Guest Singers** at VM rehearsals during the first several years of this history. I've captured those names in hopes that current and past VM members, as well as anyone who ever attended a rehearsal, can see their names in print and can pinpoint when they first started to enjoy their own version of Camelot.

A CAMELOT UPDATE!

[**Author's Note:** *Camelot Is Alive And Well Today!* Susan and I had the good fortune to attend the 2017 VM Spring Show at the **Eisemann Center** in Richardson, and I came away with the satisfaction that the Camelot experience we enjoyed back in those early years was definitely evident on that stage. Most of the 20 songs in the chorus repertoire that Saturday

evening were arranged by Jim Clancy. Both **Jim** and **Greg Clancy** took turns directing Jim's ***America Medley*** (*America The Beautiful* and *God Bless America*), and the two Clancys alternated directing the chorus throughout the evening. That image, in itself, proved to me that the second generation of Camelot was indeed doing very well.

In the early days of the organization, when I was trying to decide in my own mind what kind of a choral group I would personally like us to be, I had a secret ambition that the VM would be the type of group that could do just about *any music genre* really well – folk, pop, semi-classical, patriotic, inspirational, Broadway, and certainly Barbershop. Well, as I looked at the printed program from that Spring 2017 show, I saw that wish come true in black-and-white:

- **Barbershop**: *Harmony, When My Baby Smiles At Me*
- **Folk**: *Oh, Shenandoah, Danny Boy, When Johnny Comes Marching Home*
- **Pop**: *Close To You, Ring of Fire, I Don't Want To Walk Without You, California Dreamin', One Voice, New York New York*
- **Semi-Classical**: *Stouthearted Men, William Tell Overture*
- **Broadway**: *What Kind of Fool Am I*
- **Patriotic**: *America The Beautiful, God Bless America*
- **Inspirational**: *Bless This House, The Lord Bless You and Keep You*

How much more variety could you ask for in an evening's entertainment? Thank you, guys, for keeping your founder's concept alive and well!]

Chapter 7
WHERE THE VM CONCEPT CAME FROM

Without the *Barbershop Harmony Society,* there would be no Vocal Majority Chorus (VM) and no Dallas Metropolitan Chapter (our corporate name). If you're not aware of the history of a cappella music in general – and Barbershop-style music in particular – you really can't appreciate what I'm about to tell you. So, here's a *"Reader's Digest"* version of that history.

AMERICAN BARBERSHOP HARMONY

I uncovered a two-sided page stuffed inside a *Vocalizer* during the 1980s from the **National Archives and Records Administration** in Washington, D.C. with the title you see above. I apparently thought it might be a good idea to give those 1980s VM singers an opportunity to discover how this purely American music art form developed, and I'd like to share this interesting summary with you now by quoting directly from it.

"By the end of the 19th century, a new style of performing popular songs had developed in America – a style that ultimately captured the fancy of the Nation. The new style, which featured four male singers, was

not a formal style of musicmaking and did not require instrumental accompaniment. Indeed, it seemed to be most at home at church socials, in family parlors, in saloons, and even on street corners. It was a style that invited participation, and thousands of amateur warblers joined in. Wherever a few singers who loved to blend their voices together gathered, the musical style flourished.

"The style was so popular that songs were written specifically for these quartets. The *song 'Mister Jefferson Lord, Play That Barbershop Chord'* appeared in 1910. Thereafter, the singers were labeled 'Barbershop quartets'; the musical style, 'Barbershop harmony.' Hundreds of new

'Barbershop songs' were written for close, four-part harmony of Barbershop quartets. The musical structure of these quartets became well established: the lead, or melody line, was sung by the second tenor; the first tenor sang above the melody and the baritone below the melody; and the bass supported the whole by singing the foundation of the chords.

"Part-singing had been enjoyed in America long before the heyday of Barbershop quartets. Before the Revolution, William Billings set up singing schools in New England for the purpose of teaching the principles of group singing. During the early 19th century, church hymnals provided the major source of part-singing, blending both male and female voices. In 1842, one of the most famous family quartets gave its first performance. Known originally as the Aeolian Vocalist, this quartet was made up of Judson, John, Asa and Abby Hutchinson (brothers and sister). The Hutchinsons sang popular ballads and sentimental and dramatic songs. Their voices blended so perfectly that listeners were amazed, and their performances over several decades stimulated interest in and enjoyment of quartet singing.

"In 1843, Dan Emmett, Frank Bower, Dick Pelham, and Billy Whitlock combined their musical talents and organized the first successful minstrel troupe, the 'Virginia Minstrels.' This began a form of entertainment that soon became one of America's favorite forms of amusement. Other minstrel companies were organized, and the size of the cast in some grew to as many as 40 members. Part-singing became a bigger and bigger part of these shows as they traveled throughout the country. In the 1870s and 1880s, quartets began to be featured as a regular part of minstrel programs.

"Barbershop quartets were also a part of the form of popular entertainment known as vaudeville. It is significant that the golden days of American vaudeville – the 1890s to the 1920s – coincided with the most popular era of Barbershop harmony. The most famous Barbershop quartets of the period appeared on the vaudeville stage. And, in keeping with the vaudeville atmosphere, many quartets  were four-man comedy groups. Such 'four-acts,' as they were commonly called, combined Barbershop harmony with slapstick comedy and achieved overwhelming success from coast to coast.

"Near the turn of the 20th century, Barbershop harmony entered the American home by way of the newly established record industry. While the recordings themselves helped increase the popularity of Barbershop harmony, the Barbershop quartets gave recording studios a popular medium to record in their infancy. In 1897 a recording studio named the Universal Phonograph Company was set up in New York City, and the company's first recordings featured a Barbershop quartet and chorus.

"Barbershop harmony reached its peak from 1900 to about 1925; then its popularity began to decline. With prohibition, the term became connected with the raucous, off-key singing associated with an overindulgence of 'bathtub gin.' World War I disrupted all phases of American life as Americans moved from the farms and rural communities to the cities. The automobile and new forms of communication, such as the radio and the movies, brought changing life styles. The "Charleston" became the dance craze, and many Americans went in for the musical stage, which produced the popular songs of the era. Song styles changed, and the new tunes were hard to harmonize. The new, exuberant times were in direct contrast to the slow, homey atmosphere in American that had popularized Barbershop harmony."

In a book titled, *"Barbershopping, Musical and Social Harmony"*, edited by **Max Kaplan** and published in 1995 by Associated University Presses, Inc., we can find the reason behind the initial quirky name of the original singing organization – *The Society for the Preservation and Encouragement of Barber Shop Quartet Singing in America (S.P.E.B.S.Q.S.A).* One of the contributors to this small booklet was **Dean Atlee Snyder**, and he provided an historical perspective for the creation of the organization.

"The decade of the 1930s was the period of the Great Depression, which, in its early years, saw millions unemployed, bread lines and soup kitchens, serious labor unrest, private industry shutdown, bank failures, mortgage foreclosures, and similar misfortune. By 1938 the tide was beginning to turn. But Depression-built government-sponsored economic and employment relief programs were still relied upon by many families. Everyone recognized such initials as NRA, RFC, WPA, CCC, SSA, HOLC, FDIC, and more. Those were the alphabetical agencies of the Federal government – the 'New Deal.'

"For leisure enjoyment, enforced or otherwise, there were radio programs to listen to and movies to attend. There were parks and playgrounds, family picnics, neighborhood parties, amateur sports, and games. For those with dancing feet there were 'big bands.' There was church on Sunday for the faithful. And with changing times ordinary folk were beginning to sing again because there was something to sing about. True, there were war clouds in Europe but America was at peace.

"Out of this increasing mood of optimism came the inspiration of a forty-six-year-old lawyer and a group of his friends in Tulsa, Oklahoma. This man was O. C. Cash. He proposed to revive one of the pleasures of his youth – a pastime which required no equipment except the human voice and the love of four-part harmony. With a humorous twinkle in his eye, lawyer Cash and cofounder Rupert Hall, a banker, sought to out-rival the three and four letter New Deal government agencies by creating a new organization with longer initials – **SPEBSQSA**. Spelled out it was the **'Society for the Preservation and Encouragement of Barber Shop Quartet Singing in America.'**

"The new Society held its first meeting on April 11, 1938, attended by twenty-six men 'for a song-fest on the Roof Garden of the Tulsa Club.' [**Author's Note:** *That date happens to be the* <u>*exact*</u> *date of my birth in Cleveland, Ohio!*]

"The idea of a quartet society to revive "the good old songs" had a certain sparkle and humorous quality. The new name was an instant conversation piece. Aided by publicity in the local press, the national wire services, and by several stories in wide circulation magazines, inquiries came to Cash and his local group almost immediately asking, 'How can I join?'

"The new Society did not have any set plan of organization at first. But as momentum increased, Cash took out formal incorporation papers in late 1938 as a legal entity in order to protect its name. Early membership statistics are fragmentary. By 1941-42 perhaps 2,000 membership cards had been issued for the (then) fifty-five local chapters. The Society is now more than fifty years old (at the time of the booklet's publication). At one time, its membership reached a peak of 38,000 in the U.S. and Canada, with several thousands more in overseas affiliates."

So, with that history behind us, let's move to the 21st Century. With declining membership hovering around 25,000, and the curiosity of  the organization with the longest set of initials just a memory, the Society officially changed its name to the *Barbershop Harmony Society* in 2004. Then in 2007, the organization moved its headquarters from Kenosha, Wisconsin, to Nashville, TN, in an attempt to align itself with the town's "Music City" image. And, while Barbershop-style music has long been considered a mostly American art form, it has attracted participants and fans throughout the world. As an example, the following is a listing in the Society's official publication, *THE HARMONIZER*, of "affiliates" in places outside of North America:

- Barbershop Harmony Australia
- BHNZ (BarbershopHarmonyNewZealand)
- BABS (British Association of Barbershop Singers)
- BinG! (Barbershop in Germany)
- Holland Harmony
- FABS (Finnish Association of Barbershop Singers)
- IABS (Irish Association of Barbershop Singers)
- MBHA (Mixed Barbershop Harmony Association – Male/Female groups)
- SABS (Spanish Association of Barbershop Singers)
- SNOBS (Society of Nordic Barbershop Singers)
- SPATS (Southern Part of Africa Tonsorial Singers)

The Dallas Metropolitan Chapter (corporate parent of The Vocal Majority) is a part of the *Southwestern District* of the Barbershop Harmony Society ("Society"). Our district is one of seventeen districts included in the United States and Canada, and it has chapters in Texas, Louisiana, Oklahoma, southeastern New Mexico and southwestern Kansas – 48 chapters in all. Because of the vast distance between chapters in our district and others, elimination competitions between chapter choruses and quartets generally start out in divisions – small regions including maybe 5-6 chapters. Contest winners from these divisions then compete in a central location within the district (usually Dallas or San Antonio) and contest judges who are certified by the Society are flown in from other districts to select chorus and quartet winners who then represent the district at the annual International Convention of the Society in a large U.S. or Canadian city.

I hope I didn't lose you in all that "organizational talk". Suffice it to say that the Society has always had an extremely sophisticated contest and judging system, and consistently trains its members to become judges who are really proficient in several different judging categories.

Back in the 1970s, 80s, and 90s, the Society also tried to train its members in the more mundane duties of running a corporate organization of volunteers. Each district used to host *Chapter Officer Training Schools* (COTS) once a year,

and each chapter who could afford the expenses sent their officers to the weekend series of seminars to learn what their responsibilities were supposed to be. For many of those years, I was a faculty member on COTS, teaching Program VPs and Membership VPs from chapters throughout the country how to be successful in tackling their responsibilities. They were fun weekends of camaraderie and learning for students and teachers alike. Unfortunately, with the downsizing of the Society's

86

membership during the past 20-30 years, these training schools are mostly a thing of the past.

Going back in time to the 1960s in the Dallas area, the quality of singing in chapter choruses was not particularly high nor was it very challenging. As I mentioned in the first few pages, I had joined the Dallas Town North Chapter and sang Lead (melody) in their chorus during the late 1960s and on into 1970. I tried to learn the fundamentals of male choral harmony and certainly enjoyed the fellowship within the group and with other Barbershoppers in the area. I was elected Program Vice President of the chapter in 1970, but I was beginning to have my doubts about my long-term prospects with that particular chapter.

As I became aware of the tremendous musicality and showmanship of championship quartets and choruses from other parts of Texas and the country, I started to become disillusioned. No Barbershop chorus or quartet from the North Texas area had even won a *district* contest in recent memory, let alone a national championship. What could be done to improve that meager record and provide a worthwhile musical experience for good male singers in North Texas?

A number of other Dallas area guys had that same question. I soon began discussions with several current and former Barbershop singers in the area, and we explored the possibility of pooling the talents of the two Dallas Society chapters currently in existence – **Big D** and **Town North** – by merging the two chapters. Well, that didn't turn out so well.

The Big D group voted *for* the merger, and Town North (my chapter) voted *against* it.

As the merger proponents took stock of the situation, it dawned on us that we were looking at this opportunity all wrong. Merging two smaller and rather musically challenged organizations might have simply resulted in a larger organization but with the same musical and philosophical challenges. So, we decided on a more radical direction. We decided to petition the Barbershop Harmony Society to form a *new* chapter in Dallas that could start with fresh ideas and appeal to an entirely new, higher musical caliber of male singer.

During that same time, the Barbershop Harmony Society was itself going through quite an identity crisis. There were a lot of "old timers" in the organization who sincerely believed in the mantra of *"keep it Barbershop"* to the exclusion of any expansion of or deviation from the basic art form. To them the whole purpose of the Society was to maintain a "preservation" focus, and to not mess with any "modern" intrusions. The entire organization was trying to be all things to all its members, and was losing the membership battle. Those who proposed a more liberal inter-pretation of what the Barbershop style entailed were sometimes literally shouted down in both discussions and performances. Since that time, the Society has done a good job of seemingly keeping all sides in this debate fairly satisfied by expanding the genre to include more modern music literature, and allowing the "keep it Barbershop" crowd to be satisfied by creating several sub-groups within the parent organization.

For instance, the **Barbershop Quartet Preservation Association** (www.bqpa.com) states in its web site: *"The BQPA encourages local associations of singers and chapters to concentrate on developing quartets that choose to sing the "old Songs" reminiscent of the music of earlier years. Our style definition describes Barbershop quartet harmony as it was performed in the early days of the S.P.E.B.S.Q.S.A. and is worthy of preservation."* Another subsidiary group is the **Ancient Harmonious Society of Woodshedders** (www.ahsow.org), whose mission is laid out in its web site: *"The Ancient Harmonious Society of Woodshedders (AHSOW) was formed in 1977 with the purpose to preserve the skill of woodshedding as an art form within The Barbershop Harmony Society."*

It was obvious that the Society had to maintain the interests of its "keep it Barbershop" members, while at the same time attempting to move the rest of its membership – *musically* -- into the 21st Century.

[**Author's Note:**] Today, you can examine an issue of the Society's bi-monthly publication, *The HARMONIZER*, and see the monumental changes that have occurred. There are discussions in every issue about how chapters should focus on the partnerships forged with national and international professional music organizations, and on high school and college choral music programs. A summer 2017 issue had a full-page ad from the Society's *"Harmony Marketplace"* that encouraged readers to order "New Charts" – choral arrangements of pop songs like **Justin Timberlake**'s *"Can't Stop The Feeling!"*, **Billy Joel**'s *"Lullabye"*, and *"Africa"* by the group **Toto**. It did my heart good to see that so-called modern songs are no longer shunned by the Barbershop Society's leaders.

These last few pages were an attempt to place in context the attitudes of male singers in Dallas during the early 1970s when discussions of a new Barbershop chapter developed. During the summer of 1971, I can remember meeting a lot of men who were very interested in participating in a vocal harmony group *IF THE PURPOSE WAS TO PERFORM INTERESTING ARRANGEMENTS AND HAVE CHALLENGING GOALS*. I found out that there were some excellent professional and non-professional singers available who simply didn't find any challenge in the programs offered by the Barbershop Chapters currently operating in North Texas.

Thus was born the concept for **The Vocal Majority Chorus** in 1971.

In case you're rather unfamiliar with The Vocal Majority, I encourage you to visit the organization's dazzling web site to find some history, photos and videos, ways to purchase the group's recordings, and attend upcoming performances that you might find very entertaining and fulfilling. Log on to: https://www.vocalmajority.com/.

Chapter 8
THOSE FIRST BEAUTIFUL SOUNDS

I can still remember that cold, blustery Thursday evening in November 1971 when a group of about a dozen male singers gathered in a meeting room of a bank on Industrial Boulevard in Dallas. (Both the bank and Industrial Boulevard are no longer in existence, with the street being re-named Riverside Drive several years ago.) That was the first time I met the tall, handsome and talented bass singer named **Jim Clancy**. Others had told me that Jim was a "jingle singer" who had previously visited several existing Dallas Barbershop chapters but was not affiliated with any of them. Jim brought along a couple of his own vocal arrangements to see what we could do with them. **Charlie White**, who worked at Texas Instruments at the time and who was an on-and-off member of Barbershop chapters in the past, also brought along a couple of music charts.

Considering the fact that this small group had not sung together before, and the number of singers on each voice part weren't quite balanced, the collective sound that came from those voices was as beautiful as any of us had heard in a while. *That I remember well!*

NEWSLETTERS AS HISTORY & MOTIVATION TOOLS

At this point in my story I'll begin quoting from the file of past *Vocalizer* newsletters that I wrote and distributed for about the first twenty-five years of the VM's existence. Those newsletters were sent out WEEKLY for quite a few years as we struggled to get this fledgling organization off the ground, and they contain lots of important history that I and other VM members probably have long forgotten. They were also my way of marketing the VM "vision" to our members and prospective members in hopes that *positive reinforcement each week* in the group's bulletin would help the organization grow faster with a more focused direction.

I have always believed that INTERNAL communication is just as powerful and important for nonprofit/volunteer organizations as external messages. As the great international comedian and pianist Victor Borge once told the audience when he was performing with the

Alexandria Harmonizers Chorus in Washington, DC, "These aren't amateurs, they're *volunteers*." That's exactly what I had in mind for

these raw Vocal Majority singers in 1971. I wanted volunteer male singers who had experience singing harmony with top-notch vocal ensembles; men who could read sheet music rather quickly so that our group could learn and perform a wide variety of challenging vocal arrangements; men who could be so impressive as a performing unit so quickly that they would attract *other* talented singers; and men who could appreciate and sing a wide variety of music genres in addition to "the Barbershop style".

The Author during
founding years of
The Vocal Majority

In our meetings with those who became founding members during 1971/1972, there were some serious discussions about whether we really *wanted* to become associated with SPEBSQSA (as it was known in those days) at all! Why was that?

During that period of the early 1970s, as I recall it, SPEBSQSA didn't have a positive reputation in the Dallas area among the better singers in town. So, if that was the case, then how could this new choral group identify itself as "Barbershoppers" and attract the best talent available? There was lots of discussion about that dilemma. And the reason we opted to eventually caste our lot with SPEBSQSA was their *judging system*. With all the negative opinions among our early singers about the Society being a "preservation" organization as opposed to an organization that valued "excellent vocal harmony singing", the Society's contest judging and competition system was as professional and competent as any that existed in America. And, if we wanted to eventually boast that we were the "best in the world", how would we be able to do that without a viable system of judging the quality of our performances against similar groups? That was the major reason why the leaders of the new Vocal Majority group opted to join SPEBSQSA as the ***Dallas Metropolitan Chapter*** of the Society.

If you think about it, young men who have participated in quality choral music programs at the high school and college levels had few options to *continue* that experience once they entered their work and family lives. As spiritually satisfying as they might be, church choirs don't quite fill the void – plus they rarely provided the "applause high" that other choral singing can produce. These young singers didn't grow up listening to "the old songs" like the founders of the Society did when they started the organization. And the young singers we were after probably didn't sing those square old songs in their school or college music programs. So why *force* this antiquated style onto young singers looking for fun music and a more contemporary experience.

That was the dilemma I faced when sitting down to write each issue of the *Vocalizer* newsletter every week. How could I *not* offend the dedicated "Barbershop-only" guys in the Dallas area (and elsewhere), and yet enthusiastically promote our group as something NEW and exciting – a group that appreciated the preservation of a style of music that was truly all-American while also treating its singers to styles *outside* the limited Barbershop rules and attitudes? After all, we were going to *need* the goodwill of the established chapters in the area if we expected to "charter" as a new Society chapter. I, along with our other formation leaders, had to walk a fine line in attempting to attract existing chapter members from the other groups who might be interested in taking a new direction in their singing lives, plus attracting brand-new singers who didn't know the first thing about the "Barbershop-style" tradition.

When I opened the dusty binders containing the first year's-worth of weekly *Vocalizers*, I can see that dilemma playing out in almost every issue. But a good bulletin/newsletter writer for any nonprofit or volunteer organization has that same kind of a challenge – writing positive, uplifting articles for both their internal *and* external audiences. If you work at it and get good at it, these newsletters can become a very positive and motivating force to help the organization grow, and provide positive public relations for those outside the organization and for the news media. With my background in public relations, marketing and advertising, I felt no shame in using as many of my promotional skills as I could to motivate current members of the new VM, and entice those singers outside the organization who were looking for a new singing and performance home. You could easily say that newsletters were valuable "tools" for marketing, and I used our *Vocalizers* as such during the twenty-five years that I was marketing director/bulleting editor for the VM.

Oh, by the way, if you're not familiar with the worldwide activities of Barbershop singing organizations, you might ask: *What about women singers who enjoy vocal harmony?* Well, there are two organizations for them in north America – the ***Sweet Adelines*** and ***Harmony Incorporated***. These organizations hold chorus and quartet competitions separate from the Barbershop Harmony Society.

Chapter 9
CRACKING OPEN THE *VOCALIZER* BINDERS

Now that you know some of the history and reasons for the initial formation of the fledgling Vocal Majority Chorus, let's see what mysteries are hiding inside those binders.

You might be familiar with today's word processing software that essentially allows you to select from a variety of newsletter formats, type fonts, type sizes, imported graphics and color schemes. None of that software was available when I first began churning out *Vocalizers* in late 1971. I used an electric typewriter to physically type out and measure each column of paragraphs in inches, then I cut out those columns with scissors and pasted them onto an 8-1/2 by 14-inch sheet of paper. Any graphics/photos were pasted on to that paper also. If you wanted bold headlines, you went to an art or graphic design store and bought sheets of "press-type" that you  could rub off onto your paper format sheet. When you had completed all that cutting-and-pasting, you took the finished product to the nearest quick-print shop and had them use an offset printer to produce the finished printed and folded newsletter. After that, the grunt-work began.

That good old electric typewriter was also used to type up the master mailing lists of VM members, guest singers and VIPs on peel-off labels. I then copied off those updated mailing labels each week and affixed the copies *by hand* to the *Vocalizers*. Also, you had to purchase U.S. Post Office stamps in sheets that had glue on the back side, and then *LICK* each one to affix them to the newsletters. *YUCK!* But that was the state-of-the-art back in those days, and after all that peeling and licking each week, I got so that I could remember just about every members' address for years after that.

Some people think we *swiped* the name "The Vocal Majority" from another organization. However, our name did NOT get its inspiration from the group known as the **"Moral Majority"**. According to Wikipedia, *"the Moral Majority was a prominent American political organization associated with the Christian right and Republican Party. It was founded in 1979 by Baptist minister Jerry Falwell and associates, and dissolved in the late 1980s."* The first issue of *The Vocalizer* was published December 11, 1971. Its masthead featured the following: *"The Vocalizer, Weekly Voice of The Vocal Majority"*. Obviously, The Vocal Majority *preceded* the Moral Majority by at least eight years. (Could it be that the Moral Majority got the idea for its name from the VM after we had won two gold medals in international chorus competition by 1979???)

It was **Bill Heard**, one of our early members, who first brought up the name *"The Vocal Majority"*. Bill was a member of the Houston Barbershop Chapter before moving to Dallas. He was also fresh from singing professionally with **The New Christy Minstrels**, a large-ensemble folk music group founded by Randy Sparks in 1961, with over 20 albums to their credit. I also enjoyed Bill's professional folk trio, the Claybrook Singers, several times while visiting coffee houses in Dallas during the 1960s. And, according to my recollection of Bill's suggestion for the chorus name, the "The" in "The Vocal Majority" was very important. His opinion was that the "The" preceding a name signaled a uniqueness or singularity in the identification of an organization's or group's name. Think of other musical groups with a "The" in their name: **The Four Freshmen** (as opposed to Four Freshmen), **The Sherrels**, **The Kingston Trio**, **The Everly Brothers**, **The Oak Ridge Boys**. We wouldn't dare take the "The" from the front of those ensemble names, would we?

And yet, the VM board of directors recently voted to delete the "The" in front of The Vocal Majority, and also voted to change the

long-admired logo of The VM from the swashbuckling, bold scripted logos designed during our first few decades by VM singer and award-winning graphic designer, **Gerald Ewald**, into the softer, more "feminine" logo used today. (See the comparative graphics on the preceding page.) In my humble opinion, changes that update your image to more modern times are sometimes good for an organization. However, I'm not sure I agree with those changes. But perhaps my opinion is colored by my investments and relationships in the past.

That first issue of **The Vocalizer** (there's that "The" again!) was interesting from two perspectives -- one musical and the other administrative. The bulletin listed three songs that the first group of VM singers tried to sing during their second rehearsal: *"Their Hearts Were Full of Spring"*, a **Four Freshmen** arrangement, and **Buzz Busby**'s arrangement of *"September Song"*. During those first couple of rehearsals, we were also privileged to first sing **Jim Clancy**'s inspired arrangement of *"The Lord's Prayer"*. That arrangement is still in the chorus repertoire today, and is sung at virtually every VM singer's funeral/memorial – as well as possibly hundreds of others around the world that that we have no knowledge of.

Also announced was an upcoming **Clancy** arrangement to be unveiled at the next rehearsal: *"By The Time I Get To Phoenix"* in a medley with *"It's A Blue World"*. Those arrangements of popular American songs signaled to everyone who attended those rehearsals and/or read that *Vocalizer* issue that *this was not your father's Barbershop chapter meeting or repertoire!*

Because this new group was not yet an official chapter organization, we established its first "Interim Executive Committee":
- Chairman: **Bob Arnold**
- Director-Finance: **Jim Allen**
- Director-Promotion: **Bill Heard**
- Directors of Music: **Bill Thornton, Jim Clancy, Charlie White**
- Director-Properties: **Art Haynes**

That issue also came with an apology to other Barbershoppers in the area. I had obtained lists of other area Barbershop chapter members and sent them the first pre-issue of The Vocalizer so they could be aware of what was going on with this new Vocal Majority group. Well, I had to reassure everyone in the area that we were not after "proselytizing" existing chapter members; we simply wanted to extend the invitation to come and visit to find out what we were all about.

The motto of **SPEBSQSA** during that time was *"Keep America Singing"*. Well, to promote the VM's pending affiliation with the Society, and focus on our goal of being a departure from "business as usual", each *Vocalizer* issue during the first six months of 1972 ended with the tag line, **"KEEP AMERICA SINGING (WELL)"** – an obvious reference to doing things better.

The second edition of **The Vocalizer** on December 16, 1971, indicated that the new meeting format and music philosophy was starting to pay dividends. More and more experienced and talented area singers came out of the woodwork to see what was going on. Two men who were to have an important part of the initial success of the chorus showed up: **Ray Anthony** and **Charlie Lyman**. Ray was already a semi-legend in Barbershop Society circles, having directed the **San Antonio Chordsmen** to an International Gold Medal in 1960. Since moving to Dallas, Ray had visited with both the **Dallas Town North Chapter** and the **Big D Chapter**, and was trying to decide whether to direct either chorus. Then he found a VM rehearsal one night in 1971, and the rest is history (which you'll learn if you stay with me during the next several chapters).

Because of a conflict with his military reserve duties, **Charlie Lyman** had to drop out of his Monday night rehearsals at Town North. That left him open to Thursday night rehearsals with the VM, and he flourished from then on. He was an experienced quartet tenor, a super piano player for our future Dixieland Band group, and a valuable member of our board of directors for many years, rising to chapter president in 1975. As a lifetime IBMer, Charlie was an extremely valuable VM member during our early years.

To end the year, I published the final edition of *The Vocalizer* for 1971 with the headline, **"WHATTA WAY TO END THE YEAR!"** We had established a pay-as-you-go method for members to donate funds to pay for a rehearsal site, printed music, coffee at rehearsals, and bulletin publication and mailing. The year's final rehearsal saw an arrangement that became a cornerstone for the chorus for decades: *"Today (While The Blossoms Still Cling To The Vine)"*. It was also sung at Susan's and my wedding several decades later, along with *"The Lord's Prayer"*. The latter arrangement is still in the VM repertoire today, and is sung at virtually every VM singer's funeral or memorial.

That last rehearsal of 1971 saw quite a few new singers who became long-time members of the organization: **Frank Harkness, Harrold Grogan, Don Dochterman, Buddy Holiday, Gene Butterfield, John Olson** and **Larry Roseborough.** We were all looking forward to 1972 as the year our organization would officially become a chapter of SPEBSQSA and grow to a size that could be competitive in chorus contests as soon as possible.

Chapter 10
1972: OFFICIAL CORPORATE STATUS

The first *Vocalizer* issue of 1972 boasted *thirty-four singers* attending the year's first rehearsal, with the session lasting over three hours. A consistent turnout of members and guest singers was the norm during the next few months as everyone seemed to grasp the notion that there was something special going on. [**Author's Note:** It will be the convention during the first few chapters of the book to list new Guest Singers as their names show up in the *Vocalizer* in separate, condensed paragraphs to allow more casual readers to simply skip over these lists of names – unless *you're* one of those names!]

> **JANUARY 1972 GUEST SINGERS: Al Kvanli, Burton Jones, Don Otte, Duane Lunday, Paul Baker, Ken Willis, Harrold Grogan, Jim Carter, Bob Wessley, Jack Walter, Harry DeLipsey, Isaac & Joe Morales, Buddy Holiday (KRLD Radio), Royce Parish, John Olsen, Bill Vandivort, Clark Womack, Jim Sharples, Ken Shaver, Jerry Bean, Dan Alexander, Jim Law, Mike Everett, John Piercy, Frank Bloebaum.**

The bandwagon was started for this growing group of singers to begin collecting "dues" so we could eventually petition the Society to become a "Licensed Chapter". This is the first step to being approved as a fully chartered chapter. The new Music Committee developed the first *audition procedure*, which every singer committed to go through to maintain a consistent quality to the chorus sound. And Music VP, Bill Thornton, outlined a proposed chorus repertoire that the Music Committee had developed to enable us to produce audience-centered shows. A request was made to all singers to help us find a new, larger rehearsal facility. The little meeting room in the bank building on Industrial Boulevard was becoming cramped as the number of singers grew past thirty.

The success of our fledgling group prompted Jim Clancy to introduce music arrangements that consistently challenged all of us. He brought along an arrangement of *"(This Time We Almost Made It) Didn't We"* (arranged for the **Sundowners** by **Larry Wright**), and it was a breath of fresh air for most of us. (It was also a sad "lament" after losing an International Chorus Gold Medal attempt shortly thereafter.)

101

February's first meeting of 1972 saw several *Vocalizer* announcements that were extremely important for the growth of our organization. Rehearsals were moved to the much larger, fairly plush surroundings of the **Chapel Downs Community Center** in north Dallas. Bill Heard lived in the Chapel Downs community, and talked his homeowner's association into allowing the small but growing VM chorus to rehearse there every Thursday in exchange for performances. That facility would provide a nice location for the next decade or so until we would ultimately outgrow it also.

Another bit of good fortune fell into our laps when a brand-new Dallas Barbershop quartet decided to caste its lot with the VM. The **Dealer's Choice**, comprised of **Brian Beck** on Baritone, **Bill Thornton** on Lead, **Al Kvanli** on Tenor, and **Gary Parker** on Bass, first made its appearance at a February rehearsal. That foursome would become International Quartet Champions the following July. The individual quartet members would also go on to guide our chorus music development for the next several decades as music coaches and section leaders.

FEBRUARY/MARCH 1972 GUEST SINGERS: Brian Beck, Gary Parker, Fred Cook, Chuck Denny, Dennis Stone, Joe Singer, Gene Baxter, Clyde Eisenbeis, Norm Sebens, Jim Allen, Mike McGrew.

It was also in February that **Charlie White** was selected as the first "official" musical director of the chorus. At the time, Charlie was an International Society contest judge, a former director of the Sherman, Texas, chapter chorus, a past director of a Sweet Adeline chorus, and a long-time Barbershopper and quartet coach. **Jim Clancy** was selected as assistant director. Among the arrangements the chorus was working on at the time were *South Rampart Street Parade*, *The Lord's Prayer*, *Going My Way Baby*, *Shine On Harvest Moon*, and *Didn't We*.

By March, total auditioned charter members totaled twenty-four. The minimum number of men required to "license" as an organization with SPEBSQSA was 20. The minimum needed to CHARTER as a chapter after the license procedure was 35. So, we had our work cut out for us if we were to compete in the coming Fall chorus contest for the Southwestern District.

In April of 1972, the organization held its first Novice Quartet Contest. The participants:

1. **Clancy (Bs) Grogan (Bt) Sharples (L) Singer (T)**
2. **I. Morales (Bs) White (Bt) Bean (L) Haynes (T)**
3. **Eisenbeis (Bs) Thornton (Bt) McGrew (L) Butterfield (T)**
4. **Holiday (Bs) Roseborough (Bt) Shaver (L) Lyman (T)**
5. **Belknap (Bs) Wood (Bt) Vandivort (L) Kvanli (T)**
6. **Sebens (Bs) Allen (Bt) Arnold (L) Heard (T)**

We were also pleased to have as guests during April three-fourths of the **Stage Door Four** quartet, **Keith Houts**, **Jim Law** and **Don Dochterman**. Keith and Don eventually became very important members of the chorus for many years. Another important growth event happened in April: our very first Open House/Guest Night. And we have another visit from the inspiring man who would become the first VM director to lead the chorus in an International Chorus Competition, **Ray Anthony**.

Ray took over directing the chorus in May, and these comments during his first rehearsal were a sign of what our future was destined to be: *"This will be the nucleus around which we'll build a really fine chorus. We'll learn approximately an arrangement each week for a while. We'll sing a lot of songs and pick the ones we want to keep. We'll attempt to have most of our arrangements produced for us by Brian Beck, Jim Clancy and other talented area arrangers. We don't want to be a 'me-too' chorus, singing arrangements other choruses have done for years. And we'll have a lot of fun SINGING WELL."*

To avoid even *looking* like a "me-too" chorus, Bill Thornton designed a slick, orange jumpsuit costume for our first performance outfit, along with a long-sleeve shirt with white puffy sleeves. All this was set off by white patent leather boot-style shoes. Bill was a graphic designer at the time, and obviously had some unique ideas for our costumes.

APRIL/MAY GUEST SINGERS: George Rugge, John Good, Ken Rathjen, Bob Carwell, Phil Guthrie, George Baker, Bill Malloy, Glen Hutton, Jim Struble

The May 27, 1972, issue of the *Vocalizer* trumpeted, **"IT'S OF-FICIAL ... WE'RE LICENSED!"** We had just received letters of congratulations from board members of the Society notifying us that we had become a licensed chapter. That license was co-sponsored by the two existing chapters in Dallas, **Town North** and **Big D**.

> **JUNE/JULY 1972 GUEST SINGERS:** Sam Houston, Don Flemming, Barry Battershall, Bill Chandler, Tom Morgan, Bob Jett, George Burrell, Glen Hutton, Richard Poyner, Bill Jaynes, Jay Butterfield, Bob Wessley, Roy Prestigiacomo, Phil Leslie, Terry Diedrich, Andy Anderson, Ron Harrington, Charlie Page, Pete Mitchell, Don Colquhoun, Art Foster, Tom Wiginton, Dennis Black, Tom Eames, Ron Bowden, Ken McKee, Bob Cournoyer, Chuck Denny, Pat Carley, Tom Eames.

One of **Jim Clancy's** finest arrangements was unveiled to the chorus in June: *If I Ruled The World*. It would become a favorite of both our audiences and our singers. We also were introduced to our contest up-tune about the same time called *"At The Jazz Band Ball"*. The chorus was also visited at a July rehearsal by two of the fabulous **Four Freshmen**, **Ross Barber** and **Bob Flanigan**, who were in Dallas to perform at the Loser's Club. **Jim Clancy** and **Frank Bloebaum** joined with the two Freshmen to sing *"It's A Blue World"* for the rest of us, and then **Brian Beck** and **Clark Womack** joined both *Freshmen* for the song *"Poinciana"*. Both of those arrangements would one day work themselves into our chorus performance repertoire.

BOB JETT: Voice of The Vocal Majority

For the past 25+ years, most Vocal Majority singers and patrons became familiar with our current MC/Announcer, **Nick Alexander**. Today, hardly anyone could imagine a VM show or performance without hearing Nick's resonant voice introducing songs and making the audience feel comfortable, informed and entertained. He's also been an anchor in the VM bass section for the past three decades.

However, the man who was most recognized as "The Voice" of The Vocal Majority from 1972 through the 1990s was **Bob Jett**. Bob was at least 6-foot 4-inches tall, and it was said that he "had a voice like God". He did back-

ground research on virtually every song the VM sang, and as a result came up with some of the most interesting and amusing introductions to each song during our shows.

I first met Bob when he joined me at WFAA Radio as my newsman during my disk jockey stint at the station during the 1960s. Then later, when I became the manager of the speaker's bureau at Lone Star Gas Company, Bob was the first individual that I hired on my staff of six public speakers. It was about that time that I helped to establish The Vocal Majority Chorus, and I invited Bob to become one of its charter members. He went on to collect ten Gold Medals with the chorus, and was inducted with the chorus into the Southwest District Hall of Fame. He passed away in September 2004.

The rest of the summer of 1972 was spent preparing for our first Southwestern District chorus competition coming up September 8th & 9th in Lubbock, Texas. We had to borrow chorus risers from area schools to "stack" our first chorus lineup so we could see what we would actually look like on competition risers. And we worked on rudimentary stage presence moves to go with our two contest songs, *"At The Jazz Band Ball"* and *"I Wish I Had A Girl"*.

AUGUST/SEPTEMBER 1972 GUEST SINGERS: Pat Carley, Dennis Black, Dick Friedell, Don Peoples, Floyd Taylor, Bob Presley, Greg Page, Mike Steen, Jim Hartley, Tom Bamford.

The chorus was now large enough – close to forty consistent singers – for each of the four sections (Tenor, Lead, Baritone and Bass) to hold its own rehearsal at different sites and on different days outside of our regular Thursday evening chorus sessions. Plans were being made to finalize the fitting and purchase of our orange jumpsuits that would serve as a "mod" costume for our young chorus. And, in addition to our fabulous new quartet the *Dealer's Choice*, we were introduced to a new foursome that called themselves "the *Mod Quad*": **Bill Heard** (Tenor), **Phil Leslie** (Lead), **Clark Womack** (Baritone), and **Bob Jett** (Bass). We were indeed fortunate that the individual members of both quartets not only worked hard to shape the sounds of their own ensembles, but also worked with us "less musically endowed" singers to improve the overall chorus sound.

We were also informed by the International Society office that our official Charter Petition had been fully approved and was on its way to Dallas. *Talk about under the wire for our first formal competition!*

CHARTER MEMBERS OF THE DALLAS METROPOLITAN CHAPTER

The following names were affixed to the charter document, dated August 28, 1972, that confirmed our organization as an official Chapter of the **Society for the Preservation and Encouragement of Barber Shop Quartet Singing in America**:

Ray Anthony	**Bob Arnold**	**Brian Beck**
Ray Belknap	**Jerry Bean**	**Gene Butterfield**
Jim Clancy	**Harrold Grogan**	**Art Haynes**
Bill Heard	**Charles Lay**	**Burton Jones**
Bob Jett	**Al Kvanli**	**Charlie Lyman**
Mike McGrew	**Isaac Morales**	**Joe Morales**
Larry Roseborough	**Norm Sebens**	**Bill Thornton**
Bill Vandivort	**Charlie White**	**Jim Sharples**
Ken Shaver	**Clyde Eisenbeis**	**Bill Malloy**
Jim Carter	**Barry Battershall**	**Don Dochterman**
George Burrell	**George Rugge**	**Andy Anderson**
Phil Leslie	**Jim Allen**	**Gary Parker**
Frank Harkness	**Sam Houston**	**Bob Wessley**
Don Colquhoun	**Pat Carley**	

The September 11th issue of *The Vocalizer* headlined, **"HOW SWEET IT IS"**! Not only did The Vocal Majority capture first place in the Area Chorus Contest in Lubbock, but our two chapter quartets finished First and Second. The **Dealer's Choice** took the top spot, while the **Mod Quad** finished second. The Dallas Metropolitan Chapter was just beginning a journey that would eventually bring it to the top of the Barbershop Society world, and would create a model for other singing organizations who wanted to rise above the mediocre image of a "community chorus". *It was indeed a thrill to be there for the beginning of this monumental ride!*

A SLIGHT BUMP IN THE ROAD

To say that each member of The Vocal Majority was riding a wave of euphoria after that first victory was an understatement. We didn't think there was any way anything could stand in our way of being named the top men's choral group of the universe. You might have called us cocky. So, we prepared hard for the next level of competition – the Southwestern District Chorus and Quartet Contest in San Antonio in October. Twenty-five rooms were reserved for VM singers and families at the Gunter Hotel, and extra rehearsals were scheduled outside of our regular three-hour sessions each Thursday evening. We even managed to obtain our first paid booking! The **American Bankers Association** booked the VM chorus to sing for 10,000 of their members coming to Dallas for their annual convention in October. (That was the first of many profitable bookings I helped arrange during my years as the VM's marketing director.) And the VM repertoire was expanding. Jim Clancy and the Music Team unveiled Jim's new medley, *"It's A Blue World"* and *"By The Time I Get To Phoenix"*, along with *"On A Wonderful Day Like Today"*.

Since the organization was now an official chapter of SPEBSQSA, we had to elect our initial board of directors. Nominating Committee Chairman, **Frank Harkness**, proposed the following men to lead the chapter for 1973:

ART HAYNES, President
RAY ANTHONY, Music Director
BOB ARNOLD, Administrative V.P.
BRIAN BECK, Assistant Music Director
BUDDY HOLIDAY, Program V.P.
JIM CLANCY, Assistant Music Director
BILL THORNTON, Music V.P.
DON COLQUHOUN, Director At-Large

JIM SHARPLES, Secretary
HARROLD GROGAN, Director At-Large
GEORGE BURRELL, Treasurer
LARRY ROSEBOROUGH, Director At-Large
BOB WESSLEY, Director At-Large

"DEALER'S CHOICE is also judges' choice as DISTRICT CHAMPS!!"

That was the *Vocalizer* headline on the October 30th edition, as the Dallas Metro Chapter had its first of several quartet champions. But **The Vocal Majority Chorus** missed a first-place finish in their initial contest by a mere *27 points* out of a total of 1300 possible points. Our chorus numbered 37 singers, and earned a second-place finish to the 81-voice **Houston Tidelanders Chorus,** which didn't seem so bad. At that point, we felt we were *"the little engine that could"*. Our other quartet entry into the District contest, **The Mod Quad,** finished in 7th place, which was certainly not too bad with only a couple of months preparation before the competition.

[**Author's Note:** *That 1972 contest was the last district competition The Vocal Majority would <u>ever</u> lose right up to the publishing date for this book!*]

All in all, a joyous first weekend of District competition for our fledgling organization. It was a great learning experience about what it takes to score points in the Society's judging system, and we gave notice to a lot of people that this new *singing machine* in Dallas, Texas, certainly was something they should watch.

FIRST SHOW PRODUCTION A WINNER

Momentum really started building back in Dallas after everyone returned from San Antonio. The Vocal Majority hosted a party at the Chapel Downs Community Center for all the Barbershop chapters in the Metroplex to help celebrate the contest results from the District competitions. About 100 people showed up, including members of both Dallas Barbershop chapters, the **Arlington Chapter,** and the **Fort Worth Cowtown Chorus.** The director of the Fort Worth Chorus, **Sonny Lipford,**

THE GOLD MEDAL STANDARD

made the first of many visits to a VM rehearsal that evening, and eventually became a much-loved and respected VM chorus member, coach and an assistant director.

OCTOBER-DECEMBER GUEST SINGERS: Sonny Lipford, Ross Wise, Joe Wiggins, Bill Young, Keith Houts, Louie Mullican, Dale Butterfield, Bob Smith, Mike Osborne, Dave Shuppert, Don Otte.

The first Vocal Majority show production was scheduled for December 2 at the **Jesuit High School** auditorium, with the proceeds benefitting the **Chapel Downs Community Center** (as payment for our rehearsal facility), the **Dallas Symphony Orchestra** (as support for another Dallas arts organization), and, of course, our own organization. The show featured not only the VM chorus, but the **Dealer's Choice**, the **Mod Quad**, and the **Stage Door Four**.

December wrapped up with an early morning appearance by the chorus on **Channel 8** (WFAA-TV) doing a promo shot for host **Suzie Humphreys** on a program called *"News 8, Etc."*. It was the first time in anyone's memory – but not the last – that any Barbershop-oriented group had ever appeared on a local Dallas TV station.

The first year of existence for The Vocal Majority was certainly a success from almost any standpoint. We proved – to ourselves and those who noticed our progress – that we had the *potential* to be an outstanding choral music organization. We had talented music professionals who could teach us "amateur" singers what it takes to become professional-*sounding* musicians. We not only established ourselves as a top-notch Barbershop ensemble, but also as a contributing member of the arts community in the North Texas region. We attracted the kinds of experienced and dedicated singers who would provide the foundation for future growth. And the future certainly looked bright in December 1972. Those who were there could feel the eminent arrival of the *Kingdom of Camelot*.

Chapter 11
1973: THE YEAR THE GOLD RUSH BEGAN

After the whirlwind of incorporating as a 501(c)(3) tax-exempt nonprofit arts organization, and winning the first chorus contest we had ever entered, The Vocal Majority Chorus was set to grow – both musically and membership-wise. The January 1973 issue of *The Vocalizer* announced the organization's first annual installation banquet to officially install its new board of directors.

> **JANUARY-MARCH 1973 GUEST SINGERS – Quinn Hunter, Don Walker, Tom Bamford, Brian Belcher, Jan Arps, Buddy Shuppert, Buddy Coopwood, Bob Decker, George Shipley, Glenn Fordham, Don Peoples, Jim Cullison, Lynn Jacobs, Chuck Steward, Larry Rogers, Clay Smith, Joe Wiggins, Tom Eames, Bob French, Chris Christensen, Ron Taylor, Perry Compton, Bill Dunklau, Frank Montgomery, Dwain Brown, James Beasley, Don Knight, Ben Kiker, Jim Covey, John Parkin, Bill Elliott, Tom Cole, Barry Battershall, Carl Hathaway, Ray Hyman.**

As a new year's challenge, director Ray Anthony told the chorus that his music committee's goal was to win the Southwestern District chorus title in the fall. To do this, Ray made no bones about the fact that the chorus must DOUBLE its number of singers if we were to have a chance at the title. Quoting that *Vocalizer* issue: "Let's consider the words of Henry Ford in working toward that end: 'Coming together is a beginning; keeping together is progress; working together is success.' Success means winning . . . and winning isn't everything . . . *IT'S THE ONLY THING!*"

Rehearsals during the first several months of 1973 saw over 50 singers attending most rehearsals. Word was getting around that VM rehearsals on Thursday nights were the place to be if you were a male singer in the Metroplex who wanted a great choral music experience.

The first of many VM **Good Time Music Shows** was announced in March at the **Windmill Dinner Theater** in Dallas. If you're old enough to remember the popularity of dinner theaters during that time, you might recall that these small venues seated around 350-500 patrons, and featured Broadway and Las Vegas acts Tuesday through Sunday nights. Patrons were seated at tables surrounding a small performance area and a tiny stage. Since these theaters were "dark" on Monday nights, we worked out a deal with the theater management to sell tickets to our patrons on those Monday evenings, and the price of admission would also include beer, soft

 drinks, pretzels and chips – all served by chorus members before the show, at intermission, and after the show. The chorus was small enough at that time to fit into the limited performance area, and we invited one or two of our quartets to perform during the evening to add some variety.

Because the VM couldn't afford to rent most of the larger venues in the Dallas area at that time, we took advantage of the Good Time Music Show concept on an almost monthly basis, bringing in new quartets for each show to augment the rather limited chorus repertoire. The concept was so unique that it was eventually picked up by other chapters in the Barbershop Harmony Society, and I eventually wrote an article for the Society's *HARMONIZER* magazine about the concept.

In late March, Ray Anthony outlined the show songs we would be singing on future performances: *"At The Jazz Band Ball"*, *"Blue World/Phoenix Medley"*, *"Didn't We"*, *"I Wish I Had A Girl"*, *"If I Ruled The World"*, *"No One's Perfect"*, *"On A Wonderful Day Like Today"*, *"South Rampart Street Parade"*, *"Keep Your Sunny Side Up"*, *"Today"*, and *"All His Children"*.

We were very excited at the time about our two quartets, the **Dealer's Choice** and the **Mod Quad**, competing in the International Preliminary Quartet Contest in Port Arthur. This was a regional competition that qualifies quartets to compete the following summer in the International Barbershop Society championships. We were also rooting for another of the Dallas area quartets in that contest, the **Stage Door Four**. After the results were in, the **Dealer's Choice** overwhelmed all other foursomes in the contest and were on their way to the International competition

112

that July in Portland, Oregon. The **Stage Door Four** came in third, and the **Mod Quad** finished sixth.

> **APRIL-JUNE 1973 GUEST SINGERS** – Don Knight, Dennis Brown, James Beasley, Jim Covey, Dennis Malone, Dan Robinson, Jerry Waymire, Frank Maska, Ed Miller, Ken Logan, Dick Anderson, Ken Shaver, Mac Mckinney, John Kennedy,

The Dallas Metropolitan Chapter was honored by **Dallas Mayor Wes Wise** during April, as he proclaimed *Barbershop Harmony Week* in Dallas. (Since April 11 is the anniversary of the Barbershop Harmony Society, we figured it might be a good P.R. stunt to propose such an event to City Hall.) A photo was taken in front of city hall with the **Dealer's Choice**, **Mayor Wise**, and **this author**, and published in the April 13, 1973, issue of the *Vocalizer*.

"SOCKO!" That was the big headline on the May 22nd *Vocalizer*. It signified the reaction of the audience at the first **Vocal Majority Good Time Music Show** at the Windmill Dinner Theater. The newsletter quoted some important folks who attended that first show: *"Utterly fantastic! Outta sight!"* (**Ron Chapman**, **KVIL Radio**); *"What a spectacular show! Do you think you could do other shows in our Fort Worth and Houston theaters?"* (**Bob Mathis**, **Windmill Theaters** President); *"I'm going to write a feature article telling our readers what they've been missing! I'm also going to get you more new members than you can imagine!"* (**Floyce Korsak**, **Dallas Times Herald**); *"My wife and I were both amazed – no stunned – by the excellence of your group, both as a whole and the quartets therefrom. We've heard a lot of choruses over the years, but neither of us can recall one that had such a combination of excellent stage presence, fine intonation and absolutely superb diction. I don't think we missed a word the whole evening. Please convey to Ray Anthony and all the members of the The Vocal Majority our complete delight with the performance."* (**Dave Battey**, Manager of Operations for **The Dallas Symphony Orchestra**).

> **APRIL-JULY 1973 GUEST SINGERS:** Bill Rodgers, Fred Bolanz, Bob Hamm, Smokey Mountcastle, Dick Rothermel, Jerry Bean, Jay Butterfield, Joe McCombs, Bill Ridgers, Eddie Wall, Jack Kelly, Sonny Lipford, Ray Helal, Jim Belt, John Parkin, Jack Ware, Bill Gatlin, Jim Denton, Dennis Ferrell, Steve Dukes, Jeff Brock, Dan

Robinson, J.W. Hooton, Ernie Hawkins, Ray Hyman, Bill Elliott, Chuck McClellan, Jonathan Cooke, Glenn Huttan, Tom Canada.

You could tell the excitement was building that spring as rehearsals pointed toward a performance with the **Dallas Symphony Orchestra** in June, and the **Southwestern District Chorus Contest** in Oklahoma City in October. And, oh yes, our **Dealer's Choice** quartet was competing in its first **International Quartet Contest** in Portland, Oregon, in July. Not too bad for a less-than-one-year-old Barbershop Society chapter starting to spread its wings and give our singers some excellent rewards for the hard work they had been putting in. And to finish things off, a July **Good Time Music Show** was sold out almost as soon as tickets went on sale.

"DEALER'S CHOICE INTERNATIONAL CHAMPS" The July 16, 1973, *Vocalizer* exploded with that headline and a full-page photo

The Dealer's Choice – 1973 International Quartet Champions

of our new International Champions. It was the first time any quartet had taken the top prize in their initial attempt since 1954. A special celebration was held at a July rehearsal to honor our quartet champions, and all the excitement caused a large influx of Guest Singers and curious active Barbershoppers from throughout the Metroplex during the next few months.

114

AUGUST-OCTOBER 1973 GUEST SINGERS: John Robbins, Harold Rusk, Bill Sturgeon, Mike Everett, Tommy Gayle, Jeff Brock, Hugh Miller, Bill Wheat, Dennis Ferrell, John Davis, Steve Dukes, Jim Carroll, Sonny Lipford, Tom Canada, Ken McKee, Frank Freeman, Jack Parkin, Pat Patterson, Bob Cournoyer, Bill Martin, Ron Floyd, Bill Allen, Tommy Gayle, John Schroy, Paul Daniels, Jody Tallal, Tom Canada, Jim Martin, Wade Bennett, Mickey Bonesio, Joe Poyner, Howard Dosier, Herb Langthorp, Doug Hardman, Terry Diedrich, Jay Stone.

Ray Anthony announced the two contest songs we would be performing at the Division and District Contest: *"At The Jazz Band Ball"* and *"Laughing On The Outside, Crying On The Inside"*. The new chapter roster printed during August listed 63 active members – not nearly the eighty singers we had targeted by the time the District Contest rolled around in October. We obviously had some work to do in recruiting.

My marketing efforts to get more exposure (and income) for our organization seemed to be paying off with a **Fair Park Band Shell** performance with the **Dallas Symphony Orchestra**, a convention booking for **J.C. Penney's** regional meeting, and an appearance on **KERA-TV's** "Newsroom" (along with the **Dealer's Choice**). And a new registered chapter quartet was in the process of forming that would include **Art Haynes, Frank Harkness, Harrold Grogan** and **Dennis Malone**.

As a testament to the commitment our music team had to win the Southwestern District Contest that October, the board of directors voted to rehearse *twice each week* for the six weeks leading up to the contest. So, Monday and Thursday chorus rehearsals became the routine starting in August of 1973, with both full chorus and section rehearsals taking place on both nights. An all-day Saturday music education session was held in late August to teach each VM singer the finer points of professional voice production and performance. The faculty consisted of members of our own International Quartet Champions the **Dealer's Choice, (Al Kvanli, Bill Thornton, Brian Beck** and **Gary Parker)**, plus Audition Chairman **Charlie White** and our Musical Director and his assistant, **Ray Anthony** and **Jim Clancy**. **Keith Houts** served as "Dean" of the weekend school. We even acquired our own local choreographer, **Mickee Albert** (a Dallas Sweet Adeline), to spice up our stage presence. You could tell that our singers were craving the musical instruction, because the turnout of members was almost 100%.

Charlie White was spending almost every minute at rehearsals auditioning lots of Guest Singers in order to march toward that *"80 Singers By October"* goal. We even got our *significant others* (wives, sweethearts, mothers, etc.) involved in the excitement of preparing for the District Contest. Named the *"Vocal Sorority"*, the new ladies group was coordinated by **Bob Wessley** and **Buddy Holiday**.

As I mentioned earlier, the Barbershop Society for many years conducted **Chapter Office Training Schools (COTS)** throughout the country so all chapters could send their administrative officers to a location in their home district to learn what it takes to function in their appointed office. I was invited to Society headquarters in Kenosha, Wisconsin, during a weekend in September 1973 to learn how to be a COTS faculty member. It was quite a kick to visit with Society leaders and discover that The Vocal Majority was considered a "model" in those early days for what constitutes a growing, healthy chapter. I'll have more on my COTS experiences – both good and not-so-good – in future pages.

V.M. DISTRICT CHAMPS

That headline blasted out of the top one-third of the October 29, 1973, Vocalizer. The VM chorus beat out the **Houston Tidelanders** by a mere 18-points, but it felt like a *thousand* points to each of us who had worked so hard to reach that first milestone. Not only did the VM outsing the other competitors, but we outscored all the other choruses in the one category that everyone – including us – felt was our weakest one: *Stage Presence*.

NOVEMBER-DECEMBER GUEST SINGERS – Bill Rushing, Dick Snyder, John Grosnick, Wayne Pruitt, Jack Johnston, Jerry Underwood, Bob Pickins, Bob Lichtenstein, Gene Roberts, Dwight Cook, Earl Keel, Chuck Shelton, Ernie Powers, Bill Kennedy, Carl Hathaway,

116

Heading into the Christmas season of 1973, everything seemed to be going our way. A tremendous celebration ensued the Thursday rehearsal after our District contest victory. Some of the highlights mentioned in the November 5th Vocalizer:

- A "Chapter of Champions" trophy display, with the International Quartet trophy of the **DEALER'S CHOICE** alongside the Southwestern District Chorus Trophy of the VM.

- Lots of significant others and guests.

- A box of *WHEATIES Breakfast of Champions* presented to us with a poem by our choreographer, **Mickee Albert**.

The chapter voted in our 1973 Board of Directors:

President – BOB WESSLEY
Admin. V.P. – BOB ARNOLD
Prog. V.P. – TOM BAMFORD
Music V.P. – KEITH HOUTS
Secretary – CHARLIE LYMAN
Treasurer – QUINN HUNTER
Immed. Past Pres. – ART HAYNES
Music Dir. – RAY ANTHONY
Ass't Dir. – JIM CLANCY
Ass't Dir. – BRIAN BECK
Aud. Chmn. – CHARLIE WHITE
Music Comm. – BILL THORNTON
At Large – FRANK HARKNESS
At Large – GEORGE BURRELL
At Large – SAM HOUSTON

We were headed toward our third Good Time Music Show at the Windmill Dinner Theater, and a paid booking for the **Greenville Community Concert** organization. In a *Vocalizer* editorial by yours truly titled, ***"God Loves The Vocal Majority",*** I expressed the belief that all of us held in our united quest for excellence with the following words:

> *"We hope our headline doesn't offend any of our Barbershop Friends. It's a saying that members of our organization have had*

since we first gathered in the late fall of 1971. We used to say it out of despair when the turnout of singers was so small we wondered if our idea would every get off the ground. We used to say it after we were jolted out of despair by an exciting rehearsal session, with first-time attendance by some new and talented singers. We said it when we were officially chartered in August 1972, just one week before our first contest. We said it when we won that contest and eventually came in second in District competition. We found many occasions to say it during 1973, with our Dealer's Choice taking gold medals at International and our program of shows and singouts all being tremendously successful during the summer and fall. And we certainly said it after our miraculous victory in Oklahoma City. We believe now, more than ever, that Someone has taken a liking to us . . . or we could never have achieved what we have. And each of us should give thanks."

All of us got *REALLY* excited when I printed the future order of chorus appearances at the 1974 International Convention in Kansas City, and the DALLAS METROPOLITAN TEXAS group was listed as the **number four chorus** to perform. It was proof that *North Texas area chorus competitors would no longer be absent from that annual competition!*

Chapter 12
1974: BRAGGING RIGHTS & A NEW *VOCALIZER*

With some bragging rights now in our hip pocket because of two quartet champions and a chorus championship, *The Vocalizer* got a new "masthead" in January 1974. In publishing terminology, *a masthead refers to the flag, banner or the name of a newspaper or periodical, its proprietors, publisher, etc., printed in large type at the top of the front page* (Wikipedia). **Bill Thornton**, who was working at the time as a graphic designer, created the new masthead that read in part:

> **The Chapter of Champions**, Chartered Aug. 1972
> Home of the following Champions
> **The Dealer's Choice**, 1973 International Quartet Champions
> **The Stage Door Four**, 1970 Southwestern District Quartet Champions
> **The Vocal Majority**, 1973 Southwestern District Chorus Champions

Bill and I agreed that the new look provided some great *credibility* for our young organization. And, while only two members of the **Stage Door Four** quartet were VM members (**Keith Houts and Don Dochterman**), we claimed the quartet for our very own anyway. For two marketing guys, all's fair in love and promotional audacity!

Vocal Majority, Vintage 1974

The New Year saw our organization moving to **Granny's Dinner Theater** for our Good Time Music Shows, as we began the musical, financial and logistical planning for the International Chorus Contest in Kansas City that summer.

At the VM's first annual installation banquet that year, **Ray Anthony, Jim Clancy** and **Brian Beck** received our chapter's first *Barbershopper of the Year* awards.

Rehearsals during January and February got to be exciting as **Jim Clancy** continued to introduce clever new arrangements to our repertoire. *"Delta Dawn"* was a popular country music ditty, and Jim turned it into a rollicking, fun song for the chorus. A special guest night brought out 24 singing guests, and many of them were turned into members during the next few months. The February *Good Time Music Show* featured the **Innsiders** (current SW District quartet champs from Houston), the **Stage Door Four**, and the **Dealer's Choice**.

Since the "beer & pretzel" show format was such a success, we decided the do one each month during March, April and May of 1974. Performing as guest quartets on the March show were such well-known groups as **The Mark IV** (1970 International Quartet Champions from San Antonio), and **The Crackerjacks** from Oklahoma City. Guest quartets on the April and May shows included the **Dealer's Choice**, the **Brass Ring**, the **Folkel Minority**, and the **Tune Aces** (a crazy, funny Cajun group from Houma, Louisiana).

WHO (OR WHAT) IS/ARE THE FOLKEL MINORITY

Those VM members and show patrons who came to our shows during the 1970s and 1980s might describe the group as "wacky". In fact, I heard **Jim Clancy** once admit that he wasn't quite sure our organization should allow them on our shows. The "them" he was talking about was *MY GROUP!* After having a strong hand in forming The Vocal Majority Chorus, I secretly yearned to find a few of our singers who might enjoy forming a folk/country group within the larger organization. I also hoped they would play appropriate instruments to accompany the singing, and add some good wholesome "character" to the ensemble.

Well, I found **Jim Martin** in our Tenor Section, **Ross Wise** in our Bass Section, and **Bill Sturgeon** in the Baritone Section. And they all played guitars like me! YAHOO! And we all were fans of vocal harmony groups like **The Oak Ridge Boys, The Gatlin Brothers, Peter Paul & Mary, The Kingston Trio, The Limelighters,** etc. Now, if we could only harmonize and entertain like these groups, we might have an act that could contribute to the variety of VM shows and give each of us in the group an outlet for a different kind of music.

L-R: Jim Martin, Bob Arnold, Bill Sturgeon, Jake Greene, Ross Wise

Well, it didn't look or sound all the pretty from the get-go. But little by little, the group came together and started to perform some fairly entertaining segments on the VM's Good Time Music Shows. We needed a rhythm instrument to add some depth to the acoustic guitars, so I learned to play the electric bass guitar – not all that well, but it was good enough for us. We didn't really take ourselves all that seriously, and we encouraged our audiences to do the same.

After a couple of years, we managed to become proficient at putting together songs and medleys and comedy routines that even entertained audiences *outside* of our VM shows. We found that people and organizations would actually pay good money to hear us sing! We wrote a couple of original songs ourselves – mostly comedy material and mostly about the Dallas area and Texas topics that everyone could relate to: "A Tribute To The Trinity", "I'm A Mexican Junkfood Junkie", "Ridin' On The DART Rail Line".

One original song in particular that audiences enjoyed was **"Freeze A Yankee"**, which I wrote on a business trip to West

Texas. We received outrageous audience reactions when we sang it, so we put it on one side of a 45-rpm record and printed up a couple of hundred copies to sell at shows and bookings. It was just a silly "redneck" song about the energy crisis us Texans experienced around 1979. But then **Ron Chapman** got ahold of it and played it a couple of times on his top-rated KVIL Radio show, and all hell broke loose!

We started receiving requests for hundreds of copies from record distributors and record retail stores (remember them?). It rose to the #1 record seller in Dallas for ONE WEEK, and was a top seller throughout the Southwestern part of the U.S. Ultimately, the record sold about 100,000 copies, and the story behind the song was written up in *The Wall Street Journal* and *The Dallas Times Herald*. The song eventually generated a "cult following" for The Folkel Minority, as people all around the country treasured their copy of the record. And I still get comments today from people I meet who either have a copy or have heard about it.

Actually, the bass singer on that recording is NOT Ross Wise. Ross's job was moved to Lubbock by his employer at the time, Texas Instruments, and we had to find a replacement. About that time, a new bass singer joined the VM by the name of **Jake Greene**. Jake was super talented and fit right into the Folkel bass slot. About two years after that we faced a dilemma: Ross moved back to Dallas. Because we loved both guys personally and as musicians, we simply added Ross back into the group and became a quintet. Problem solved!

The Folkels disbanded after about eight years together when Jake moved to South Carolina in retirement and, tragically, both he and Jim Martin passed away within a year of one another in the 2014-2015 timeframe. I still miss them both a lot.

Weekly section rehearsals began in March for the intense preparation leading up to the International Contest in Kansas City in July. The two songs the VM would sing in the chorus contest were announced in February: *"At The Jazz Band Ball"* and *"Who'll Take My Place When I'm Gone"*. The latter song was one that the **Dealer's Choice** sang during their final set in their own march to the quartet gold medal.

President **Doris Thornton** was meeting monthly with her *Vocal Sorority* helpers, planning a casino party at St. Mark's Church in Plano to raise funds for the chorus costumes and travel expenses. Later, our ladies created a Vocal Sorority Pizza Sale conducted at **Saint Michael and All Angels Episcopal Church** in north Dallas.

A rare three-day seminar was held on Easter weekend, importing such Barbershop Society coaches as **Don Clause**, who mentored the **Dealer's Choice** in their stunning first-time Gold Medal title, and **Jack Hines**, a judging specialist in the Stage Presence category. Both men were scheduled to be on the judging panel in Kansas City that summer.

Speaking of the Kansas City Barbershop convention, **Frank Harkness** headed up the team that was responsible for the complex task of registering, moving, housing, rehearsing and feeding over 70 VM singers plus family members and friends in KC. That team included: **Ray Hyman, Jeff Brock, George Burrell, Bob Jett, Barry Battershall, Jim Carter, Bill Sturgeon, Charlie White, Don Knight, Wayne Pruett,** and **John Schroy**.

Several VM members signed a hefty bank note to borrow about $6,000 for the purchase of new performance outfits for the Kansas City contest. The old orange jumpsuits were relegated to performances at future Good Time Music Shows and other more informal chorus appearances. Several buses were reserved for the KC trip, and a makeup committee was established within the **Vocal Sorority** to apply cake makeup, rouge, eye liner and lipstick. All choruses competing in the International competition needed to wear makeup to prevent face colors from washing out under the bright stage lights.

New VM member **Sonny Lipford** volunteered to be the chapter *"Tongue Twister"* and fine each chorus member 25-cents for interrupting during rehearsals. The collected money went into Sonny's collection cup for the B.M.F.F.K.C. (Big Mouth Fund For Kansas City). And coach **Don Clause** made his last visit to a VM rehearsal at the end of May to see how the chorus was picking up on the vowel-matching techniques he demonstrated during his preceding visit. Ten rehearsals were scheduled during the end of June and beginning of July as the music team whipped the chorus into a performance machine. *"The Majority Rules"* buttons were produced by the VM promotions team to be worn on clothing, placed on luggage, and shared with unsuspecting Barbershoppers attending the KC convention.

VOCAL MAJORITY
OOOOOPS!
INTERNATIONAL CHAMPS!

Ooooops is right! The headline above was on the July 15, 1974, *Vocalizer*. It was meant to show the world that the best laid plans of even well prepared, musically talented choral singers could be dashed by a team of sophisticated contest judges. I don't have meticulous notes on events in Kansas City during that weekend in July, but I certainly do remember

124

that sick, stomach-churning feeling when the announcements were made naming the winning choruses. Not only did the VM NOT win the contest, we didn't even come in *SECOND!* Third Place would have been fantastic for many other chorus competitors that day, but not for a singing machine that prided itself in already being the best in the world at what we did.

I do remember that, after the winners were announced, all VM chorus members gathered in our assigned rehearsal room to assess the feelings of each singer and those of our leaders. Curiously, our director, Ray Anthony, was nowhere to be found. Undoubtedly, Ray was feeling the tremendous let-down that all leaders feel after an emotional build-up over the past several months, and went to soothe his emotions somewhere quiet and alone.

I remember gathering with the other chorus members in that rehearsal room, most of us with tears in our eyes, as we listened to the musical leader we most respected out of all the talented men we had at our disposal – **Jim Clancy**. While Jim was *technically* our Assistant Director, he was, in most of our eyes, the person with the most natural musical talent and credibility when it came to the more "technical" aspects of music making. Jim gathered us together and said some very encouraging words about our performance that day, and our devotion to the goal of being extremely proficient at our craft. He then taught the chorus a new twist on an arrangement that we knew quite well ("Delta Dawn"), and promised us two new challenging arrangements when we got home to Dallas. We all knew better things were to come, and our new leader was now *Jim Clancy*.

WHERE DO WE GO FROM HERE?

To quote from that July 15th *Vocalizer*: *"It didn't work exactly as we had planned . . . but we all know that The Vocal Majority was the best SINGING chorus in the contest . . . even though the judges gave us a Third Place Medal for our overall performance. I am personally proud of that Third Place Medal! But we apparently have to 'pay our dues' for the next year just like Louisville did. They came in second last year, and then paid the price AGAIN to come back and win the contest. And the Peninsula, California, chorus was just magnificent in taking second! So be proud to have lived up to the reputation which the VM had in Kansas City before anyone even heard us. Now they know that all those rumors about a fantastic singing chorus in Dallas were absolutely true! "*

*"We have so many individuals and groups to thank for their con-tributions to our ambitious efforts. The Contest Committee and its chair-man, **Frank Harkness**, made me feel absolutely pampered during the last few weeks. Our music specialists had us up to a perfect pitch . . . both musically and psychologically . . . for the competition. And our good-looking, hard-working **Vocal Sorority** was just amazing with their organ-ization and support! Lastly . . . the chapters of the Southwestern District who contributed financially (and morally in K.C.) toward our efforts. Our financial contributors included: HOUSTON'S TIDELANDERS, SAN AN-TONIO, SABINE AREA, MIDLAND, OKLAHOMA CITY, CHICKASHA, ARLINGTON, and DALLAS BIG D. Thanks, from the bottom of our hearts, guys and gals!"*

We were also blessed with thoughtful telegrams while we were in Kansas City from THE GREATER DALLAS SWEET ADELINES, GRANNY'S DINNER PLAYHOUSE, THE SCHLITZ BREWING COMPANY, and the BIG D CHAPTER.

The big question was: *Where do we go from here?* It was obvious that The Vocal Majority would be aiming to again knock off Houston and San Antonio in the coming fall District Contest, which was to be conven-iently held in Dallas and hosted by the **Town North Chapter**. The VM board of directors would have to re-group and find a way to lead us back into contention, and also replenish our destitute chapter treasury. To help solve that problem, a well-paid **Mary Kay** Convention Spectacular at the new **Dallas Convention Center Theater** was scheduled, and a new series of Granny's Good Time Music Shows made it on to our calendar. Would these and other performances brush away the sad memory of a third-place finish at our very first International competition? Read on and find out how the VM gathered itself together and eventually captured its first inter-national chorus Gold Medal.

In an informal celebration hosted by our Vocal Sorority shortly after our return from KC, **George Burrell** came up with a great theme for our drive to the International chorus competition in 1975 at Indianapolis: *"THE INDIANAPOLIS 100"*. That theme signified 100 singers on stage the following summer, which meant more ambitious recruiting of new singers, and holding down the natural attrition of current members. A more realist goal was for 90 singers on stage at the Southwestern District

126

contest in October, which wasn't far away. And a great community exposure opportunity came our way when I was contacted by the **Dallas United Way** Campaign for the chorus to perform at their September kickoff luncheon. (As the marketing director for the chorus, I was the contact person for any organization that wanted to book the VM for a paid or pro-bono performance.)

One of the most import and far-reaching decisions the VM made after the Kansas City competition was the transition from **Ray Anthony** as chorus director to **Jim Clancy**. The *Vocalizer* issues during that time don't shed much light on this change-over, but I remember the mountain of discussion that went on regarding the future direction of our music program. As I recall, Ray decided on his own that he didn't quite have the necessary musical knowledge and abilities to lead the chorus to any greater heights than we had already achieved. His charisma and emotional-style of directing, apparently, weren't enough to move the chorus to the next level of musical sophistication necessary to win a gold medal. He and Jim had some serious discussions about why Ray felt that Jim could, with continuing help from Ray and the other members of the VM music team, develop into a Gold Medal director. Ray volunteered to stay on the music team and tutor Jim on the basics of directing a choral organization. Jim, however, wasn't so sure. While he had a tremendous musical background and outstanding talent, and had taught the chorus the music to his own arrangements which he had gone on to direct, he still didn't appear confident that he could take over such an important role. The board of directors, however, felt confident enough in Jim to name him the VM's new chorus director. And, the rest as they say, is history.

JIM CLANCY: PRODIGY IN A MUSICAL FAMILY

I first met Jim at the initial rehearsal of the group that was to become the VM chorus in December 1971. Guys I'd known told me he was a "jingle singer", which meant to me that he was a professional musician and someone we'd love to have join our merry group of wannabees.

127

I've since learned that Jim is known throughout the recording industry as America's most recorded bass singer in jingles and commercials on radio and television. (If you're from around the North Texas area you might have heard his deep voice on the **Westway Ford** jingle for many decades singing, *"Wah wah Westway Ford"*.) He also was once considered as the replacement for the **Tony The Tiger** voice on the TV ads for **Kellogg's Frosted Flakes**. (*They're grrrrrreat!*)

Jim was raised in a very musical family in Shreveport, Louisiana. You can Google his mother's name – **Martha Moore Clancy** – and find that her career in music spanned 50-plus years as a music teacher, choir director and as a music professor at Baptist Theological Seminary in Fort Worth, Texas. She was one of two women on the 35-member committee that prepared the 1956 edition of the Baptist Hymnal that is still used today in America. While Jim's mom was teaching in Fort Worth, his dad, Jack, took over directing her church choir back in Shreveport.

Jim said this about his dad: "My father, Jack, was very instrumental in my musical development and love of vocal harmony. He was himself a wonderful director and baritone soloist. He taught me so many of the great old songs, many of which we have sung or heard in Barbershop circles. He had as much to do with my love of vocal music as Mom did. Several of the songs Mom and Dad taught me have been Gold Medal ballads for the VM. Mother passed up an operatic career to go into church music. With parents like this, how could I not have loved music."

Martha Clancy attended many VM shows and rehearsals until she passed away in 2000, just short of her 91st birthday. But the one visit that is etched in my mind was when the chorus was rehearsing in the Mormon Tabernacle in Salt Lake City just prior to our second joint appearance with the world-famous Tabernacle Choir in 1986. She appeared at our rehearsal site inside the Tabernacle and said these immortal words: *"This is my beloved son in whom I am well pleased."* That's something you just don't forget.

Jim has conducted the VM in performances throughout the United States, Canada, Scotland and England, and directed VM performances for two United States Presidents, at national athletic events, with major symphony orchestras, and before hundreds of national conventions. Jim is often called upon as a coach with national and international choral groups, having directed multiple concerts for the American Choral Directors Association and Music Educators National Conference. He has understudied American greats such as Fred Waring, Madeleine Marshall, Paris Rutherford, Martha Moore Clancy, Warren Angell, and B.B. McKinney, in addition to pursuing academic work at Baylor University, Centenary College, and the University of North Texas.

His discography with Vocal Majority includes 25 albums of popular, jazz, classic, Barbershop, inspirational music along with a DVD, *A Vocal Majority Christmas*, released in 2003. As a guest conductor with the famed **Mormon Tabernacle Choir**, Jim combined the Utah ensemble with The Vocal Majority in a joint album, *Voices In Harmony*, for CBS Masterworks. He has also performed on stage with many legendary artists including **Jimmy Dean, Bob Flanigan, The Four Freshmen, John Gary, Lee Greenwood, The Lettermen, Johnny Mann, The Oak Ridge Boys**, and the **Suntones**.

In October 2000, Jim was honored by the **Barbershop Harmony Society's Southwestern District** when a new Chorus Champion trophy was unveiled and named in his honor – the *Jim Clancy Chorus Champion Award*. And, in 2005, he was inducted into the *Barbershop Harmony Society Hall of Fame*.

As primary arranger for Vocal Majority, Jim has shaped its rich harmonies and distinctively elegant sounds in his years as its director. His legacy goes on now as his son, Greg, has taken over the baton and has stamped his own creative imprint on the chorus. However, Jim continues to churn out unique and challenging arrangements for the chorus and other choral organizations around the world. For more information about Jim, visit his web page at jimclancyarrangements.com.

Since Jim has was named Executive Music Director for The Vocal Majority Chorus, then his wife, **Judy**, should probably have the title of *"Creative House Mother and Cheerleader"*. Judy and Jim were married in 1988 after carrying on a short distance romance between Dallas and Oklahoma City. She has since become the organizer and inspiration behind the **VMW** (**V**ocal **M**ajority **W**omen), an organization of our significant others that supports the activities of the chorus in myriad ways. Judy is herself a gold medal quartet singer with Sweet Adelines International, winning with the **Ginger 'n Jazz** quartet in 1987. Judy explains her reasons for creating the VMW: *"It was important to me to unify the women into an organization of support and give back to our men. Thus, VMW – Vocal Majority Women – was born. The guys are gone rehearsing a lot, particularly the last month before contest, and it's vital to me for the ladies, especially women new to the organization, to feel a part of this incredible family. I want VMW to embrace one another in a sisterhood and provide them fun memories and their own involvement at conventions, too!"*

THE BEAT GOES ON AFTER KANSAS CITY

An ambitious membership recruitment campaign began in late July 1974. This concentrated two-month campaign had a point system for recruiters, incentive prizes, special business cards printed, and media publicity.

Good Time Music Shows were scheduled for September and November with featured performers that included the **VM Dixieland Band**, the **Dealer's Choice**, the **Stage Door Four**, the **Brass Ring** (reconstituted Mod Quad), and the **Folkel Minority**. The Dixieland Band became quite popular at most of our shows during the late 1970s and early 1980s. It was composed of VM members **Charlie Lyman** on piano, **Ray Helal** on Trumpet, **Jim Sharples** on bass, and other area musicians at various times on drums and other instruments. Other VM singers who cycled in and out of the band included **Brian Beck**, **Red McDonald**, and **Jeff Brock**. In fact, the band was a part of the entertainment package we offered to the United Way executives for their kickoff event.

Fifteen new members were recruited and passed their audition as a result of the membership campaign, with several more in the wings waiting for their obligatory three chorus rehearsal visits before they became eligible for an audition. After the VM's surprising success at Kansas City, plus all the local publicity surrounding the Good Time Music Shows and the United Way appearance, good singers were coming in droves to lend their talents to this relatively new singing organization.

And that's exactly what we had hoped for since the founding of the organization only three years prior. The September 27th Vocalizer captured the progress the organization had made in such a short amount of time by declaring: "*From about a dozen singers in early 1972, The Vocal Majority has grown in both reputation and size. Chapter Secretary, CHARLIE LYMAN (a co-founder of our chapter) reported last Thursday night that our paper membership has now risen to over 100 singers! What's even more important . . . most of those singers will be on stage with us for District!*"

To move the organization forward for the next important year, the chapter nominating committee named the following men to take the reins of management and create the organizational atmosphere for a Gold Medal chorus:

President – CHARLIE LYMAN
Administrative VP – NORM SEBENS
Program VP – BILL STURGEON
Music VP – BILL THORNTON
Public Relations VP – BOB ARNOLD
Secretary – EDDIE WALL
Treasurer – BARRY BATTERSHALL
Immediate Past Pres. – BOB WESSLEY
Directors At-Large   ROSS WISE
                    JOE POYNER
                    JIM DENTON
Chorus Director – JIM CLANCY
Assist. Chorus Dir.   BRIAN BECK
                    CHARLIE WHITE
                    RAY ANTHONY
                    GARY PARKER

During the final week prior to the District contest, the chorus rehearsed four nights a week – all in full costume – at Highland Park High School's auditorium. The headline on the October 28th *Vocalizer* gave proof that this tremendous amount of preparation was worth it:

"WE DID IT AGAIN!"

The VM beat the second place **Houston Tidelanders** by 71 points in the Southwestern District Contest, and we were on our way to our second consecutive appearance in the "super bowl" of chorus competitions the following year in Indianapolis.

Some more challenges for the board of directors to look forward to: The purchase of new risers; a new schedule of Good Time Music Shows at Granny's; a new and bigger recruiting campaign; and a stunning direct mail piece to get the chorus more lucrative convention bookings. Jim Clancy wasn't idle in coming up with some new, fun arrangements for our public performances. One, *"Who's In The Strawberry Patch With Sally?"*, was a rollicking **Tony Orlando and Dawn** song that fit right into our "good time" atmosphere at Granny's shows.

The December annual installation and awards banquet saw **Frank Harkness** and **Charlie White** win co-*Barbershopper of the Year* Awards,

132

and **Ray Anthony** was presented with the special award of *Chorus Director Emeritus* for his impassioned guidance in bringing the chorus along to its present high standard. Special guests at that event were former International Society President **Ralph Ribble**, Southwestern District President, **Dave Sjogren**, Town North Chapter President, **Duane Lunday**, Big D Chapter President, **Bob Engle**, and Arlington Chapter President, **Jerry Lux**.

Among the many decisions by VM leaders for the coming year included settling on our two contest songs for the next summer's International Contest, revising the format and production of future Good Time Music Shows, and planning the first chorus record album.

Chapter 13
1975: *"THE INDIANAPOLIS 100"*

The January Good Time Music Show at Granny's Dinner Theater featured a beautiful new arrangement taught to us and directed by **Ray Anthony**, *"Deep River"*. And the much-awaited new chorus contest up-tune was introduced at a January rehearsal, *"I Never Knew/You Were Meant For Me Medley"*, arranged by the well-known Sweet Adeline coach and director, **Renee Craig**.

February was named *"Bring-A-Singer Month"*, as we geared up to put at least 100 singers on the risers for the late June Indianapolis contest. We also had visits from high profile vocal coaches **Renee Craig** and **Don Clause** during those Springtime months. And we were now able to rehearse on our first *fully-owned set of chorus risers* as the chapter exercised a $1,600 line of credit to obtain them. Up to this point, our rehearsal and performance risers were borrowed from various schools and other organizations.

Section rehearsals for all four sections prior to rehearsals began in March. Since we were still cramped into the Chapel Downs Community Center for our weekly rehearsals, those section rehearsals had to be held at members' homes an hour prior to the regular 8 o'clock rehearsals. Another visit from acclaimed vocal coach **Don Clause** happened in April, along with a visit from choreography coach **Arnie Bauer**. There was a continuation of section rehearsals prior to every Thursday rehearsal, and a *Good Time Music Show* that audience members said, "was the best ever!".

Chorus members were asked to devote an enormous amount of time to both chorus rehearsals and performances during April and May. Monday rehearsals were added in addition to regular Thursdays, and the VM was booked for paid performances for **Dallas Federal Savings & Loan, "Artfest"** for a nonprofit arts organization called **The 500, Inc.**, and the **Texas Association of Insurance Agents** in the Great Hall of the Apparel Mart. It was going to be expensive transporting 100+ singers, families and guests from Dallas to Indianapolis, so we all had to grit our teeth and hope our families would understand the challenges we had to undertake to be the best in the world.

Who were those three kids who passed the VM audition that April? Why, none other than **Greg Clancy, Chuck Denton** and **Jody Denton.** Jody and his brother **Chuck** were both the sons of VM Charter Member **Jim Denton.** Jim, unfortunately, passed away far too young one month prior to the 1982 International Chorus Contest. But his son Chuck is still a front-row member of the chorus to this day, and is a great legacy to honor his father.

Greg was later immortalized in the chorus photo from the 1975 Indianapolis contest as the "cute little kid with the long curly hair standing in the middle on the front row". He also later turned into an outstanding chorus director and International Quartet Champion tenor (Max Q, 2007). He currently has more *combined* chorus and quartet gold medals than any other member of the Barbershop Harmony Society. *I think it's safe to say that cute little kid on the front row has done OK for himself!*

The Max Q Quartet took the quartet gold medal in 2007 after finishing second the previous three years. From L-R: **Greg Clancy, Tony De Rosa, Jeff Oxley, Gary Lewis**. The group won the gold despite its members living some distance apart. Greg and Jeff were in Dallas, Tony in Florida, and Gary in Ohio. They were a welcome addition to VM shows before and after their championship victory.

Since bursting onto the VM front row in 1975, Greg has been a first-call studio vocalist, jingle singer and composer of image music for some 25 years. He is now GM/VP Creative for TM Studios. (It's the same studio where his dad was once employed as a jingle singer for many years.) Greg composes imaging music for stations around the country including KABC in Los Angeles, WMAL in Washington, D.C. and WLS in Chicago.

"MANUFACTURING CARROTS" TO GROW THE ORGANIZATION

May's first *Vocalizer* tried to hold that "carrot-on-a-stick" in front of VM members with the following motivational declaration: *"Before we discard our current show package of songs, we'll cut a Vocal Majority record album to preserve these great arrangements. After that, it's another*

136

great package of new music, more Granny's shows, and more profitable convention and show bookings. All designed to make the second half of 1975 just as exciting as the first half!" I've always believed that nonprofit organization newsletters need to address the motivational needs of BOTH its customer/client base AND its own members and employees. Or maybe I've said that already . . .

Beginning in mid-May, chapter leaders scrambled to find additional rehearsal facilities because the Chapel Down Community Center was not available four nights each week to accommodate the heavy rehearsal schedule for contest preparations. Travel Chairman, **Quinn Hunter**, put together a convention registration packet for all registered VM members, and Transportation Chairman, **Jim Denton**, arranged for busses to travel from Dallas to Indianapolis. The **VM Dixieland Band** would also make the trip with the chorus, so room needed to be made on the busses for drums and musical instruments. Treasurer **Barry Battershall** reported that the chapter did much better financially then the board of directors previously thought, and that each member would receive a stipend of $80 to help defray the costs for the trip. That doesn't seem like much of an incentive in today's dollars, but it seemed pretty darned great back in 1975.

"THE END IS IN SIGHT NOW!" was the blazing headline of the May 30, 1975, *Vocalizer.* Two-a-week rehearsals were in full swing, with section rehearsals prior to each Thursday evening session. Much needed funds came in the form of a Good Time Music Show format for the **Texas Insurance Agents Association** in the Great Hall of the Apparel Mart featuring the **VM, Dealer's Choice, Folkel Minority**, and the **VM Dixieland Band**. In early June, our pair of respected Barbershop coaches, **Don Clause** and **Ernie Bauer,** made their final journey to Dallas to give some last-minute advice to our music team and to the chorus. Dress rehearsals were scheduled for TWO nights at Highland Park High School in late June, as we made final adjustments in costumes, choreography, and vocal interpretations for the two contest songs and our other show material.

Two rehearsals were scheduled on the Friday we arrived in Indianapolis, with each chorus doing a "run-through" at the contest stage location on Saturday mid-morning. The VM was scheduled to be the 12th chorus in the contest lineup out of fifteen choruses competing. Rumors from around the country indicated that the **Phoenicians** from Phoenix, Arizona, were the chorus to beat in the contest. A Saturday morning VM chorus breakfast for singers and family members was scheduled at our headquarters hotel, That family breakfast became a decades-long tradition for VM choruses at international competitions that still exists today.

The stage was set. Would all the hard work, the long hours of rehearsals and planning, and the sacrifices of both singers and family members be enough to bring home Gold Medals for each VM chorus member?

THE MAJORITY RULES
AS INTERNATIONAL CHAMPS!

That *Vocalizer* headline pretty much said it all. Not only did The Vocal Majority win that contest in June of 1975, but there were reports that we rang up the highest score of *any* chorus (up to that time) in the history of the Society, and the largest winning margin (120-points) of any chorus so far. The VM got a standing ovation from the 10,000 people in the convention audience that afternoon during the contest, and again when we performed on the evening "show of champions". That *Vocalizer* went on to capture some experiences that I'll never forget as a member of that chorus with these words:

> *"The personal congratulations and complements of competing chorus members . . . the very touching ovation and handshake line formed by members of the Phoenicians as we exited from the recording room after we had won . . . the marvelous song composed and sung by JIM CLANCY at our breakfast Saturday morning ('No Thanks, Louisville, Thanks A Lot') . . . the touching words by TOM BAMFORD at the same breakfast . . . the warm and thoughtful assistance of our wives, sweethearts and family during our entire stay in Indy . . . the absolute best afterglow/hospitality room, with the likes of THE SUNTONES, INNSIDERS, REAGENTS, SOUND ASSOCIATION, QUASARS, and our new International Quartet Champs, THE HAPPINESS EMPORIUM . . . the glowing personal comments from almost every quartet appearing at the hospitality room, the fine accommodations at the Quality Inn. All this and much, much more will remain with us as memories of our victory."*

138

That Gold Medal was the first of ten that I had the pleasure of winning as a member of the chorus, but it had to be the most memorable one of all. From the time we first met 3-1/2 years earlier, to winning the recognition as "the best chorus in the world", it was a beautiful ride to remember and savor. I had 91 other brothers on that stage in Indianapolis, and I loved every last one of them.

After all of us got back to Dallas and the euphoria had died down amid a return to our everyday lives, we seriously wondered whether chorus

members would feel deflated. After all, we had just spent the past six months focusing on the chorus to the detriment of our family life, our careers, and our bank accounts. Contest preparations had not only drained our personal lives, the chapter's treasury was in tatters with zero on hand for operations, and bank debt looming due to performance outfits, risers, and travel expenses. Could it be that we had unwittingly snuffed out the flame that had been burning so fiercely in all our hearts?

As a concerned member of our organization's leadership team, I put those feelings into print in the July 7th *Vocalizer* with the headline,

"WHERE TO FROM HERE?" I've always been a firm believer that personal motivation must be ongoing, with a new *carrot* being manufactured and tied to a new *stick* every time a major goal is achieved. [**Author's Note:** In fact, *"Manufacturing Carrots"* was the title of the motivational weekend seminar that I provided to interested Barbershop and Sweet Adeline chapters who brought me into their towns during the next few decades. They all wanted to know the secrets to raising their chapter organizations up to the level attained by the new sensation Vocal Majority Chorus. It was around this time that Susan and I formed a new company for the purpose of providing these workshops called **Arnold Marketing Associates.**]

In that first *Vocalizer* after returning to Dallas, I laid out what I hoped would be sufficient motivation and activities to engage current and future members. That ambitious calendar of events was conceived in hopes it would keep members and guests coming back for the foreseeable future:

- Good Time Music Shows in July and August
- A VM appearance at the regional quartet and chorus contest in Arlington to show area Barbershoppers what an International Champion Chorus looks and sounds like;
- An appearance on the Fort Worth Chapter show in October;
- A homecoming appearance for our own Southwestern District Convention in Abilene during November;
- A December benefit concert in Houston featuring the VM, the Houston Tidelanders, and the San Antonio Chordsmen;
- A printed ad promoting paid bookings on behalf of the VM and the Dealer's Choice in the *Whitmark Talent Directory*, which was sent to all advertising agencies in the Southwest;
- Two record albums to cut – one for ourselves and one side of an album for the Barbershop Harmony Society;
- A KVIL Radio night with The Vocal Majority.

All our fears about whether our singers would show up at our first rehearsal after the big competition week were laid to rest as *100 VM members and guest singers* gathered to learn new songs and see souvenir pictures of the Indianapolis experience. The most media exposure the VM ever was a two-night **KVIL Radio-** sponsored show at the NorthPark Inn. We were aware that anytime KVIL got behind an organization or event, it would automatically be a sellout. And the September shows were no exception. **Ron Chapman**, who was known to be one of the top radio personalities in the U.S., and certainly the number one DJ in North Texas, let loose with over *100 radio spots* during the week promoting the shows to his listeners. We put on a "Good Time Music Show" format, and the KVIL audience loved it!

The new chapter board of directors was introduced and voted into office in October, with a new leadership team consisting of:

President – FRANK HARKNESS
Administrative VP – CHUCK SHELTON
Program VP – BOB JETT
Music VP – JIM CLANCY
Public Relations VP – BOB ARNOLD
Secretary – JACK JOHNSTON
Treasurer – CHRIS CHRISTENSEN
Immediate Past Pres. – CHARLIE LYMAN
Directors At-Large   JIM DENTON
                        JIM CARTER
                        GEORGE BURRELL

A big surprise was unveiled at a mid-September rehearsal: A rough edited version of our very first audio recording from our last Good Time Music Show. It was the first time that chorus members had the opportunity to hear themselves in a local live performance. The Music Team promised to have the rough tape completely edited and post-production completed to release our new LP called *"Standing Room Only"* by Christmas. Also on the way from our Society's headquarters were 150 LPs, 25 cassettes and 25 eight-track tapes of our winning contest performances from Indianapolis. It was looking to be a very nice Christmas for VM singers!

A DEVESTATING BLOCKBUSTER

You couldn't have invented a worse scenario for our budding organization than we experienced in late October 1975 when **Jim Clancy** and **Brian Beck** *both* announced that they had decided to move to Los Angeles. Jim and Brian were both first-call jingle singers in the Dallas

141

recording industry, and that industry segment was undergoing some unfortunate down times. Consequently, they made the difficult decision to move to LA and try to revive their careers. *BOTH Jim and Brian!* The news just deflated the VM's collective psyche after the euphoria of winning the coveted International Chorus Gold Medal.

Reading the *Vocalizer* from October 24, 1975, I could just FEEL the air being let out of a beautiful balloon as that edition began with the opening words of a Dealer's Choice ballad, *"Everything must have an end / So the poets say."* Chapter leaders certainly had plenty of competent musical directors they could turn to who might be able to see us through this monumental challenge – **Ray Anthony, Charlie White, Bill Thornton, Sonny Lipford, Denis Conrady**. But how could you possibly replace the arranging, coaching and directing talents of Jim and Brian? Well, in the next few months, *we were about the find out.*

Fortunately, we got *some* relief from that devastating blow when we found out that **Jim Clancy** would be back to direct us for the remainder of 1975, and maybe for a considerable amount of time during 1976. And we desperately *needed* his talent and expertise for an important recording project. The VM had made an agreement with the Barbershop Harmony Society to record one side of an LP album during the month of February, with the **Louisville Thoroughbreds** recording the other side – each chorus doing the production on their home turfs. This was an experimental project cooked up by the Society's Director of Music, **Dr. Bob Johnson**, and could significantly increase the exposure of the chorus to more members of the Society. But there was a catch: We had to *only* sing songs approved by the Society.

We submitted the following songs for approval: *"At The Moving Picture Ball", All Alone", An Old Fashioned Girl", "Sing Me A Good Old Mammy Song", "Welcome Back To Dixie Land"*, and *"Alexander's Rag Time Band"*. Yep, all of them good old square Barbershop-style arrangements, with nary a Four Freshmen "modern" chord among them! But we agreed to do it because of the recognition it inferred that The Vocal Majority was now considered on the same level of competence among Barbershoppers as the legendary **Louisville Thoroughbreds**. And it was some great P.R. for us with the staff of the Society when the album's title was announced: *"Champions: Back-To-Back"*. You might say it was a *changing of the guard* for preeminence in Society chorus competitions.

142

Louisville never again dominated future competitions like they had once done.

The annual installation and awards banquet was held at the Empire Room of the Executive Inn near Love Field, and I was honored with the ***Barbershopper of the Year*** *Award.*

Our Vocal Sorority also elected new officers for 1976:

President: **Shell Bonesio**
Vice President: **Betty Sturgeon**
Sec. & Treas.: **Judy Wall**

And to show you how ambitious and active our female support group was, here are the committee members who volunteered to contribute their time:

SOCIAL
Rose Ann Burrell
Pat White
Inez Walter
Sue Lyman
Nancy Crinnion

WAYS & MEANS
Sharon Hawkins
Charlotte Shelton
Mary Ann Rogers
Joyce Hunter
Olivia Barstow

CONTACT
Evelyn Anthony
Karen Reid
Jan Moseley
Kathy Barrow

MEMBERSHIP
Mary Poyner
Candy Cox
Doris Wessley
Evelyn Denton

The six months ahead of us in 1976 appeared to be busy ones. One Good Time Music Show a month was scheduled from January through June, as well as paid bookings for the **Ex-Braniff Stewardesses Association** (remember them?), and the **National Secretaries Association**. And then there was the matter of returning to the annual Barbershop Society convention in July at San Francisco to "give away the trophy" to the new chorus champions. (In case you are not aware of the chorus competition rules, a winning chorus had to "lay out" of the competition for two years and then re-qualify through their district contests once those two years had expired.) The VM leadership team debated the wisdom of making such a heavy time and money commitment to return to the San Francisco convention ever since we had returned from Indianapolis. How could we possibly ask our singers to follow up the sacrifices they had made and go through the same arduous build-up for the 1976 event in San Francisco? We would soon find out.

Chapter 14
1976: A DIFFICULT SAN FRANCISCO DECISION

1976 began with a tremendous amount of enthusiasm for the tentative trip to San Francisco. The first few *Vocalizers* blared, *"California Here We Come!"*. But there were still strong doubts about a large segment of VM singers being able to *afford* the time and financial commitments necessary to travel for the performance. It was a long-standing tradition in the Barbershop Society for gold medal choruses to return the year after winning the title to present a "swan song" show at the annual convention.

January was filled with section rehearsals prior to each rehearsal to get new material ready for the San Francisco convention and our recording session for the *"Back To Back"* album. One Good Time Music Show was planned each month at Granny's Dinner Theater. A "San Francisco Savings Program" was set up by VM member **Chris Christensen**, a vice president at Dallas Federal Savings, so members would have sufficient funds to make the trip. Vocal Sorority members were cooking up pot luck suppers to raise additional funds.

February not only saw another sold-out show at Granny's, with the **Quasars** from Austin being the featured guest quartet, but the Society's Director of Music Education, **Bob Johnson**, came to Dallas to supervise a recording session that would put the VM on one side of an LP album and the Louisville Thoroughbreds on the other side as a Society fund-raising project. Sixty VM singers got up early and appeared for a Channel 8 (WFAA-TV) morning show appearance. And planning continued for the San Francisco trip, with deposits collected for rooms at the San Francisco Hilton Hotel and for convention registration fees. With all that activity, it sure looked like the convention trip was a "go".

March was an exciting month for VM activities. Guest quartets for our Good Time Music Shows included our old friends the **Stage Door Four**, a reconstituted version of one of our crowd favorites, the **Beau Jesters**, along with the **Innsiders** from Houston, our own **Folkel Minority**, the **Vocal Oakies** from Oklahoma City, and our own Gold Medal foursome, the **Dealer's Choice**. We also looked forward to taking our Good Time Show on the road to New Braunfels, where the **Austin Chapter** had invited us to headline their annual show.

145

One of **Jim Clancy's** classic arrangements was also unveiled along the way – *"How Deep Is The Ocean"*. Jim's comment to us when he provided the arrangement: *"You're probably the only chorus in the world that could sing this well"*. A new sound system for our Good Time

THE BEAU JESTERS was a comedy quartet that was just heading toward retirement when the VM was founded. From L-R: **Ernie Boring, Wally Bradford, Don King,** Art Haynes. They won the Southwestern District quartet contest in 1949, and appeared on some of the first Good Times shows produced by the VM.

Shows was also being constructed by **Brian Belcher, Jim Martin** and **Bill Sturgeon**. Plus, the word was put out that the chorus needed a travel trailer to haul around our risers and other equipment. Our organization was not only growing in numbers, but also in equipment that had to be stored, moved and maintained by our volunteer group.

Finally, March ended with a feature story in *The Dallas Morning News* by entertainment opinion writer **Bob Brock** that mentioned The Vocal Majority Chorus from Dallas being featured in a new PBS special documentary about the 1974 Kansas City Barbershop Society convention. He also said that the VM had won the gold medal in Indianapolis the following year. Nice publicity that's been very difficult to obtain in recent years.

The Barbershop Society's publication, *The HARMONIZER*, also featured a story about the VM, written by me. [**Author's Note:** While doing research for this book, I came across a history of *Harmonizer* articles submitted by various Society members. I was frankly amazed that I had *thirteen* articles published about the VM between 1973 and 1988. That's almost one a year, but I guess that's what a marketing director is expected to do, right? However, the article in the *HARMONIZER* edition shown on the next page was NOT written by me.]

Through the cooperation of a lot of VM singers, the month of April saw quite a bit of public relations activities. The Barbershop Society was celebrating *"National Harmony Month"* commemorating the found-

ing of the organization on April 11, 1938. *(So nice of them to do that on my birthday!)* Public service sta-tion-break slides were sent to each of the network TV stations in Dal-las-Fort Worth, custom cassette tapes with an accompanying bro-chure touting the VM as great con-vention entertainment were sent to convention groups throughout the country, and **Bill Barstow** headed up a team that personally made phone calls to each of those conven-tion organizations to pitch the VM as entertainment.

We lost **Buddy Holiday**, one of our charter members, to a job transfer in April. Buddy was one of the top radio personalities in the Metroplex for many years, working at **KLIF, KRLD, KVIL** and **WFAA** among others.

A three-day performance weekend had chorus members scram-bling to start the month of May. It began with a Saturday night a paid performance for the **National Secretaries Association** at the Inn of the Six Flags in Arlington, continued with another Good Time Music Show at Granny's Dinner Theater on Monday night, and a get-up-early Tuesday morning booking at the Dallas Convention Center for the **Texas Hospital Association** – paying us the unheard-of fee of $5,000! [**Author's Note:** After our performance for the Texas Hospital Association, I received some very complementary remarks from the executive director for that organi-zation. Included in those remarks was her eye-opening statement: *"And you saved us so much money for entertainment!"* Well, after that revela-tion, we increased our performances fees for future association bookings significantly.]

During that same week in May, **Jim Clancy** unveiled his spectacular new arrangement of *"The Star Spangled Banner"*. That custom version of **Our National Anthem** is, of course, still in the chorus repertoire to this day, and has been responsible for the VM being invited to sing at dozens of sporting and special events over the years, including appearances before two U.S. presidents.

We tried a little experiment during the spring of 1976 by dividing the chorus up into two *mini-choruses* – the **White Chorus** and the **Orange Chorus**. The active membership was now close to 80, and the thinking was that more paid performances could be acquired by having two smaller choruses available for certain events rather than the entire group. Well, it eventually fizzled out. Unfortunately, when each chorus was introduced as "The Vocal Majority", the audience was not REALLY experiencing the power and majesty of the total chorus experience. It was one of many innovations we tried over the years that didn't quite work out.

The chorus was booked for a July 5th appearance at **Arlington Stadium** to sing *"My Country 'Tis Of Thee"* and the *"Star Spangled Banner"* before the **Texas Rangers** game. Family members were also invited with free tickets, so it was a wonderful night of family fun and baseball.

The Difficult San Francisco Decision

I was very surprised when I went through the *Vocalizers* during the Spring of 1976 that NO mention was made of the chapter's vote NOT to attend the San Francisco convention. All Barbershoppers pretty much EXPECTED an outgoing chorus champion to attend and perform at the Society's convention the year after winning the Gold Medal. However, a vote of the entire VM membership confirmed the board's suspicion that the preceding Indianapolis contest had drained members' finances, family life, work schedules, and enthusiasm. We voted, reluctantly, to withdraw from performing at the 1976 International Convention, and we so informed the Barbershop Society. I expect that this decision was so traumatic for all of us – myself included – that I simply chose to leave this very important event out of the *Vocalizer* publications entirely.

Even though the VM would not be going to San Francisco to the Barbershop Society Convention in July, and were not yet eligible to compete at that fall's Southwestern District chorus competition in San Antonio, we were invited by the San Antonio Barbershoppers to put on a special show at the district convention. And, like all other times – past and present, competing or not – when the VM appeared on a Barbershop convention stage, we felt certain that we were being compared with other major choruses anyway. So, **Jim Clancy** prepared us throughout the summer months of 1976 just like we were going into full competition mode. After all, we were the highest scoring SPEBSQSA chorus in the history of the Society, so we felt people would be *expecting* the very best sound they had ever heard. And that's the way the organization approaches it to this day.

It should be noted that I, along with about 18 other VM singers *did* make the trip to San Francisco for the Society convention. The **Phoenicians** from Phoenix won the chorus contest, with Houston's **Tidelanders** finishing fourth in the scoring. Houston did us Texans proud by providing the gold medal quartet for that year, the **Innsiders**. Our performance coach, **Don Clause** padded his success resume by having coached three out of the top four quartets – including his *4th straight quartet winner* – and two out of the top four choruses. Because the entire VM chorus couldn't make the trip to San Francisco, the 18 chapter representatives gathered at the chorus run-through the morning of the contest and presented each of the fifteen competing choruses with a small trophy to commemorate their appearance at the event.

Even though we weren't eligible to compete in San Antonio, **Jim Clancy** and **Bill Thornton** combined to initiate choreography and interpretive expression for our two possible future contest tunes, *"My Lady Loves To Dance"* and *"An Old Fashioned Girl"*. We figured both would be great public performance numbers for general audiences, and we could get some feedback from the judges in San Antonio about the contestability of both songs.

THE SECOND HALF OF 1976

116 paid members were on the Dallas Metropolitan Chapter's roster as of August. Our coach **Don Clause** was scheduled to come to Dallas from New Jersey in September for an all-day Saturday coaching session, section rehearsals picked up once again, and guest singers were starting to

visit VM rehearsals in big numbers. And the fall performance calendar saw us doing several Good Time Shows at **Granny's Dinner Theater**.

The first *New Member Orientation* took place that summer, when sixteen men who had recently passed our audition spent a Saturday morning learning about the organization they had recently joined. Four general areas were covered in the session:

1. History and purpose of the VM, and basic information about our International and District organization (**Bob Arnold**);
2. The Society's contest and judging system, and singing qualification requirements for all VM singers (**Charlie White**);
3. VM Chapter officers, structures and responsibilities, along with special committees the new recruits may wish to volunteer for (**Frank Harkness**);
4. Where does your chapter dues money go, and what items are included in the chapter budget (**Chris Christensen**).

The new *"Back To Back"* record album the VM recorded that spring – along with the **Louisville Thoroughbreds** – was finally made available to the general public for just $4.00. Being our first *real* record album, even if we had to share it, was quite an exciting event, and spurred us on to covet our own album which arrived in the near future.

For the first – and only – time in the history of the VM, *five quartets* from our chapter competed in the Division Quartet Contest which, at that time, qualified foursomes for the District Contest in the fall. It might seem a small item in the overall history of our organization, but it might be interesting to those who were active during those days.

- **SIDE STREET RAMBLERS** (Houts, Malone, Law, Hagn)
- **THE PLAYBILLS** (Haynes, Harkness, Gatlin, Dochterman)
- **NEW VARIATION** (Horine, Van, Wessley, Belcher)
- **CHORD RUSSLERS** (Clarke, Anderson, Battershall, Johnston)
- **MINT CONDITION** (Denton, Bush, Rogers, Reid)

The Ramblers came within two points of first place, and went on to great success in the next several years in both shows and competitions.

Preparations were well under way by September for our chorus performance at the District Convention in San Antonio in October. Being the past year's International Chorus Champions, the VM was not going to be eligible to compete at the district level for another year. But that didn't stop our music leaders from treating our San Antonio appearance any different from a competition performance. Important Barbershop Society representatives from throughout the country would be present, along with a judging panel who would be there to enjoy our presentation – and be judging us *informally* anyway.

So, to prepare for this "unofficial competition" appearance, **Jim Clancy** and his music team ran each rehearsal just like we were competing for an International contest. And they added an all-day Saturday HEP (Harmony Education Program) School to our September schedule, plus bringing to Dallas our vocal coach, **Don Clause**, for a Thursday night rehearsal session.

But, all work and no play certainly doesn't make for happy singers. So, our **Vocal Sorority** hosted a Mexican Fiesta social event. And, as fund-raising projects, our Sorority was also collecting aluminum cans as well as selling pizza coupon booklets. Anything that could help cut members expenses to future contests and performances.

The new chapter officers for 1977 included:

President.........................BILL STURGEON
Admin. VP.......................PHIL HAWKINS
Program VP......................CHUCK NESTER
Budget/Operations VP...........JOE WIGGINS
Music VP.........................CHARLIE WHITE
Public Relations VP..............BOB ARNOLD
Secretary.........................JACK JOHNSTON
Treasurer........................JOE HOLLOWAY
Members-At-Large................DAVE BARROW
                               JIM MARTIN

GARY REID
Immediate Past President..........FRANK HARKNESS

VM RECORDINGS GET OFF THE GROUND

Over the years, recording sessions for VM albums have been some my most memorable experiences. Rehearsals leading up to these sessions were a bit more exciting because we knew those songs would be available for our enjoyment and that of our fans for decades into the future. So, throughout the first half of 1976, the chorus spent several weekends employing sound engineers to set up their equipment in an appropriate church sanctuary and laying down tracks of some of the more entertaining arrangements we had in our repertoire.

What resulted was *"Standing Room Only"*, the first album that was *totally produced by The Vocal Majority!* We were still a pretty young organiza-

tion and we didn't quite have enough songs in our chorus repertoire to completely fill an album. So, we called on our entertaining quartets to fill out both sides of a vinyl LP – the **Dealer's Choice**, the **Side Street Ramblers**, and the **Folkel Minority**.

So now we had two sides of our own album *("Standing Room Only"*), one side of the Barbershop Society's album *("Back To Back"*), and in the near future we had been booked to provide a substantial part of a third album for the **National Geographic Society** and their millions of subscribers throughout the world. It seemed like the sound and reputation of The Vocal Majority Chorus was gaining attention quickly.

And the competition honors just kept coming. **Our Side Street Ramblers (Keith Houts, Bill Thornton, Dennis Malone, Earl Hagn)** won the Southwestern District quartet title, and then went on in 1983 (with a lead singer change to **Brian Beck**) to win the International Quartet Gold Medal.

Proof positive that the creation of the VM was having positive effects on Barbershopping activity in the Dallas area was the fact that in October 1976, the **Dallas Town North Chapter** had over 100 members, and the **Dallas Big D Chapter** was over 60 members. Neither organization had membership numbers near those prior 1971 when the VM was founded.

Vocal Sorority president **Shell Bonesio** announced the new 1977 officers:

President...........................SHARON HAWKINS
Vice President.....................MARY ANN ROGERS
Secretary...........................KAREN REID
Treasurer...........................CHARLOTTE SHELTON
Immed. Past President...........SHELL BONESIO

The VM produced our very first Christmas show in December at Granny's Dinner Theater, with **Jim Clancy** breaking out new arrangements to *"Oh, Come All Ye Faithful"*, *"Joy To The World"*, and *"Silent Night"* – all still in our current seasonal repertoire.

Jack Johnston received the 1976 *Barbershopper of the Year* award at the VM's annual installation dinner for being the chapter's secretary, handling the duties of *"Sunshine Chairman"*, handling the chorus performance outfits, and running the successful mini-chorus program. Special recognition for outstanding service to the chapter during the year was provided in the form of handsome desk pen sets to **Jim Clancy, Bill Thornton, Gary Parker, Dave Barrow, Carl Johnson** and **Bob Arnold**. (I'm sitting here writing this book and looking directly at that desk pen set that's been on my desk for all these many years.)

Chapter 15
1977: JIM CLANCY WAS GONE!

The first issue of the *Vocalizer* in 1977 saluted the new members who joined in 1976: **JAKE GREENE, BOB SHUPE, KEN McKEE, JAY STEINFELD, BILL SMEAD, SANDY SMITH, DON ALBERT, JIM JENNEY, JOHN HENDERSON, DAVE HANDY, BUD HORINE, DAVID ANDERSON, ROBB OLLETT, CHARLES BAKER, TOM TAHLBEE, GREG LYNE, HARRY BURGESS, WALT MORRIS, LONNIE POPE, LARRY EDENS** and **DON ADKINS**.

The chapter goals for 1977 were set as the following:

1. Stay the #1 competition chorus in the district . . . and point to the same distinction in International competition in 1978;
2. Have *fun* while learning to become even better singers;
3. Add many more good singers while keeping our present members active;
4. Purchase new chorus costumes, while holding their cost down;
5. Raise sufficient funds to finance competition travels;
6. Form and encourage several new quartets for our shows and competitions;
7. Perform a sufficient *variety* and *volume* of shows and other performances to interest every singer.

This could actually be the list of priorities for virtually *every* future year of the VM's existence, and I would certainly encourage you to consider them for YOUR choral organization.

The first rehearsal of 1977 got off to a fantastic start, with the headline blasting off the *Vocalizer* page: "**WHAT A START!**" Music Director **Jim Clancy** made a proposition to the chorus that night: *"I'll make a deal with all of you; I'll write new arrangements as fast as you guys can learn them!"* And to start the new year off right, Jim unveiled his newest fun arrangement of the popular country song, *"Won't You Play Another Somebody Done Somebody Wrong Song"* – purported to be the longest song title ever.

155

In February, the VM took on its biggest financial challenge to date. The chapter was responsible for a budget of $6,000 to produce a massive show at the 3,400 seat **Music Hall at Fair Park** to benefit the Society's charitable sponsorship of the **Institute for Logopedics**. *("We Sing That They Shall Speak"* was the underlying motto for this joint venture.) Top Barbershop choruses and quartets from throughout the State of Texas would travel to Dallas for the February 12ᵗʰ show. Participants included the **Dallas Big D Chorus, Dallas Town North Chorus, Vocal Majority Chorus, Side Street Ramblers Quartet, San Antonio Chordsmen Chorus, Sound Association Quartet, Houston Tidelanders Chorus, Dealer's Choice Quartet,** and a massed chorus of over 400 singers for a grand finale. Over $8,000 was eventually sent to the Institute of Logopedics from the show's proceeds. Mission accomplished!

A late February Good Time Music Show and a big performance with the **Mid-Cities Symphony Orchestra** in the **Great Hall of the Apparel Mart** were on the early year's schedule, as well as Granny's Good Time shows in March and April. The VM earned an impressive performance fee from the symphony show of $2,000. Credit for the event went to **Nancy Crinnion**, wife of VM member, **Jim**, who was a member of the sponsoring organization, *The Clipped B's* (former Braniff Airlines hostesses). From my perspective as the VM's marketing director, I felt it was my responsibility to get as much exposure for the chorus and our other ensembles as possible during the first part of the year when competition was not an immediate priority. I was also responsible for raising considerable amounts of dollars through shows, bookings and record sales so that new costumes, new risers, a new equipment trailer, and future chorus member transportation costs could be absorbed through our chapter treasury.

Jim Clancy unveiled two more arrangements that would add to our country & western repertoire: *"The Green Green Grass of Home"* and *"Lone Prairie".*

A real "downer" was announced in the February 21ˢᵗ *Vocalizer*: **Granny's Dinner Theater** would no longer be available for Monday night Good Time Shows after April 25ᵗʰ. Members were asked to scout for a new venue so we could continue with our very popular "beer & pretzels" shows and report any possible locations to new Show Chairman, **Ken**

McKee. *(Could God be telling us that we needed to move to a larger theater format for our regularly scheduled chapter shows?)*

The **Mid-Cities Symphony** joint concert on March 19th featured the most varied and extensive repertoire by the VM to date. The lineup of songs includes:

- My Lady Loves To Dance
- On A Wonderful Day Like Today
- Who's In The Strawberry Patch With Sally
- Sweet Gypsy Rose
- Somebody Done Somebody Wrong Song
- I Never Knew/You Were Meant For Me Medley
- Who'll Take My Place (When I'm Gone)
- All By Myself
- Asleep In The Deep
- An Old Fashioned Girl
- How Deep Is The Ocean
- The Intermission Song
- Brigadoon (Bagpipe Comedy Song)

To demonstrate how much the VM repertoire had expanded during this time, a March *Vocalizer* noted: *"The songs we'll be doing on the last Granny's show which are different from or in addition to those for the symphony show include:*

- At The Moving Picture Ball
- It's A Blue World
- Didn't We (Almost Make It)
- Green Green Grass of Home

And to demonstrate how well things were going during this time in the chapter's history, *twenty-six Guest Singers* registered at a March rehearsal!

As spring was winding down, the Music Team got serious about competition once again as section rehearsals were scheduled each week for a different section leading up to the September 17th Region 4 Chorus and Quartet Contest in Sherman. That event qualified choruses and quartets for the Southwestern District contest in Houston October 22nd.

To layer more icing on our cake, the May issue of the Society's *HARMONIZER* publication had *four pages of articles* devoted to the VM – including a full column about my **Folkel Minority**. And about that same time, **Jim Clancy** excitedly introduced a new contest ballad, *"Broadway Rose"*, on a recommendation from our vocal coach, **Don Clause**. The *Vocalizer* was sparkling with exciting news as the VM headed into the Fall calendar.

At a June rehearsal, one of our favorite quartets got a rousing send-off to the International Quartet Contest scheduled for July in Philadelphia, **The Side Street Ramblers**. The Ramblers (**Keith Houts, Jim Law, Dennis Malone** and **Earl Hagn**) were the past year's Southwestern District Quartet Champions, and had qualified to compete at the International level. They wound up finishing a disappointing 28th in the quartet competition. Shortly after that contest, **Brian Beck** replaced **Jim Law** as the lead singer, and that foursome went on to capture the quartet **Gold Medal** in Seattle in 1983.

BRIAN BECK NAMED CHORUS DIRECTOR

Jim Clancy was gone! The musical and inspirational leader of the chorus since its inception bid a tearful farewell to the VM at a July 1977, rehearsal, as he explained he had received a job offer "he couldn't refuse" from recording producers in Los Angeles. Jim had been on-again-and-off-

again on his pending move to California, but he had finally made the decision that would affect the VM music program for at least the next year – and possibly longer. **Brian Beck**, recently returned from his temporary move to California, was named by the board of directors to be the new VM chorus director. Brian certainly had the experience and the musical talent to be a great director. But the question was: Could he hold the chorus in the palm of his hand at rehearsals and performances like Jim could always do? Could he inspire them to sing above their talents and limits like Jim could always do? Could he be a leader of men as Jim could always do? And what about the new, custom arrangements that VM singers had come to look forward to and challenge them from Jim? Where would those come from? So many questions that only time would answer.

Our chapter president, **Bill Sturgeon**, introduced Brian to the chorus as its new Music Director at a July rehearsal with these words: *"Brian's personality is different from Jim Clancy's, and we all must realize that. The approach of each man is somewhat different, but we're extremely fortunate to have musically trained men of Brian's caliber available for selection."*

Besides continuing section rehearsals, twice-weekly chorus rehearsals, and an all-day Saturday craft workshop in late August, the chorus worked hard to adapt to Brian's directing techniques after years of experiencing those of Jim Clancy. And – wonder of wonders – a NEW Good Time Music Show venue was located at the **Windmill Dinner Theater,** and a show was scheduled for late August. The latest computer printout from the International Society office showed that the VM was now officially up to 119 members, which was 16 members over the same month the past year. Things seemed to be going along pretty well even with all the chorus director turmoil.

The lineup of entertainment at the new Good Time Show location was a knockout that summer: The **Side Street Ramblers, Forty Acre Four, Folkel Minority, Vocal Majority Chorus, VM Dixieland Jazz Band,** and **Brass Ring**. Plus, the VM got the good news that the **Music Hall at Fair Park** was making available a January 1978 date for the VM to hold an ambitious 3,400 seat show at that location.

However, there were some signs that discipline was beginning to become a problem at rehearsals. In a rare move, I took the liberty of publishing an "editorial" in the August 19th issue of the *Vocalizer: "Each of us is going to have to concentrate MUCH better on the risers if we're going to have everything in shape for our two contests. There's absolutely NO excuse for talking or not giving your attention to our directors and coaches during rehearsals. Conversely, all us common singers will also require planning from music leaders before each rehearsal to eliminate as much confusion as possible. It's a two-way street, and both singers and directors/coaches of the Vocal Majority require confidence in each other to do their jobs correctly."*

I have no idea whether that directive did any good or not after the long passage of time. But I believe it's the responsibility of an organization's bulletin/newsletter editor – just like the publisher or editorial board of any major newspaper – to occasionally remind the organization or community about the philosophical direction that needs to be established.

The new slate of chapter officers was duly elected at an October rehearsal, and included:

President...........................PHIL HAWKINS
Admin. VP.........................PHIL ANDERSON
Program VP.......................BILL SMEAD
Public Relations VP..............BOB ARNOLD
Secretary...........................JACK JOHNSTON
Treasurer...........................JOE HOLLOWAY
Music VP...........................GARY PARKER
Members-At-Large................RED McDONALD
　　　　　　　　　　　　　　MIKE O'NEAL
　　　　　　　　　　　　　　CHARLIE WHITE
Immediate Past President.........BILL STURGEON

This group of chapter leaders would be charged with the complex task of leading the organization through the money-raising activities and musical improvements necessary to compete for a second gold medal in Cincinnati in 1978. But as the following excerpt from the October 7th *Vocalizer* warns: *"Some of us more experienced, 'sophisticated' singers assume that the VM will repeat as Southwestern District champions in Houston on October 22[nd.] Very frankly . . . the scores in the Louisiana contest (where the VM competed in the Region contest) were among the highest in our four-state district. And the* **San Antonio Chordsmen***, while competing in a different region contest with different judges, scored just 21 points less than the VM. The Chordsmen have gone through a difficult re-auditioning of their entire chorus. Also, the new* **Mardi Gras Chorus** *from New Orleans will probably put close to 100 men on stage with a big sound, and El Paso's* **Borderchorders** *has a new director and new enthusiasm. It ain't gonna be easy!"*

It seemed apparent that the success of Dallas' Vocal Majority in rising to national and international prominence had a strongly *positive* effect on the rest of the Southwestern District during 1976-1977. The merger of the two New Orleans chapters raised the **Mardi Gras Chorus** membership count to 136, making it – for the moment – the largest chapter in the district. The **Houston Tidelanders** membership totaled 128, with the

VM showing up at 125. The **San Antonio Chordsmen's** membership was 88, and the **El Paso Borderchorder's** total was now 81 members. The Barbershop Society had good reason to point with pride to the growth spurred by the establishment of the successful Vocal Majority in Dallas.

A BUMPY ROAD ON THE WAY TO CINCINNATI!

The VM chorus struggled during the two months leading up to the Southwestern District Chorus Contest in Houston. It took quite a number of chapter-produced shows and outside bookings to raise the funds to make the Houston trip. And the change of music directors from **Jim Clancy** to **Brian Beck** certainly had some challenges. But even with all those negatives tugging at us, the chorus easily won the contest in Houston, winning over second place New Orleans by 97 points. And the **Forty Acre Four** (two of whom were VM members) won the quartet contest. However, there was one person in that Houston audience who was *not* very impressed with our contest performance. Jim Clancy.

Jim had returned to Texas from his work in the Los Angeles jingle studios kind of discouraged by the volume and quality of work they offered. We learned shortly after the Houston contest that Jim was returning – for the time being – to Dallas, and would be available to help our chorus with coaching and arrangements. Jim didn't mention his less-than-enthusiastic response to our contest performance to too many people. He thought the contest presentation was sloppy and not up to the VM's standards. But, being the Texas gentleman that he is, he didn't spread that opinion around. He just knew that we had to experience better discipline if we were to have a chance at another gold medal the next year in Cincinnati. And, looking at other district chorus champion scores from around the country, it was obvious that several other choruses had scored *as high or higher* than the VM did in our own district competition.

As the end of 1977 approached, the *Vocalizer* issues that I'm reading from that era begin touting not only the **Cincinnati International Contest and Convention** the following summer, but our very first large-scale show production at a venue that had seen many Barbershop chapter shows in past decades – **McFarlin Memorial Auditorium** at Southern Methodist University in Dallas. (That was the theater where I first performed as the MC for the Dallas **Town North Chapter** Barbershop show about a decade earlier, and where I was introduced to my first Barbershop show production.) McFarlin Memorial Auditorium was first opened on the SMU campus in 1926 and, of course, has had quite a bit of updating since that time to be able to accommodate some pretty impressive show business luminaries – **Sheryl Crow, the Grateful Dead, Elton John, Barry Manilow, Prince, Pink Floyd, The Doors** – and now The Vocal Majority.

The theater seated over 2,300 on three levels, and had excellent sight lines from virtually all seats. Which meant we had to sell considerably more tickets to each show than we were used to selling for our 350+ seats at our Good Time Music Shows. This prompted the chapter leadership to establish a *super show management team* that would lead our successful productions for the next two decades. **Ken McKee** took on the responsibilities of Show Chairman, **Bill Smead** took leadership of Show Production, and **Phil Anderson** headed up promotion and ticket sales. (Ken retired from active participation in the chorus in about 2004 with the title of *"Show Chairman Emeritus"* for his many years of service, and passed away in his 80s in 2016. Bill now has an annual award named for him, the *"Bill Smead Show Production Award"*. Unfortunately, Bill was killed in a highway robbery attempt in his second decade of being our show production leader.)

The February 1978 show at McFarlin Auditorium was set to feature the **Dealer's Choice,** the **Side Street Ramblers,** the **Folkel Minority,** the **VM Chorus,** and the **VM Dixieland Jazz Band**. What a blessing of talented ensembles we had to offer the public in those heady days! And, to top things off, our *"Standing Room Only"* album was featured in our first-ever *HARMONIZER* ad and was beginning to draw buyers from throughout North America. Finally, in the latest summary of data from the Barbershop Harmony Society, the Dallas Metropolitan Chapter ranked *third* among all chapters of 100 members or more. The VM "brand" seemed to be on the rise.

As a personal note, the December 3, 1977, *Vocalizer* noted that my **Folkel Minority** group recorded two comedy songs we had written which had been receiving some great audience feedback recently: *"Freeze A Yankee"* and *"A Tribute To The Trinity"*. The 45-rpm record that came out a few months later with those songs on it eventually sold over *100,000 copies*, and the "Freeze A Yankee" comedy song about the national energy crisis would eventually be covered by *The Wall Street Journal* and *The*

162

Dallas Times Herald. **Ron Chapman** on **KVIL Radio** played it so often that it became the #1 selling record in Dallas for ONE WEEK. And it got me fired from my job at Lone Star Gas Company. But that's a whole other story. You can actually see and hear both songs from that record today on **YouTube** (not necessarily a moving experience!) by using the search term "Folkel Minority". [**Author's Note**: Susan happened to be listening to the radio in her car one day before we even met and heard "Freeze A Yankee". She said to herself, 'I have to see that group someday.' She eventually did, and we've been married for 32 years!]

Our Vocal Sorority president, **Sharon Hawkins**, announced her new board of directors for 1978:

President........................... MARY ANN ROGERS
Vice President.................... NADINE McDONALD
Secretary...........................JOYCE HUNTER
Treasurer...........................CHARLOTTE SHELTON
Immed. Past President............SHARON HAWKINS

The annual installation and awards banquet was more emotional than usual in December. I'd like to quote again from the December 16, 1977, *Vocalizer* to capture what transpired: *"It was an emotion-filled evening. The banquet had even more drama than usual with the announcement that JIM CLANCY was returning as Director of The Vocal Majority, with BRIAN BECK graciously reverting to his previous position as Assistant Director. Brian received a standing ovation from wives, sweethearts and members last night when he was honored by outgoing president, BILL STURGEON. As Bill said, 'Brian did exactly what we expected of him in leading the VM to the District Chorus Title and qualifying for International in Cincinnati next summer.' It was a most difficult, but highly rewarding, past six months for Brian."*

Sonny Lipford was awarded the ***Barbershopper Of The Year*** trophy at the banquet for his contributions to the Music Committee, as an assistant director, voice coach, quartet coach, and constant advisor to the other directors and administrators. It seemed that a very serious detour into mediocrity had been avoided by the chapter leadership, and the new year seemed to portend great things for the chorus. However, as **Jim Clancy** warned everyone at the banquet: *"The chorus is further behind than it should be at this point in time, and I am going to be interested to*

163

see the turnout of singers at Thursday's rehearsal. It will be an indication of the determination of the chapter members to win another International title." He let everyone know that he would be flying to New York in the next week to meet with VM vocal coach, **Don Clause**, and to explore music options for the upcoming contest.

Jim's ominous assessment was a warning that would come true during the next summer in Cincinnati.

Contrary to how things are done today, regular VM rehearsals took place throughout the Christmas and New Year holidays of 1977. It was an indication of how *desperate* our Music Team was to re-establish a culture of discipline and renewed music learning. Jim came back from his visit with Don Clause carrying three new arrangements that he said were ABSOLUTELY NECESSARY to learn quickly: *"On A Wonderful Day Like Today"*, *"Looking At The World Through Rose Colored Glasses"*, and *"For The Sake of Auld Layng Syne"*. (The latter two songs were arranged by Ed Waesche, prolific Barbershop Society arranger.) We had our marching orders, and we took them seriously as we ended 1977.

Chapter 16
1978: CAN CLANCY'S RETURN RIGHT THE SHIP?

The new year of VM activities started with Monday AND Thursday evening rehearsals in preparation for February's first large theater show at McFarlin Auditorium. Rehearsals for all sections preceded each Thursday rehearsal, and the push was on to sell 2,500 tickets to the upcoming show. Music VP **Gary Parker** posted the arrangements the Music Committee expected the chorus to know for the 1978 performance year:

- For the Sake of Auld Lang Syne
- Rose Colored Glasses
- On A Wonderful Day Like Today
- Give Me A Good Old Mammy Song
- Who's In The Strawberry Patch With Sally
- It's A Blue World
- An Old Fashioned Girl
- My Lady Loves To Dance
- How Deep Is The Ocean
- The Lord's Prayer

Our first big show at McFarlin Auditorium was a *virtual sellout*, stocking our treasury with valuable dollars we desperately needed to make the long trip to Cincinnati in July. Because of that show's financial and artistic success, the Show Committee began plans to hold a TWO-night performance in February the *next* year.

Two possible contest songs were unveiled in February by **Jim Clancy**, and they weren't even his arrangements. Prolific Barbershop Society arranger, **Ed Waesche**, came up with a great contest up-tune, *"Looking At The World Through Rose-Colored Glasses"*, along with a ballad, *"For The Sake of Auld Lang Syne"*. It was quite late in the contest cycle for adequate preparation, but the decision was made – for better or worse.

The five months of preparation leading up to the July competition were filled with Saturday workshops, visits from **Don Clause** and our visual interpretation coach **Arnie Bauer**, section rehearsals each week, a performance for the Region 4 District Convention in Euless, another Logopedics spectacular benefit in San Antonio, Saturday workshops, and many hours on the risers learning the words, performance moves, facial interpretation, and practice singing on pitch and on tempo. Lots of work! And lots of fun, fellowship and good feelings about where we were headed artistically. But was there sufficient time to do all that and out-perform all the other choruses we would be competing against who were *also* working just as hard. We hoped we were working *smarter*, not just harder. But only time would tell.

Show Chairman **Ken McKee** uncovered a new location for a rare *Good Time Music Show* at the **Inn of the Six Flags** in Arlington, seating about 450, and scheduled a performance there in April. [**Author's Note:** Back in the 1970s, the Texas liquor laws permitted organizations like the VM to bring kegs of beer and wine into a venue and serve it themselves while offering "free" snacks and soft drinks. That made it very enjoyable – both for our performers and for our patrons – to have VM singers serve beverages and snacks before the show and at intermission, and mingle with our patrons at each of those shows. All this for the economical price of $7.00! Those liquor laws changed a couple of decades ago, and these days it's against the law to operate like that. I guess that's why us old-timers now call it "the good old days".]

A *Dallas Morning News* half-page ad appeared in a June 1978 *Vocalizer* edition that promoted a series of shows at NorthPark Center sponsored by the **Dallas Symphony Orchestra**. July 14th promised a *"100 Voice Barbershop Bonanza"* featuring the **Vocal Majority, Dealer's Choice** and **Folkel Minority**. Other lesser-known performers on the NorthPark series included **Bill Cosby, Sergio Mendez, Tammy Wynette, Pete Fountain, Pearl Bailey, Helen Reddy, Dionne Warwick, The Fifth Dimension, Hank Thompson** and **Joel Grey**. Pretty good company, I'd say.

The *Vocalizer* editor must have been feeling the pressure of rehearsing for the International competition as I read in the June 5, 1978, issue: *"Singing with the Vocal Majority and preparing for International competition are almost athletic events, aren't they? Standing on risers for several hours and singing correctly take more stamina than most amateur singers would normally put up with. But we're NOT like most amateur singers, are we? The dedication and time put in by Clancy, our coaches and our singers will, I firmly believe, result in the VM winning another Gold Medal at Cincinnati a month from now. All the hard work NOW to*

166

win the top prize is certainly better than having to gear up again next year, right?"

A DEVASTATING BLOW – AND A NEW BEGINNING!

No one could have prepared us for the gut-punch of losing the Cincinnati contest to the **Louisville Thoroughbreds** – *by just 10-points!* Everyone in our chorus family was devastated. The headline on the July 10, 1978, *Vocalizer* said it all: **"VM Wins Battle . . . But Loses The War"**. Quoting the first paragraph of that edition: *"Even after capturing the highest score ever awarded to a chorus in the Sound Category, the Vocal Majority came away as the second best to the mighty **Louisville Thoroughbreds** last Saturday. The scoresheets enclosed with this Vocalizer tell the story of how we were simply 'outperformed' by most of the medalist choruses."*

I recall that the VM was scheduled to appear immediately after the intermission in the Saturday afternoon chorus contest. Each chorus had quite a long walk from their warmup room at the headquarters hotel to the performance auditorium outside in the sweltering summer heat of Cincinnati. For some reason, the intermission lasted longer than anyone expected, and the VM chorus had to wait *outside* in the heat for quite a while before being led into the air-conditioned contest auditorium. As a result, every singer was dripping with sweat before ever going on stage. It also threw off our concentration for the job ahead, and the performance just didn't "feel" right after it was all over.

After we sang, we all meandered back into the performance hall to find our seats, and all of us had a bad feeling about the outcome. When the announcement was made awarding The Vocal Majority SECOND place, all the frustrations of the past year – the temporary change of music directors, the lateness of getting our contest preparations under way, a contest up-tune that we received a bit late to have sufficient time to "live" with it – all came back to haunt us.

Clancy then asked **Sonny Lipford** to blow the pitch for a song we had been singing for a while that seemed to capture all the feelings we had at that moment – *"This Time We Almost Made It, Didn't We"*.

This time we almost made the pieces fit, didn't we?
This time we almost made some sense of it, didn't we?
This time I had the answer right here in my hand,
Then I touched it, and it had turned to sand.
This time we almost sang our song in tune, didn't we?
This time we almost made it to the moon, didn't we?
This time, we almost made our poem rhyme
And this time we almost made that long hard climb.
Didn't we almost make it this time...this time.
Lyrics & Music by Jimmy Webb

As we sang that song with more emotion than we ever had before, I remember standing next to **Jim Martin** and both of us softly grabbing each other's hands with tears welling up in each of our eyes. Jim would go on to become one of my closest friends, my personal family attorney, Dallas County family court judge, and the wacky tenor in my folk/country group, **The Folkel Minority**. Mere words couldn't describe the emotions of Vocal Majority singers in the room that afternoon in Cincinnati.

And then **Jim Clancy** said something to the assembled chorus that I'll never forget. *"I promise each of you that this will be the last time the Vocal Majority will ever finish out of first place."* And, for three decades after that, he kept his promise. *The VM won every contest for which they were eligible for the next 30 years until 2009.* My last contest with The VM was in 2003, and that was in Montreal.

It was difficult getting the taste of that bitter defeat out of our collective mouths when we got home to Dallas. But the schedule of activities for the next few months took some of the sting out of our psyches as we tried to decompress from the horrible Cincinnati experience. The July 17, 1978, *Vocalizer* brought some cheery news to VM members in the form of a party to celebrate our excellent performance in the contest and at the *"Summertop"* concert series at **NorthPark Center**. Jim Clancy promised a new arrangement we could sink our collective teeth into (*"With A Song In My Heart"*), a new record album was to be recorded in September, a special Vocal Majority evening with **The Four Freshmen** was scheduled at the Venetian Room of the Fairmont Hotel, and an August Good Time Music Show was just around the corner. What's not to like about that schedule?

168

[**Author's Note:** You'll notice that lots of "carrots" are dangled from lots of "sticks" throughout this Vocal Majority early history. As I've previously mentioned, *"Manufacturing Carrots"* was the title of the series

MANUFACTURING CARROTS

A Unique Weekend of Profitable Marketing Ideas for Barbershop and Sweet Adeline Chapters

of weekend marketing workshops I delivered to dozens of Barbershop and Sweet Adeline organizations during my first thirty years of active VM participation. Writing about exciting and challenging activities coming up is an amazing way to make sure that, no matter how many disappointments your organization may experience, there's always another interesting "carrot" coming up that will keep your volunteers coming back for more week in and week out. It's certainly worked for this bulletin editor/marketing director over many decades.]

The special Vocal Majority night with **The Four Freshmen** turned out to be forever memorable. About 160 VM singers, friends and relatives descended on the Venetian Room of the Fairmont Hotel to help stack the audience with a bunch of "ringers". **Bob Flanigan**, the tenor voice of the quartet, introduced the group's premier hit song, *"It's A Blue World"*, with these words: "A lot of you probably think that some of our songs have such close harmony that it's pretty difficult to sing, right? I'll bet you a lot of folks in our audience tonight could probably sing that song without any trouble. And we'll prove it to you by inviting the audience to sing with us." And without much coaxing, the VM singers in the audience chimed in with the Freshmen on the chorus of the song, much to the amazement and enjoyment of the rest of the audience.

The event was arranged by a fairly new member of the chorus, professional photographer **Bob Rice** and his wife **Rose**. After the Freshmen were finished with their act that night, Bob and Rose hosted a party at their home for many VM singers and family members, with the Freshmen in attendance also, until the wee hours of the morning. Those are the kinds of memories that last forever!

169

We didn't have much time to prepare for the upcoming Southwestern District chorus contest in October, so the Music Committee decided to compete with the same two songs we did in Cincinnati. A new Good Time Show was introduced to our schedule in October, and Channel 8 (WFAA-TV) was in the process of doing a feature about the **Folkel Minority**'s *"Freeze A Yankee"* recording and its regional popularity, while also featuring the Vocal Majority chorus in a program called *"PM Magazine"*. The "new" **Side Street Ramblers** unveiled their new lead singer, **Bill Thornton**. And **Clancy** unveiled his newest arrangement that he was VERY excited about, *"For Once In My Life"*. Things seemed to be ramping up very nicely after the downer of a Cincinnati debacle, so we eagerly looked ahead to the district chorus competition in October.

Nominating Committee chairman, **Bill Sturgeon**, presented his committee's slate of new officer candidates for 1979:

President............................JOE HOLLOWAY
Membership. VP...................JIM CULLISON
Program VP.........................JOHN SCHROY
Public Relations VP...............BOB JETT
Secretary............................JACK JOHNSTON
Treasurer............................EDDIE WALL
Music VP............................GARY PARKER
Members-At-Large.................BILL BARSTOW
　　　　　　　　　　　　　　MIKE O'NEAL
　　　　　　　　　　　　　　TOM HALVERSON
Immediate Past President.........PHIL HAWKINS

Betty Sturgeon, chairperson of the *Vocal Sorority*, placed the following names in nomination for that organization's board:

President............................ SHARON MARTIN
Vice President.................... ELAINE BELCHER
Secretary............................ROBY DECKER
Treasurer............................SUE IMMEL
Immed. Past President............MARY ANN ROGERS

CHAMPIONS IN EVERY WAY!

That was the headline on the October 30, 1978, issue of the *Vocalizer*, which went on to enumerate the reasons why the headline said it all: *"With possibly its most inspired performance in history, The Vocal Majority captured the hearts of the judges and the audience last Saturday afternoon. And in the process captured its fourth straight Southwestern District Chorus Championship. One of the more satisfying aspects of the victory was the fact that we captured EVERY category . . . including Stage Presence . . . by 33-points over the runner-up in this category."*

With the chorus once again headed in the right direction and our ticket punched to the International Chorus Contest in **Minneapolis** the following July, the rest of 1978 was a whirl of victory parties, shows and financially rewarding bookings. **Jim Clancy**'s return to the director's helm, along with the improved discipline by both our singers and music team, were rewarded with a redemption trip to the "super bowl" of Barbershop competitions. Was another gold medal in the VM's future? Let's find out what the next eight months of *Vocalizer* memories reveals.

A *benefit* Good Time Music Show for **Ursuline Academy** (and the VM) took place in the Fall at W.T. White High School, along with our own Good Time Show at the Inn of the Six Flags in Arlington, followed by the "social highlight of the year" – the annual Installation and Awards Banquet in December. (**Ken McKee** won *Barbershopper of the Year* honors at the banquet for his untiring efforts in being the Show Chairman for all our Good Time Shows and for our expanding February shows at McFarlin Auditorium.) And our **Dealer's Choice** quartet bid farewell as they made their final appearance in England for the **British Association of Barbershop Singers (BABS)** convention. And finally, the next VM record album had its first recording session at the **Northlake Baptist Church** in Dallas. The new album would be called, *"With A Song In Our Hearts"*, and would be released in 1979. It not only featured The **Vocal Majority Chorus**, but also the **Dealer's Choice, Side Street Ramblers, Beau Jesters,** and **Folkel Minority**. Liner notes (remember those?) on the LP jacket were written by **Bob Flanigan** of **The Four Freshmen**.

Chapter 17
1979: THE GOLD MEDAL MAGIC RETURNS

As the new year dawned, all eyes were on our most ambitious local show production yet – a two-night extravaganza in February at **McFarlin Auditorium**. Were we biting off too much to sell out *two nights* of shows at 2,500 seats each night? Traveling to Minneapolis with a projection of a much larger chorus would require more dollars than we had ever raised before. So, it was mandatory that we sell as many tickets to this huge show weekend as possible.

And what about the two songs we would be competing with in Minneapolis in July? It's generally NOT a good idea to repeat the songs you did in a losing performance the preceding year, since the judges and audience had already judged them to be, well, not worthy of first place. So, what did our music team and their contacts throughout the Barbershop world have up their collective sleeves for contest material? We would soon find out.

The VM's second self-produced album, **"With A Song In Our Hearts"**, was released in January 1979, and sold over 200 copies at the big 2-night show production at McFarlin Auditorium in February. Ads for the album in the *HARMONIZER* magazine of the Barbershop Society were bringing in record orders from throughout the U.S. and even from some foreign destinations where Barbershop music was beginning to take hold.

That first 2-night show produced over $16,000 in income for our struggling treasury, and treasurer **Eddie Wall** said it was "right on budget". That show moved the VM out of the small venue dinner theater category into the big-time proscenium theater venues that eventually expanded into 4-5 shows over a weekend by 2017.

Recognition from the Barbershop Harmony Society continued its lavish praise of our organization. Executive Director, **Hugh Ingraham**, wrote to the VM president: *"Congratulations! It is my pleasure, on behalf of 1978 International President Roger Thomas, to pass on the good news that your chapter has won 1ˢᵗ Place in Plateau 6 (the larger chapters) of the 1978 International Achievement Award Program. Your chapter scored 2ⁿᵈ in number of points among all chapters in the Society."*

It was obvious that we were cramped for rehearsal space in the low-slung confines of the Chapel Downs Community Center. It was OK for 50-60 singers on risers, but we were beginning to approach 100+ singers on some rehearsal nights, and things were getting a bit tight. So, we explored several facilities – including the Ridgeview Presbyterian Church meeting hall in north Dallas – during the Spring of 1979, as we prepared for that Summer's competition in Minneapolis.

Speaking of that competition, the two songs the music team selected for us were *"How Could You Believe Me/It's A Sin To Tell A Lie Medley"* and *"For The Sake of Auld Lang Syne"*. Both were challenging numbers to choreograph, and we knew we were going to have to bring in some outside coaches to help us translate them into winning material. However, we found that we had two *in-house* choreography coaches who could do the job – **Bob and Rosemary Calderon**. Bob was a recent transfer member from the El Paso Chapter, and Rosalie was a Sweet Adeline singer and choreographer. Bob and Rosemary were the first real "professional" choreographers to help shape our stage presence, and remained as our coaches for eighteen years and beyond.

I wrote an article for the **Dallas/Fort Worth Business** magazine about that time titled, *"S.P.E.B.S.Q.S.A.: Unique Entertainment"*. It

helped to spur recruitment during that Spring when we were trying to mount as large a chorus as possible for the Minneapolis contest. Saturday workshops were a regular part of our rehearsal routine from January through July, as well as a final Good Time Show in Arlington. Then, another stroke of good luck came our way in the person of **Jimmy Dean**. He was headlining a VERY special Muscular Dystrophy benefit concert at the Anatole Hotel. In addition to Jimmy

174

and the VM, the event featured appearances by **Larry Gatlin, Chet Atkins, Boots Randolph, Trini Lopez, the Dallas Cowboys Cheerleaders, Evil Knievel** and **Tom Landry**. Those names might not bring much recognition these days, but they were show business and sports royalty in 1979!

Until he passed away in in 2010 at the age of 81, Jimmy was a huge fan of The Vocal Majority Chorus. He even appeared as our MC on one of our McFarlin Auditorium shows a few years later when he introduced the VM as *"one of the greatest singing groups in the world, and they're from right here in Dallas, Texas, and I want the entire world to know about them. They are the most American group you will ever see."* Jimmy also volunteered to write the liner notes for our next album.

Jimmy Dean gives Susan a hug for being his personal makeup artist!

[**Author's Note**: When Jimmy appeared on our shows in 1981, Susan was coordinating the makeup for the chorus. As soon as Jimmy spied the attractive blonde with the blue eyes, he asked her to do HIS makeup *personally*. Now there's something to make a husband a little jealous!]

VM Champs Again!

That was the blaring headline adorning the top of the July 9, 1979, issue of the *Vocalizer*. The first paragraph of that issue said it all: *"The scores on the back of this Vocalizer show the 'mechanics' of what happened last Saturday. But there will never be a score sheet to describe the emotional experience the members of The Vocal Majority went through along the way to our second International Chorus Championship."* Those scores showed that the VM beat out the Alexandria HARMONIZERs by 99-points for the Gold Medal. Our **Vocal Sorority** raised over $1,000 through various fund-raising activities in Dallas prior to the Minneapolis trip, which helped us reserve the largest conference meeting room in our Radisson Hotel for rehearsals. Popular Chicago quartet **Grandma's Boys** won the quartet contest, and our own **Side Street Ramblers** finished a strong 7th out of 48 quartets.

After a wild victory celebration party back in Dallas after the trip, **Jim Clancy** was excited to unveil some new arrangements he'd been keeping undercover, and thoughts of VM singers once again turned to renewing acquaintances with family members and co-workers after a grueling contest preparation build-up. The rest of the year would be a blur of chorus bookings and benefit appearances – a paid gig for the **American Bar Association** at the **Hyatt Regency Hotel**, three Good Time Shows at the **Inn**

1979 INTERNATIONAL CHAMPIONS

The VOCAL MAJORITY
Dallas (Metropolitan), Texas

I've Been a Liar All My Life/It's a Sin to Tell a Lie Medley
For The Sake of Auld Lang Syne

of the Six Flags in Arlington, an appearance at the **Southwestern District Convention** in New Orleans as International Chorus Champions, plus another **Logopedics Spectacular** benefit show in Houston.

New Clancy arrangements that summer included *"Pass Me By"* (with choreography by the Calderons), *"Have A Little Talk With Myself"* (a pop favorite made famous by **Gordon Lightfoot** with a four-part vocal arrangement by our own **Gary Parker**), *"An American Trilogy"* (originally arranged by songwriter **Mickey Newberry**, with snippets of *"Dixie"*, *"All My Trials, Lord"*, and *"Battle Hymn of the Republic"*), plus

176

a favorite for decades in the VM repertoire, *"Danny Boy"* (which eventually turned into an inspirational contest ballad for the chorus in their 2017 International Contest in Las Vegas).

One unfortunate result of choosing to pay for members' travel to Minneapolis was that our treasury hit rock bottom after the trip. We had to take out a short-term loan of $3,000 and, as a result, ask members to self-fund the obligatory trip to New Orleans coming up that fall to perform for the fall District Convention. I've made it a point to include some negatives in this history to show that even successful profit and nonprofit organizations must have good business and accounting strategies to see their way through the down times, as well as celebrating the good times.

The Dallas Morning News sent reporter **Leslie Barker** and a staff photographer to a July rehearsal to follow up on a story about our Gold Medal success in Minneapolis. That article showed up in an August edition of the newspaper, and reprints of the story became a great recruiting tool for chorus members during the remainder of 1979.

One of the most challenging arrangements ever sprung on the chorus by Big Jim happened one night in September – *"Their Hearts Were Full of Spring"* – a **Four Freshmen** arrangement. That one may have been a bit TOO challenging; even after recording it for a future album, I'm not sure I ever *really* locked in on some of those close-harmony chords. As far as almost-impossible arrangements for the chorus to learn was Gene Puerling's *"Stardust"*. Now THAT was a weird one!

The nominating committee for the 1980 Board of Directors – **Phil Hawkins, Frank Harkness** and **Bill Sturgeon** – came up with the following names to be placed in nomination:

President – JIM CULLISON
Imm. Past Pres. – BILL STURGEON
Membership VP – JACK JOHNSTON
Program VP – TOM HALVERSON
Music VP – GARY PARKER
Public Relations VP – BOB JETT
Treasurer – EDDIE WALL
Secretary – CLAYTON COOK
Members At-Large – DAVID GREEN

MICKEY BONESIO
BOB COURNOYER

We were also fortunate to get some international publicity for our newest album, "With A Song In Our Hearts", in the newsletter of **The Four Freshmen**. **Bob Flanigan** is quoted in *The Fifth Freshman*: *"Jim Clancy made The Vocal Majority national champs in a very short time. They are 110 guys who love to sing. This love shows on the album. I know Four Freshmen fans will want to hear 110 voices sing 'Blue World'."* The article went on to give the price of the album and our address. I don't think that kind of publicity would have happened if we had stuck with square Barbershop songs on that album, do you?

With the Fall season heading into October, my Marketing Director's mind began turning to the *next year's* International Convention in Salt Lake City. I began exploring some additional paid performances during that trip by contacting the Salt Lake City Chapter of the Society and inquiring about other venues that might help pay for our trip there as outgoing chorus champions. Possibilities such as a joint performance with the **Mormon Tabernacle Choir**, and maybe the **Osmond Brothers** was discussed. I pursued those leads for the remainder of 1979 and into the new year. *Could this Utah opportunity really turn out to be something spectacular?*

CLOSING OUT 1979 WITH EXCITEMENT

October featured a chorus trip to New Orleans for the Southwestern District Convention, where director Jim Clancy was a no-show due to an unfortunate and rather serious auto accident that necessitated 70+ stitches to his handsome head. However, he bounced back the next week with one of the most iconic arrangements that will ever be in the VM repertoire – *"One Voice"*, with words and music by **Barry Manilow**. That 8-part arrangement played a huge role in our inspirational repertoire for the next 35+ years, and turned into the leadoff song in our **Mormon Tabernacle** appearance in Utah the next summer.

The year closed out with Good Time Shows in Arlington, a Log-opedics Spectacular in Houston, the Annual Installation Banquet at Chandler's Landing in Rockwall (show production ace **Bill Smead** was presented with the ***Barbershopper of the Year*** *Award*), and planning for the newest VM record album in early 1980, ***"Here's To The Winners"***. **Jim Clancy** and **Renee Craig** joined their arranging talents on the title song for that album, *"Here's To The Winners"*. Jim added another arrangement to bolster the theme of the album when he introduced *"Let A Winner Lead The Way"*.

The decision was also made to move VM rehearsals to the more spacious **Churchill Way Presbyterian Church** in north Dallas. We had finally outgrown the Chapel Down Community Center.

Chapter 18
1980: A NEW ALBUM – PLUS THE TABERNACLE CHOIR

Our new rehearsal facility got quite a workout during the first two weeks of the new year – *Monday, Thursday and Saturday* chorus rehears-

als in preparation for the new record album which wrapped up recording sessions in late January. A change in calendar year also saw a return of several wayward former members: **Jerry Bean, Ross Wise, Clark Womack, Bill Heard, Bill Martin, Brad Nichols, Terry Diedrich** and **Larry Rogers**.

January rehearsals were also spiced up with our chapter quartets performing some songs they'd be doing on our Spring Good Time Music Shows: the **Folkel Minority, Buffalo Gap Close Harmony Gang, Beau Jesters,** and **Side Street Ramblers**.

Our show patron mailing list now numbered some *4,000 names*, and flyers for our February Spring shows and our new record album were mailed out. Because of our nonprofit status, the U.S. Post Office allowed our mailings to be sent at the much lower Non Profit Bulk Rate, savings lots of dollars through the years. And VM president **Jim Cullison** presented the chapter with a much larger budget for 1980 -- $110,000, up from $64,000 the previous year. More travel expenses, more local show production costs, recording of the new record album, repayment of a bank loan – all contributed to a greatly expanded budget for a larger and more active organization. That, in turn, meant more pressure on the marketing team to sell The Vocal Majority more aggressively to a wider potential audience base.

A HOTLINE newsletter I sent to "members only" during the first part of 1980 laid out the strategy: *"The absolute easiest funds we can obtain to satisfy our $110,000 budget goal is to perform often in our community for convention and business meeting groups. YOU can help obtain these important bookings by keeping your eyes and ears open for opportunities in your business, associations and personal contacts. Another way*

181

you can help: ASK MEN YOU KNOW TO ATTEND REHEARSALS! Our goal this year is to have 200 members on the rolls by December 31. With more members, we'll have more singers on the risers for every performance . . . and ultimately more contacts in the community to help obtain paid performances, to sell show tickets, and to enhance the image and prestige of The Vocal Majority. YOU are the secret to reaching our $110,000 goal!"

Some other important events that kept VM singers busy and engaged that Spring included a special appearance at the **Dallas Advertising League**'s Banquet hosted by **KVIL's Ron Chapman** at the Fairmont Hotel; a two-night annual VM show at McFarlin Auditorium; hosting the Region 4 competition in Dallas for the Southwestern District (including a Good Time Show at the **Dallas Dunfy Hotel**); a two-night paid performance in Houston for **Kraft Foods**; two paid performances at the **World Championship of Tennis** at Reunion Arena; and a well-paid VM appearance at the prestigious **Military Ball** at the Sheraton-Dallas Hotel (with the Texas governor and mayor of Dallas in attendance).

Company employee newsletters were a focus of publicity for the VM during this time. A strategically-placed article in the **Texas Instruments** newsletter brought to our attention the fact that this internationally known North Texas corporate citizen was also home to quite a number of VM members when we read the following:

"Nine TIers (employees of Texas Instruments) from the Dallas-Lewisville-Sherman area are members of The Vocal Majority – a men's chorus which is a part of the Society for the Preservation and Encouragement of Barber Shop Quartet Singing in America. Members of the group who are TIers are **Phil Anderson, Barry Battershall, Jerry Bean, Parker Lowrance, Dick McCarty, Joe Poyner, Gary Reid, Bob Shupe and Charlie White.** *Two other members of the chorus are* **Lou Moseley,** *now based in Colorado Springs, and* **Ross Wise,** *currently based in Lubbock."*

That kind of exposure is rather easy to obtain for nonprofit organizations if you know where to look for it.

In late Spring 1980, we were informed by friends and contacts in Utah that the VM was being considered to perform on a huge annual

Fourth of July celebration for the City of Provo. Included in the offer was an all-expense paid trip to the area, as well as transportation while we were there for a *FULL FIVE DAYS!* We were also contacted by the **Osmond Brothers Production Company** to do a TV pilot video of our Good Time Music Show format. No guarantees that it would turn into anything in the future, but *it sure was fun to imagine TV stardom!* But that wasn't the full extent of the wonderful events that VM singers and their families might experience in Utah that summer. The reality was actually beyond our wildest dreams!

Some of those wild dreams were pretty well dashed later that Spring when the Provo invitation fizzled out, and the Osmond TV pilot didn't go anywhere. But one thing *did* sound absolutely fantastic – aside from the VM performing for 10,000 Barbershoppers in the Salt Palace Saturday evening in Salt Lake City to "win" another chorus contest in which we were not entered. We were notified that we had been invited to perform on a Sunday morning with the world-renowned **Mormon Tabernacle Choir** in the Salt Lake Tabernacle. It was the first time in anyone's memory that a non-Mormon performance group had been invited to sing in that magnificent building. Which meant that the chorus had to prepare a completely *different* music program on Sunday morning from the one on the previous Saturday night.

A May 1980 *Vocalizer* listed NINE VM chapter quartets. (Not bad for a Barbershop chapter that many in the Society consider to be totally devoted to chorus activities.) Some of those foursomes included **Class of the 80s, Beau Jesters, Buffalo Gap Close Harmony Gang, Side Street Ramblers, Folkel Minority, Trinity River Authentic Singers of Harmony (TRASH),** and the **Stage Door Four.**

THE HAND OF GOD MOVES IN MYSTERIOUS WAYS

The July 15, 1980, *Vocalizer* was the first issue after we had returned from the amazing trip to Salt Lake City. As I read that issue, I could tell that the emotion was still coursing through my veins as I recounted the previous weekend: *"After the greatest performance in the history of The Vocal Majority on the Saturday night show at the Salt Palace (for Barbershoppers), it seemed almost incomprehensible to expect anything as fulfilling the next morning. But it happened, didn't it? After experiencing 10,000 Barbershoppers – and three standing ovations – on the Saturday*

183

night show, could there be anything more thrilling in store for the VM the next morning? As the chorus members filed onto the risers in the Tabernacle, with the Mormon Tabernacle Choir and audience members singing

'Nearer My God To Thee', *VM chorus members took their places and gazed into the faces of nine thousand beautiful people who had gathered for the event. If you managed to keep your composure through that experience, you were indeed unusual."*

It still gives me goose bumps to read those words and remember the strong feeling of the hand of God in that holy place. It was hard to perform in that setting for two primary reasons. First, it was difficult for me to sing the first notes of our opening song, *"One Voice"*, with all the emotion choking my throat. Second, our chorus was situated on risers out in front of the huge organ pipes and the Tabernacle Choir, so we had no chorus "shell" or other hard surface to bounce our sound off of to hear each other sing. It was certainly not our best performance, *but it was so INTENSE!* Unknown to VM singers at the time, we were treated to a standing ovation by the members of the Tabernacle Choir after completing Jim Clancy's arrangement of "The Lord's Prayer". And I remember seeing hundreds of people in the audience openly weeping after finished that magnificent hymn.

I hope I've captured for you, dear reader, a little of the *intensity* of that morning in the Tabernacle. Both the members of the Tabernacle Choir and The Vocal Majority established a symbiotic bond that day which would be re-established a few years later with another appearance in the Tabernacle, a joint record album between the two groups, and a two-night joint appearance in Dallas.

And to prove that the hand of God *does* move in mysterious ways – consider the fact that IF the VM had *not* lost the chorus contest in Cincinnati in 1978, we would have never experienced the beginning of our relationship with the Mormon Tabernacle Choir in 1980.

HOW DO WE FOLLOW THE UTAH EXPERIENCE?

The real challenge for chapter leaders after that Utah experience was how to keep the enthusiasm flowing for the rest of 1980 and on into the following year. We were pretty sure we would have some member drop-outs after such a hectic build-up to Utah. That meant we had to not only establish an interesting and exciting calendar of events and performances, but continue to recruit new singers to combat possible turnover.

After a rollicking afterglow party at Pizza & Pipes Restaurant in July, the VM calendar exploded with:

- An August **Novice Quartet Contest** (17 quartets from within the chorus participated in that event);
- A Saturday **Summer Jamboree** in August that brought together Barbershoppers from throughout the Metroplex for an outdoor picnic and barbeque;
- An August Good Time Music Show at the Dallas Dunfey Hotel;
- Hosting a special Music Educators & Choir Directors Night at a Thursday VM rehearsal;
- Another VM appearance on **WFAA-TV's** *"PM Magazine"* program;
- A pre-game VM appearance (along with the **Dallas Cowboys Cheerleaders**) at the **Dallas Cowboys** vs Philadelphia Eagles game at Texas Stadium;
- A chorus appearance at the **Southwestern District Convention** in October at the Dunfey Hotel hosted by the Town North Chapter;

185

- Another Logopedics Spectacular in November with choruses and quartets from throughout Texas, hosted by the VM;
- A December Installation & Awards Banquet at the Ramada Inn downtown Dallas;
- Recording a new record album sometime in early 1981;
- April 1981 annual two-night show at McFarlin Auditorium;
- May/June/July 1981 – A possible **trip to England** hosted by British Barbershoppers??? (Notice the *carrot* in the calendar?)

That last bullet above was something I call "blue sky". If you're in charge of drumming up excitement and anticipation for members of your profit or nonprofit organization, what better way than to *tease* them with future events to encourage their continuing participation. I certainly don't encourage outright lies. But the possibility of that England trip wasn't pure fabrication. Several of our singers had had conversations with **BABS** (British Association of Barbershop Singers) members about bringing the VM to Great Britain for the past year or two. After our Salt Lake City performances, these conversations became a bit more serious. Thus, the "tease" to members about something that *could* possibly become reality was a lot more than just fabrication. (And it eventually DID happen!)

The Vocalizer was generally sent out weekly to not only VM members and Guest Singers, but also to other Barbershop chapters and Society leaders around the country. When something needed to be discussed in writing with members only, a *"Hotline"* was mailed to only paid members. I came across such a **Hotline** in August 1980 that notified VM members that I (Bob Arnold) had just been appointed the organization's Marketing Director by the board of directors. It was the first "paid" position other than the chorus director, and the position would be an annual appointment by the board with no voting privileges. According to the Hotline: *"This would include promotion for and booking of chorus performances; record production, advertising and distribution; show publicity; development of gifts and grants from corporations and foundations; publicity for member recruiting campaigns; coordination of artwork themes for shows, programs, advertising, flyers, etc.; and media relations."*

This was a big step for our organization back then, and a real challenge for yours truly. The board didn't always agree with my promotional ideas, and we clashed quite often over creative directions. But it worked quite well for about the next 20 years as the financial needs of the chapter expanded and my responsibilities for generating several hundred thousand dollars each year came to fruition.

Gearing up for a new record album became the primary focus of our music team, as Jim Clancy broke out *four* new arrangements during the Fall months: *"Ten Feet Off The Ground"*, *"From The First Hello To The Last Goodbye"*, *"Beautiful Girl Medley"*, and the blockbuster of all Clancy arrangements up to that time – *"The Texas Medley"*.

Total VM membership at this point was 164, according the Membership VP **Jack Johnston**. As the chorus requirements for more risers, performing outfits, and other equipment expanded, so did our need to transport all that equipment to performances and rehearsal sites. The chapter eventually invested in a truck for this purpose, and to serve as a moving "billboard" as it traveled the highways throughout the country. (See the old and current truck photos below and you'll see the new "wrap" sign adorning the truck on the right featuring a full color shot of the chorus.)

New truck photo courtesy of Vicki Brackett

The nominating committee (**Bob Arnold, Art Haynes, Frank Harkness** and **Bill Sturgeon**) announced the slate of officers to handle board responsibilities for 1981:

President – MIKE O'NEAL
Membership VP – TOM HALVERSON
Program VP – NICK ALEXANDER
Music VP – BOB COURNOYER
Secretary – DON HACKETT
Treasurer – DICK McCARTY
Directors At-Large – BRIAN BELCHER
　　　　　　　　　　DON DOCHTERMAN
　　　　　　　　　　TERRY DIEDRICH

JIM MARTIN
Immed. Past Pres. – JIM CULLISON

VM singer **Dick Couch** along with wife **Dianne** started being responsible for all record sales, distribution, and mailing. It was noted in a September 1980 *Vocalizer* that Dick and Dianne were responsible for selling over $13,000 worth of albums at VM shows, conventions, and through the mail during the past year. The Couches held down that responsibility for the next *TWENTY YEARS*, with annual record sales eventually topping $100,000.

Our Good Time Music Shows continued to be a fun, viable way of producing smaller shows where we could interact with our show patrons by serving them drinks and munchies at show intermissions. As a matter of fact, we started selling out those shows so easily that we began looking for a LARGER show venue. In December 1980, we moved our Good Time Shows to the **Wintergarden Ballroom** in East Dallas with a capacity of around 1,000 seated at tables.

Proposed budget for the chapter for 1981: $200,000. And our Vocal Sorority announced its slate of officers for the next year:

> Dianne Couch – President
> Nikki Hotchkiss – Vice President
> Evelyn Denton – Secretary/Treasurer
> Connie Erwin – Social Chairman

THE BUMPER STICKER CRAZE

Back around 1980, bumper stickers and back window hangers (remember *"Baby On Board"*?) were all the craze for vehicles. I guess if you

count political bumper stickers, things haven't changed all that much to-day. We were fortunate that one of our newest members, **Gerald Ewald**, was a very successful artist and graphic designer, having created logos for some of the best-known companies in America. Gerald created the first of the swash-looking VM logos that you see on the bumper sticker above. He said it looked bold and masculine, much like he envisioned the chorus it-self. He always said that he patterned our logo after the popular band *Chi-cago*. Years later Gerald updated our logo to a more modern version which incorporated the word "Chorus" into it, which is featured below.

One of the goals of the VM's newly appointed Marketing Director (me) was become more deeply involved in the Dallas arts community. Part of that endeavor included membership in the **Dallas Chamber of Commerce** and the **Dallas Visitors and Conven-**

tion Bureau. Fellow area Barbershopper and a close friend of the VM, **Greg Elam**, worked as VP at the Convention Bureau, and we deftly used that connection to obtain annual lists of business meetings and conventions coming to Dallas so we could send solicitations to the larger groups who had booking and entertainment dollars to spend. Mining those lists even-tually brought the VM quite a number of lucrative $10,000-$15,000 book-ings. It also enabled us to attend Chamber and Visitors Bureau meetings and banquets to meet other members able to help our VM organization get significant publicity.

One example of how those connections benefitted us was one day in November of 1980 after the **Dallas City Council** approved the con-struction for the new **Dallas Museum of Fine Arts** downtown. Shortly after that meeting, I got a call from the director of the museum asking The Vocal Majority to perform at the groundbreaking ceremonies in a couple of weeks. It was another great opportunity for civic and media exposure because of being involved in our community organizations.

A NEW *VOCALIZER* FOR A NEW ERA

As you might imagine, writing, printing, folding, and mailing a newsletter to around 200 individuals EACH WEEK for ten years was not only a time-consuming venture, it was also expensive. While I strongly believed a weekly bulletin had been instrumental in motivating members and helping the group to grow in numbers, I – and our board of directors – eventually decided that a more realistic and economical process might be considered. So, in November of 1980, the

newsletter format you see on the next page was initiated and sent out every *two* weeks. Our in-house graphic design team of **Gerald Ewald** and **Bill Thornton** created the new look and color scheme. Smaller, letter-size *"Hotlines"* were sent to members in between regular *Vocalizers* if emergency communication was necessary.

Keep in mind that 1980 was a time before emails, Facebook and texting. So, regular communication with a large group depended on paper, ink and the U.S. Postal Service. These days, our *"eVocalizer"* is sent to members and others electronically via email whenever communication is needed, with little or no cost to the organization. (Gary Hennerberg does a PHENOMINAL job with it!)

[Author's Note] Along with the change of *Vocalizer* design and delivery schedule, the next 15-years of VM history will be much more condensed to keep the size of this book from becoming completely unmanageable.

Chapter 19
1981-82: THAT GOLDEN TOUCH AGAIN

The 1981 calendar year started with the announcement that **Gary Parker** had won the ***Barbershopper of the Year*** *Award* at the annual awards banquet. Gary was "Mr. Everything" during our initial decade, and *still performs in the chorus to this very day.* He was a VM charter member, a bass section leader, craft school instructor, Gold Medal bass singer with the **Dealer's Choice** quartet, assistant chorus director, Music Vice President, and arranger for several songs in the chorus repertoire. And he still writes occasional choral craft articles for the Barbershop Society's *HAR-MONIZER* publication.

Due to the Society's chorus competition rules, the VM was not yet eligible to compete in the 1981 Summer contest. But we had to qualify for the next year's International contest by competing with other choruses in the Southwestern District contest that Fall. So, the chorus calendar for the first half of 1981 was filled with lots performances geared to provide exposure and bring in the big bucks necessary for travel to the International competition in **Pittsburgh** in 1982:

- Banquet performance for members of the **Lakewood Country Club**;
- Paid entertainment for the **Scottish Rite Temple** in Dallas;
- **Channel 8** appearance in support of the Society for Crippled Children hosted by **KVIL's Suzie Humphries**;
- A Good Time Music Show at the large Wintergarden Ballroom;
- **Channel 4** telethon for Crippled Children;
- A March Good Time Show at the Dunfey Hotel in Dallas;
- Booking for executives of **Southland Life Insurance Co**.
- Hosting the International Quartet Preliminary & Small Chorus Contest in Dallas;
- Paid performance on the **Shreveport, Louisiana, Chapter** show;
- First multiple Spring Shows in the chapter's history – two nights of performances at McFarlin Auditorium;
- A July 4th performance with the **Dallas Symphony Orchestra** for 15,000 people for *"Starfest"* at the Dallas EDS campus (with **Ron Chapman** MCing);

- An August Good Time Show at the Wintergarden Ballroom;
- Appearance at **United Way Kickoff Banquet** with the **Dallas Mayor, Governor William Clements** and **U.S. Vice President George H.W. Bush** in attendance;
- VM competes in October in Houston for the right to go to the International Chorus Competition in Pittsburgh in 1982.
- For the first time, the VM produces THREE Christmas Shows during a December weekend at McFarlin Auditorium.

We have found that it helps us "politically" as a chapter of the Barbershop Harmony Society to have individual members involved with the judging program and in the administration functions of the district and at the International level. During 1981, the VM organization had several members who were certified judges or judging applicants in the competition program: **Charlie White** (Contest Chairman of Judges), **Bill Thornton** (Interpretation Category), **Keith Houts** and **Bob Jett** (Stage Presence Category), **Denis Conrady** and **Pete Rupay** (Arrangement Category). VM members have served on both the Southwestern District and the International boards of directors. We've always encouraged this kind of participation so that Barbershoppers everywhere can get to know our singers as individuals who reflect positively on our entire organization.

The chorus also embarked on one of the most exciting recording projects up to that point. **Jim Clancy** sprung a monumental medley arrangement on us during the first half of 1981 that would impact both a future record album and show performances – *"THE TEXAS MEDLEY"*! This medley, consisting of: *"The Theme From the Movie 'Giant'", "Yellow Rose of Texas", "San Antonio Rose", "Houston", "Deep In The Heart of Texas", "Abilene", "Lukenbach, Texas", "Home On The Range", "We're From Big D", "The Eyes of Texas Are Upon You", "Giant (Reprise)"*, and was the cornerstone for the next VM album, *"From Texas With Love"*.

Liner notes (remember when we had enough room on those large LP albums for lots of background information?) were written by both **Ron Chapman of KVIL Radio** and **Gene Puerling of The Singers Unlimited and The Hi-Lo's**. The unique painting that adorned the album cover was created by our own **Gerald Ewald**. [**Author's Note**: A large framed copy of that painting now hangs in the Arnolds' home office.]

Jim Jenney got the mythical *"Commuter of the Year Award"* in 1981 for traveling from Albuquerque, New Mexico, to Dallas each Thursday night for VM rehearsals. (He happened to work for **American Airlines**!) He had to give up that imaginary award several years later when **Graham Smith** flew in from Great Britain (where he grew up) each week for rehearsals.

One of the highlights of 1981 – and a marketing coup for our organization – was an affiliation with **Southwest Airlines** to help celebrate their 10th anniversary. (It also happened to be the VM's 10th year since first meeting in the Winter of 1971.) The market-ing people at Southwest bought 2,000 of our *"From Texas With Love"* albums to give away during their anniversary celebrations in Dallas, San Antonio and Houston. What was REALLY exciting about this joint venture was that we "traded-out" our performance fees for **The Vocal Majority** and **Folkel Minority** in exchange for $10,000 worth of trips for VM singers and families to the Southwestern District contest in Houston in October. And, because *"From Texas With Love"* captured Southwest Airlines' advertising theme, they promoted that album with an ad in their inflight magazine. It just shows that being in the right place at the right time with the right merchandise can turn into a marketing director's dream!

The Society's International Office reported that the 1981 membership total for the **Dallas Metropolitan Chapter** (our corporate name) was now 171. And the marketing effort for corporate donations to our nonprofit chapter was beginning to show some results, with donations coming from **Diamond Shamrock Corporation, Penn Resources, Dresser Industries,** and the **Texas Instruments Foundation**.

PITTSBURGH HERE WE COME!

The above headline adorned the front of the October 26, 1981, *Vocalizer*, announcing that the VM chorus had *not* done its best job in the Southwestern District contest, and yet still beat the **Houston Tidelanders** by almost 100-points to qualify for 1982's International Contest in Pittsburgh. With some 120 VM singers on stage, we enjoyed inspirational stage presence coaching from relatively new member **Chuck Mitchell** for the first time – but certainly not the last time.

[**Author's Note**: The **Vocal Sorority** nominated Susan to be in charge of stage makeup for chorus members during the District Contest. She recruited about 25 wives/sweethearts to handle this responsibility. She was also put in charge of a Vocal Sorority committee that was responsible for luncheons prior to the 1982, 1985 and 1988 International Contests to bring together our wives and sweethearts for social interactions. The first committee consisted of **Susan, Barbara Haythorn, Diane Couch, Elaine Belcher, Shell Bonesio, Evelyn Denton** and **Donna Wall**.]

As we approached the Christmas season, we received some more good news from **Southwest Airlines**. Because of how well our performance worked out for their 10th anniversary celebration, the airline agreed to underwrite the cost of producing 80,000 of a small "singing Christmas card" which included a 45-rpm recording of the VM singing "The Secret of Christmas". About 50,000 of the records were inserted into the airline's in-flight magazine in December, and another 10,000 were given away by airline personnel in the Dallas, San Antonio and Houston airports during the holiday season. Southwest even paid for an additional 20,000 cards and envelopes that VM members and families could sell to friends and show patrons. Now *THAT* was a win-win-win for all parties concerned!

For being an "off-year" competition-wise, 1981 turned out to be a VERY exciting year!

1982: THE MISSING VOCALIZERS!

I had a life-changing event in 1982 that resulted in the *Vocalizer* newsletter being discontinued (or lost in several household moves), even though I participated in Vocal Majority activities throughout the year. I wish I had a razor-sharp memory to reconstruct all the exciting events of

194

that year, leading up to the VM winning its THIRD Gold Medal in Pittsburgh. The photo below is taken from the Barbershop Society's *HARMONIZER* magazine in September 1982. It shows the VM banner in the background with three white flags attached beneath the banner signifying the three chorus championships attained up to that point.

The VM put 132 singers on stage in Pittsburgh, winning by an impressive *103 points* over the second place Cincinnati **Western Hills Chorus,** with the **Alexandria Harmonizers** coming in third. We started our set with a **Dealer's Choice** contest ballad, *"You Can Have Every Light On Broadway"*, and finished with a rousing rendition of *"Redhead"*, arranged by **Ed Waesche** and our own **Jim Clancy.**

Even though I don't have *Vocalizers* to remind me of the events leading up to our performance in Pittsburgh, I will always remember the VM's Saturday evening show as the new chorus champions. There were about 10,000 Barbershoppers and their friends/families in the auditorium that night. This would be the first time such a large audience would hear and see our *"Texas Medley",* and our MC **Bob Jett** was especially brilliant when he introduced that monumental medley with a "Swearing-In Ceremony" that was an audience pleaser. His monologue went something like this:

"We sincerely appreciate winning this championship in Pittsburgh, and tonight we'd like to express our gratitude by swearing all of you in as Honorary Texans! (Audience laughter and applause.) So, I would like each of you to raise your right hand. Uh, judges, RIGHT hand. Thank you. Now, repeat after me: I – say

195

your name. (And the VM chorus members echoed the response, 'I, say your name' – more audience laughter and applause). Will love ALL things Texan . . . Like oil and gas wells . . . Bluebonnets . . . Armadillos . . . Aggies (Chorus: Aggies???). I swear that I will wear my hat INDOORS . . . at dinner. I swear that I will root for the Dallas Cowboys at all times . . . unless they play your team, and then, well, you're on your own. I swear to do all these things . . . so help me J.R. Ewing! (Thunderous audience applause!) I now pronounce each of you Honorary Texans. (More applause) And now we'd like to honor each of you Texans with a special tribute called 'The Texas Medley'."

And with that pronouncement, the VM regaled the audience with a spirited 10-minute medley that earned the chorus a long-standing ovation.

[**Author's Note**: Some things can't be explained by logic. One month prior to that 1982 contest, **Jim Denton**, one of our founding members and the father of **Chuck** and **Jody**, passed away from cancer. We were obviously all devastated. But something unusual happened on stage during that Pittsburgh contest. It is the responsibility of one of the contest judges to count the number of men on stage for each competing chorus. The judge counted 133 Vocal Majority singers, but there was in reality only 132. *We all knew that Jim Denton was there in spirit.*]

Chapter 20
1983-84: CAN THE GOLD RUSH CONTINUE?

The results of that third Gold Medal victory in Pittsburgh resulted in two outstanding opportunities for our organization the following year.

It set in motion a long West Coast weekend trip for our chorus and quartets that was monumental in its concept and execution. In February 1983, Two Barbershop chapters and a Sweet Adeline chapter invited the VM to bring our brand of entertainment to **San Francisco** for a Friday night show, a Saturday evening performance in **Los Angeles**, and a Sunday afternoon Good Time Show at the state fairgrounds outside of **Boulder, Colorado**. You can well imagine what an *exhausting* weekend of travel it was for chorus members – and for our recording sales people who had to transport boxes of LPs, cassettes and 8-tracks from airplanes to each of the venues and back again. But what a great memory for those West Coast organizations, and for each of us who experienced a real show business performance "tour".

One of the most famous members of the Los Angeles show audience at the Shrine Auditorium was **Meredith Willson**. You'll recognize that name as the creator of the Broadway and movie musical, *"The Music Man"*. Mr.

197

Willson wrote a very nice letter of appreciation to the members of the VM, which is included on the previous page.

The second opportunity that arose from the Pittsburgh victory was to create an album that captured the excitement of our West Coast trip with a "live" record album called, *"A Decade of Gold"*, with songs from our performances in California and Colorado. Along with the chorus, the album included selections from our two former Southwestern district quartet champions, **Class of the 80s** and the **Side Street Ramblers**. The Ramblers

 would go on that summer of 1983 to win the International Quartet Championship in Seattle. As you can see from the front of the album jacket, a **Southwest Airlines** plane was prominent as VM chorus members gathered around the airplane for the photo shoot (although we actually used **American Airlines** for the West Coast trip because Southwest wasn't yet cleared to serve any cities outside of Texas).

Without a year's worth of *Vocalizers* to lean on, that about wraps up what I can tell you about 1982.

PASSING ON THE TROPHY IN SEATTLE

An unfortunate lack of *Vocalizers* for 1983 will necessitate a rather short summary of activities for the VM chorus and quartets during that year. But, as outgoing chorus champions of the Barbershop Harmony Society, the VM got to present a special show performance in **Seattle**, site of the 1983 International Convention. **Phil Anderson, Pete Rupay** and other creative folks came up with a 17-minute *"Tribute To O.C. Cash Medley"* for the event, celebrating the Barbershop Society's 45th anniversary. (If you'll recall, O.C. Cash was instrumental in starting the Society in Tulsa, Oklahoma, in 1938.)

The VM medley memorialized the songs associated with the Society's top quartets over the past 45-years. And, with pictures of the quartets shown on slides behind the VM chorus as we sang each of their signature songs, it made for a beautiful and nostalgic presentation that received a long-standing ovation at its conclusion.

[**Author's Note**: To promote our Saturday night O.C. Cash extravaganza to the convention in the days leading up to that event, VM singers, wives and significant others distributed pins, flyers – and we even rented a helicopter pulling a banner with the theme slogan for our presentation: "Thanks, O.C. Cash!" It signified another milestone for our chorus that set a new standard for our International Convention appearances that we were challenged to exceed in future conventions.]

In October of 1983, the VM was honored to perform at the Registry Hotel in Dallas for **President Ronald Reagan**. It was the first of *four times* our chorus has since sung for President Reagan and later for President George H. W. Bush.

A new VM-spawned quartet, **Gatsby**, won the **Southwestern District** contest that Fall. The group was comprised of some very experienced singers – **Bill Thornton, Greg Clancy, Jason January,** and **Gary Parker**.

Finally, the new Board of Directors for the chapter was elected to serve during 1984, and included the following:

President – Bill Barstow
Membership VP – Ric Haythorn
Program VP – Vann Norwood
Music VP – Charlie Lyman
Corr. Secretary – Larry Hearn
Record. Secretary – Prentice Barnett
Treasurer – Dan Deters

Immed. Past Pres. – Frank Mahnich
Members At-Large – Bud Miller
                  David Harris
                  Jim Croley
                  Terry Diedrich

But what about that trip to England? Well, we'll see if that transpires next year.

ANOTHER PRESIDENTIAL APPEARANCE

Unfortunately, the number of *Vocalizers* from which to glean information was again few in number for 1984, but there was one event that all of us who were there will remember for the rest of our lives. I'd like to quote from the August 27th *Vocalizer* to capture the moment:

"To be within a hundred feet of the President of the United States, Ronald Reagan, as he waved his approval of your performance. To raise your voice in praise of your country and your God with more than 2,000 other singers. To perform a Jim Clancy arrangement with the Dallas Symphony Orchestra, and be rewarded with applause by over 17,000 very appreciative audience members. To impress some of the most influential civic and religious leaders in the Metroplex with your outstanding

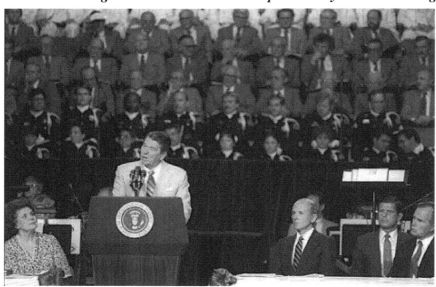

singing. To have participated in the most prestigious internationally-viewed event in our city's history. What a marvelous memory for all those Vocal Majority singers who participated in the past week's events!"

What magical event was I talking about in that newsletter? The VM and several area church choirs were invited to sing inspirational songs -- individually and as a massed chorus -- at what was called *"An International Prayer Breakfast"* at **Reunion Arena** in Dallas. Instigated by Dallas oilman **Ray Hunt**, who was also a huge Republican fund raiser and supporter, the event was telecast throughout the U.S. and in several other countries. Two of the biggest hits at the prayer breakfast were Jim Clancy's arrangements of *"An American Trilogy"* and *"God Bless America"*.

Nothing could match the thrill of being thanked profusely by our Commander in Chief for our contribution to the event. All this happened with just nine weeks to go before the VM would enter our district chorus competition in New Orleans to see if we would once again represent the Southwestern District at the International Convention the next year in Minneapolis.

And, by the summer of 1984, Membership VP **Ric Haythorn** reported that the chapter had acquired *27 new members* since the first of the year. I'm sure you could attribute a lot of that growth to the exposure we received from events like the Prayer Breakfast, several large Good Time Music Shows at the Wintergarden Ballroom, and being featured for the second straight year on **KVIL Radio**'s annual Christmas album.

Speaking of Christmas albums . . . December was penciled-in on the VM calendar to begin recording our first album of all Christmas and inspirational music – *"The Secret of Christmas"*. And the VM's mailing list of album buyers and show patrons had zoomed to over 10,000 names.

ON TO MINNEAPOLIS!

From that headline at the top of the October 29, 1984, *Vocalizer*, I'll bet you can guess that the VM scored another first place at the Southwestern District Chorus Contest. And you would be correct! But it was a scary close chorus contest, with the VM winning by *just 39-points* over the Houston Tidelanders.

 Two separate chorus record-ing sessions in November are important to note here. One session was for the **United States Air Force**, who brought recording engineers to our rehearsal site and rec-orded **Jim Clancy**'s arrange-ment of *"The Air Force Hymn"*. That recording was duplicated and sent to virtually every television station in the U.S. Viewers who stayed up late for their local station's sign-off could watch the beautiful aerial photography of an Air Force jet plane streaming across the horizon at sundown, with the VM's *"The Air Force Hymn"* playing in the background. You might even find that sign-off on TV stations *today* – if stations even have a sign-off any more.

The second recording session later the same November day was a commercial for **Southwest Airlines**, who indeed were a valuable benefac-tor for the chorus during the 1980s. And we finished 1984 with a two-night Christmas Good Time Music Show at the Wintergarden Ballroom, with the first show underwritten by **KVIL Radio** – another long-term benefac-tor of the VM for many years.

We couldn't end the year without electing the new Board of Di-rectors for 1985 – a most important group who would steer us through the rigors of financing and planning our trip to Minneapolis in quest of our fourth Gold Medal. The board members included:

President – Ric Haythorn
Membership VP – John Beck
Program VP – Larry Hearn
Music VP – Charlie Lyman
Treasurer – David Harris
Record. Sec. – Prentice Barnett
Corresp. Sec. – Bob O'Day
Members At-Large – David Hitt
　　　　　　　　Brian Belcher
　　　　　　　　Bud Miller
　　　　　　　　Rick Casey
Imm. Past Pres. – Bill Barstow

Chapter 21
1985: A TEXAS BIRTHDAY & MORE GOLD

The first paragraph of the January 1985 *Vocalizer* caught my eye. *"VM singers who have participated in preparations for an International Gold Medal know what's ahead of us. Lots of work on two contest songs IN ADDITION TO our regular busy schedule of shows, bookings and learning new show material. It ain't easy, but not many men have the opportunity in their lifetime to look forward to being judged 'Best In The World' at something. You have to realize, 'It's not for everyone.'"*

As I'm sitting at my laptop writing these words, I wonder if you think I'm sounding a bit too "ominous" in laying out that challenge to all VM singers? My intent was to be realistic. I estimate that there have been around 2,500 men – give or take – who have been members of the Dallas Metropolitan Chapter at one time or another. Some joined more than once in their lives. So, yes, there is turnover due to business, personal and work schedules. And some, like me, have had to retire due to the physical limitations that creep in as you get older. But on the other hand, there are a few VM singers today who have been with the organization since the beginning, and are still being fulfilled by participating fully in the rigorous schedule of activities. What man wouldn't sacrifice some of his life to enjoy the fruits of being the best in the world at *something*?

Ric Haythorn was presented with our *"Barbershopper of the Year Award"* at the January 1985 Installation Banquet. There probably

was never a more popular chapter officer and incoming president than Ric, who went on to become the Southwestern District President, and served on the International Board of Directors for the Barbershop Society. Quite a guy who passed away much too soon.

As a side note, that January Installation Banquet was also the venue for my marriage to **Susan**, with our own VM bass singer, **Rev. Prentice Barnett,** doing the ministerial honors at the wedding. Also, with a great chorus singing a couple of wedding songs, Champaign from the **Los Rios Country Club**, and a beautiful blonde bride, *what's not to like?!*

As I explained at the beginning of this book, I've been an adjunct professor with the **Dallas County Community College District** for 50+ years. And, through some connections with the college district and one of its campuses, **Brookhaven College** in North Dallas, we were invited to move our weekly rehearsals to Brookhaven. It entailed some "creative registrations" by the college registrar. **Jim Clancy** was certified as an instructor for the college, and our chorus members were registered for the "classes" that were in fact our Thursday rehearsals. It worked out quite well for several years, and provided extra rooms for section rehearsals, and even an auditorium with a stage for student concerts and contest preparations. A really nice win-win for everyone concerned.

Things were certainly looking up for us as we looked forward to the July 1985 International Convention in **Minneapolis**.

According to a March *Vocalizer*, **KVIL Radio** had Dallas Cowboys quarterback **Danny White** for an interview one weekend, and somehow the subject of the VM came up. Danny gave us a nice tribute: *"I'm a big fan of The Vocal Majority because of their unique sound and their very special treatment of lyrics in the songs they sing."* And to cap off the good news, total chapter membership was now close to 200!

A VM member ticket sales contest for our Spring Shows started showing some great results. For the first time in VM history someone made the magical $2,000 club in ticket sales: **Rev. Prentice Barnett**. Close behind was another "older" bass singer in the organization, **Royce Parish**, with over $1,500 in ticket sales. And, through one of our member contacts, we actually got a BILLBOARD advertising our shows donated by the billboard company. It was located on Central Expressway at the Forest Lane exit.

We were starting to become educated about how a nonprofit organization like ours could gain local exposure to market our shows and record albums like the more established **Dallas Symphony** and the **Dallas Summer Musicals**. And for the first time ever, the VM purchased radio ads promoting our shows on **KVIL** and **KRLD** (with our own **Nick Alexander** doing the radio voice and production work).

204

The annual Spring shows at McFarlin Auditorium were near sell-outs, and it was *rumored* that "ticket scalpers" were out in front of the theater trying to do business. *Now THAT'S when you know you've made it as performers in Dallas, Texas!*

EXCELLENCE

That was the one-word headline on the July 8th *Vocalizer,* symbolizing the results of the Minneapolis chorus contest. These are the observations I wrote back then:

> *"What happened this past weekend in Minneapolis was the result of 'A Commitment To Excellence' made over 14 years ago by a small group of Dallas singers. Luck certainly had something to do with the success of The Vocal Majority – luck in finding and holding the musical and administrative talent we've come to depend on. But the love and admiration the VM received from the 9,000+ Barbershoppers in Minneapolis made the hard work and dedication well worth the effort."*

1985 INTERNATIONAL CHAMPIONS
THE VOCAL MAJORITY
DALLAS (METRO), TEXAS
Jim Clancy, Director

Come Take Your Place In My Heart
Raise Your Baton Mister Leader Man/Strike Up The Band

The Vocal Majority won the chorus contest – and a **fourth Gold Medal** – by *36-points* over the **West Towns Chorus** from Lombard, Illinois, and the **Big Apple Chorus** from New York City – both tied for second place. Our quartet, **Gatsby**, came in 6th in the quartet contest.

When we returned to Dallas, not only were we treated to one of the biggest victory celebrations we've ever had, but were informed that we were invited to perform at two out-of-state locations in 1986 – **Salt Lake City**, where the next International Convention would take place, and **Toronto, Canada**, where the **Dukes of Scarborough Chorus** had invited us to perform on their annual show. What a treat to look forward to the next year, *and we weren't even finished with 1985 yet!*

As a matter of fact, things got VERY busy after that Minneapolis trip. The very first of many VM Christmas albums was unveiled during the second

half of 1985, *"The Secret of Christmas"*. The cover art was designed by a relatively new VM singer, **Nelson Coates**. After a few years (and several Gold Medals) as a VM singer, Nelson moved on to Hollywood. You may have seen Nelson's name on the credits as a production or set designer for some of the most popular movies to come out of Hollywood during the past twenty years. He was also nominated for an Emmy Award in 1994 for his art direction of the miniseries *The Stand*.

As I wrote in one *Vocalizer* published especially for our patrons and important contacts during the First Quarter of 1986, *"The Vocal Majority's 'THE SECRET OF CHRISTMAS' became the largest selling album of the Christmas season . . . even outselling Barbra Steisand in the stores where our albums were stocked!"*

And while the board of directors was contemplating two or more out-of-state trips the next year, they were also discussing something that could be the most ambitious project yet for this organization – the construction of a new $2 million Vocal Majority rehearsal/storage facility on the campus of Brookhaven College. *You might say ambition was NOT something we lacked in those days.*

Finishing out 253 was a busy schedule that we hoped would keep any VM singer who loved to perform quite busy and satisfied:

- A local benefit for Ronald McDonald House
- A $10,000 performance in Oklahoma City for the **Oklahoma Lumberman's Association**;
- A noon performance for 1,600 civic leaders in the Great Hall of the Apparel Mart for the **United Way** kickoff luncheon;
- An appearance on the **Richtones Sweet Adelines** show in Dallas;
- A 9 a.m. kickoff performance for the **Texas Association of Broadcasters**, underwritten by **KVIL Radio**;
- A Saturday/Sunday Octoberfest Good Time Music Show at the Westin Hotel in Dallas;
- A paid performance for the **National Heating & Airconditioning Wholesalers** at the Hyatt Regency Hotel in Dallas;
- Friday/Saturday Christmas shows at the Majestic Theater in downtown Dallas;
- A national TV appearance during the **Cotton Bowl Parade** in downtown Dallas singing the official Texas State Song, *"No Place But Texas"* (a **Jim Clancy** arrangement); and then doing our *"National Anthem"* for a packed Cotton Bowl Game audience. (That performance was carried by the **CBS Radio Network** to a worldwide audience.)

Chapter 22
1986: TRIPS TO RHODE ISLAND AND TORONTO, TEN DAYS IN UTAH, AND A ONCE-IN-A-LIFETIME RECORDING OPPORTUNITY

That heading can't even *begin* to sum up the whirlwind performance calendar that faced the VM at the start of 1986. There is SO much activity to cover, so I'll try to be brief. It might be best to present those activities in a "bullet" format – except for the Utah experiences – to squeeze in as much as possible in a small amount of valuable space:

- The January Installation & Awards Banquet at the Harvey House Hotel saw **Jim Patterson** receive the coveted *Barbershopper of the Year Award*; (Jim is still a member today at 96 years old, and *still drives himself to VM shows!*);
- A pro bono chorus performance at **Lewisville High School** to benefit the Lewisville School System music programs; long-time VM chorus and quartet member, **Steve DeCrow,** is now the head of choral activities for Lewisville High School;
- A late-March Good Time Music Show at the **Sheraton Park Central Hotel** in North Dallas;

- An invitation from the Mayor of Dallas, **Starke Taylor**, and U.S. Vice President, **George H.W. Bush**, to sing our *"Texas Medley"* at a special **Texas Independence Day** ceremony at Fair Park with over 60,000 Dallas citizens; [**Author's Note**: Its worth quoting the *Vocalizer* in describing the reaction to our *"Texas Medley"* on that day: *"Vice President Bush was so moved by the performance that he invited Jim Clancy to the stage area and presented him with Mr. Bush's own tie bar – a beautiful gold bar with the Vice Presidential Seal and Mr. Bush's signature – as a memento of the occasion."* That bulletin also noted that it was great for the VM to be seen and heard on the 10 o'clock news on three Dallas area TV stations that Sunday night. See *The Dallas Morning News* article on the preceding page.]
- The largest performance fee up to that point ever paid to the VM -- $7,500 – was provided to us for the opening of the **National Association of Broadcasters** convention in April;
- An exciting late-April paid chorus trip to Rhode Island to perform on the annual show of the **Narragansette Bay Chapter**; [**Author's Note**: A Sunday morning review of our performance by **Don Fowler** of the **Warwick Beacon** newspaper described it this way: *"The Vocal Majority has to be one of the most professional musical groups I have ever heard. Whether they were singing the traditional 'feel good' music of the twenties, a goosebump rendition of 'Danny Boy' or a choreographed 'Strike Up The Band,' I just knew I was listening to the best choral arrangements I could ever expect to hear."*]
- A two-night May show at McFarlin Auditorium titled, *"No Place But Texas"*, celebrating the 150th birthday of the State of Texas;
- A paid trip and three performances in one weekend in late May with the **Dukes of Scarborough** at Roy Thomson Hall in Toronto, Canada;
- A mid-June benefit performance for the **South Garland High School Choir** at the Garland Performing Arts Center.

And that just covers the first five months of 1986. *The most exciting trip was yet to come!*

It was about this time that my responsibilities as Marketing Director for the organization kicked in big-time. Part of my job entailed finding  additional support dollars through corporate gifts and foundation grants. I was fortunate to write and receive my very first foundation grant – but certainly not my last – when we obtained a $16,500 grant from the Dallas-based **Meadows Foundation**. I proposed that the money would be used to partially underwrite The Vocal Majority's trip to Utah to represent Texas during the start of the *Texas Sesquicentennial Year Celebration*. More to the point, the funds would be used to buy custom-tailored "western" performance outfits for the chorus, including custom leather cowboy boots and belt buckles from **Nocona Boot Company** located just north of the Dallas area. It was quite a sales pitch if I do say so myself.

And, through another grant from the **IBM Corporation**, I was able to start publishing the *Vocalizer* with a brand-new computer/word processor.

Because of the deluge of performance and recording opportunities coming our way, the board of directors decided (for legal and tax purposes) to incorporate a new, separate organization called **SOA Productions, Inc**. The new group included **Jim Clancy** and representatives from the **music staff**, **show planning**, **ticket sales** and **marketing** functions of the chapter. While all the weekly activities, performances and out-of-town adventures were taking place, this new organization was feverishly communicating with individuals and organizations in the Salt Lake City region for up to FOUR important performances there, including a joint record album with the world-famous **Mormon Tabernacle Choir** on the CBS Masterworks label.

All in all, our Utah trip-planners had arranged for VM singers and family members to spend TEN DAYS together in the Salt Lake City area, from June 28th through July 7th. During that time, our chapter organizers had developed four important venues that would test our music learning capabilities – *and our stamina!* But how often do opportunities like the following events transpire during an organization's lifetime? You will see by the following busy itinerary we had to pull off the many Utah events that were scheduled:

- **Mid-April** – I, along with **Frank Mahnich, Phil Anderson,** and **Nick Alexander,** spent three days in Utah meeting with our main  contacts with **Park City, Utah,** town leaders, the **Utah Symphony Orchestra,** the leadership team at **Brigham Young University** in Provo, and leaders of the **Church of Jesus Christ of Latter Day Saints** and the **Mormon Tabernacle Choir;** a lot of legal and logistical details had to be worked out if the VM trip to Utah was to be an artistic and financial success;

- **Saturday, June 28** – 152 Vocal Majority singers, family members and guests arrived at Park City, Utah, on a "vacation weekend" in this charming ski resort; it wasn't all R&R, however; we performed on **Sunday** at an outdoor park for patrons and friends of the town in exchange for meals and room discounts. (You could hear the beautiful sounds of the chorus echoing through the distant mountains.);

- **Tuesday, July 1** – Move to Salt Lake City, 45 miles away, for a morning rehearsal with the **Utah Symphony Orchestra** in the luxurious gold and silver Abravanel Hall. The performance that featured a first-time VM/symphony performance of the Barbershop Society's arrangement of a **"George M. Cohan Medley"** of old-time songs like *"The Old Songs", "Give My Regards To Broadway", "Mary", "I'm A Yankee Doodle Dandy",* and

"You're A Grand Old Flag". The *Vocalizer* following that week indicates *"several standing ovations"* from symphony patrons.

- **Wednesday, July 2** – Several buses took the VM entourage to Provo and the campus of **Brigham Young University** where we produced an evening performance for the **BYU Music Department** in their outstanding performance hall;

- **Saturday, July 5** – The VM performed in **The Salt Palace Arena** (where the Utah Jazz play their basketball games) in Salt Lake City as outgoing chorus champions for about 10,000 Barbershop families/fans/friends;

- **Sunday, July 6** – We began the day at about 6:30 a.m. to dress, warm up, and perform with the **Mormon Tabernacle Choir** for their weekly worldwide radio broadcast at 8:30 a.m.; then, about 10:00 a.m., we do the same program for about 9,000 Barbershoppers who squeeze into every available seat in the massive Tabernacle; both performances were recorded by **CBS Masterworks** to provide material for a planned joint album; Sunday afternoon, we had a brunch with many of our friends and contacts in the Salt Lake City area; but our commitments were not yet complete;

Photo courtesy of *LDS Church News* | Shows Jim Clancy directing the combined Vocal Majority and Mormon Tabernacle Choir in the Tabernacle.

- **Monday, July 7** – The VM gathers one more time in the Tabernacle with **CBS Masterworks** to record the solo chorus songs for the album without the Tabernacle Choir; later that afternoon we fly back to Dallas tired but so thankful for all the experiences.

"But there's more" . . . as the TV infomercials say when you think they've finished their pitch. *Four days* after returning to Dallas, the VM and our **Stage Door Four** did a joint concert at **North Texas State University** for a regional workshop of the **American Choral Directors Association** – a rare invitation from this prestigious organization.

The joint album with the **Mormon Tabernacle Choir** was called *"Voices In Harmony"*, and was released the following year on the **CBS Masterworks** label. We worked out a special arrangement with CBS to enable us to market the album at a discount so we could make some money for the chapter on this project.

"But there's even more" . . . quoting those infomercials again. Our relationship with the Tabernacle Choir really blossomed during our stay in Salt Lake City. I remember walking out of the Tabernacle and shaking hands with the choir members and their president, **Wendell Smoot**, and saying (among other nice things), *"We're gonna bring y'all to Texas next year!"* And we did! But that's an amazing story for our next chapter.

You may be wondering about the rest of 1986. Well, catching my author's breath after covering the first half of the year, I have to say that the second half didn't quite live up to the dizzying pace of the first half as far as performances go. Here's the rest of the year's calendar:

- Performing on the **Greater Dallas Sweet Adelines** show;
- **Brookhaven College Performing Arts & Lecture Series**;
- **Channel 39** live telecast for 100th Anniversary of the State Fair of Texas on the Coca-Cola Stage at Fair Park;
- Octoberfest Good Time Show at the Registry Hotel;
- Appearance at exclusive **Lone Star Ball** at the Registry Hotel;
- $7,500 show for **International Iron & Steel Institute** at Loews Anatole Hotel;
- Annual VM Christmas Shows at the Majestic Theater.

Chapter 23
1987: THE TABERNACLE CHOIR COMES TO DALLAS

A season-ending *Vocalizer* in 1986 described the past year as one of extensive TV exposure for the VM: **CBS-TV** stations throughout the country viewing our **Cotton Bowl Parade** and football game performances; our joint performance with the Mormon Tabernacle Choir that was telecast through **KSL-TV** worldwide; coverage by local TV stations when we entertained **Vice President George H.W. Bush** for the **Texas Sesquicentennial Celebration**; **WFAA-TV/Channel 8** coverage of our work on behalf of the Institute of Logopedics; our TV commercials were seen on **Texas Association of Broadcasters** member stations promoting our Christmas albums at participating **7-11 Stores**; and our two-hour *"Secret of Christmas"* holiday special on **Channel 39** was seen by viewers in three states. And VM recordings sold more than 50,000 copies of albums and cassettes to every state in the U.S., as well as to Canada, Great Britain, Sweden, Germany, Singapore, and Latin America.

Now our biggest challenge *ever* was facing us in 1987: Transporting the 350+ members of the Mormon Tabernacle Choir and their entourage to Dallas and filling the huge downtown **Reunion Arena** TWICE

reunion arena

with paying customers! The arena's capacity was 18,000, and was home to the Dallas Mavericks Basketball Team and the Dallas Stars Hockey Team. Had we bitten off more than we could chew?

Well, the stars began aligning for us right after we returned from Salt Lake City the previous year, and continued into the start of 1987. We locked in a June availability with the Reunion Arena planners; the Tabernacle Choir was willing to work with us to clear those dates on their calendar; a VM music and logistics committee was set up to plan the event; we petitioned **CBS Masterworks** to move up their release date for our joint record album to May from the original October; we established a relationship with the regional LDS (Mormon) church hierarchy to obtain their interest in supporting and promoting the project; one of the Dallas area's leading orchestral leaders, Anshel Brusilow, was enlisted to help put together a symphony orchestra to enhance the performance appeal; and we hired a PR/marketing agency to work with us in promoting and producing the event.

Were we kidding ourselves? Could our local nonprofit Barbershop chapter actually pull this off?

We knew we couldn't just rely on our own show patrons to fill such a large volume of seats twice. We needed a huge turnout of Mormon Tabernacle Choir supporters from the North Texas region, AND some fa-

vorable publicity from the local news media to make this event a financial success. After our Salt Lake City experience, we were pretty confident the *music* part of the program would be great. But how could we carry the message to the hundreds of thousands of potential attendees in North Texas – especially with a projected budget of *$400,000* for this unique project?

One great bit of news: We were notified that we could officially use the logo to the left of this page which was provided by the **Commission on the Bicentennial of the United States Constitution**. Our *"We The People"* concerts were designated as an *official event* on the Commission's 1987 calendar.

It would be correct to say that the VM administration was living in a *parallel universe* during this time. We knew we had to carry on the week-to-week activities like rehearsals, learning new music, obtaining paid bookings and pro-bono performances, and running the chapters' administration. And, at the same time, planning for the biggest event in the organization's history – all the while doing it all with just a part-time music and administrative staff.

It was somewhat fortunate – depending on your point of view – that I was "between jobs" during much of this time. It left me more time to work on coordinating the many facets of this huge concert. It was our good fortune that the United States was celebrating its 200th Anniversary, its bi-centennial, in 1987. This was a huge benefit in establishing the Reunion Arena event as a patriotic spectacular that celebrated our nation's history.

A press conference was held in mid-January to officially announce the *"We The People"* concerts that June, and the story was carried by several Dallas radio and TV stations, as well as both daily newspapers. The press conference was coordinated by **John Weekley** of the public relations firm of **Weekley/Gray/McKinney** who would also be the executive producer for the event.

To handle the week-to-week administrative functions, the chapter elected the following members to its Board of Directors:

President – Larry Hearn
Membership VP – Kevin Keller
Program VP – Joe Spiecker
Music VP – Mike Charles
Corresp. Sec'y – Joe Frazier
Record. Sec'y – Bill Powers
Treasurer – Rick Casey
Members At-Large – Vann Norwood
　　　　　　　　　Jim Martin
　　　　　　　　　Bill Chester
　　　　　　　　　Mike Estrada
Immed. Past Pres. – Ric Haythorn

At the VM's annual Installation & Awards Banquet that January, **Frank Mahnich** was presented with the *"Barbershopper of the Year Award"*. I was also honored at that event with a new permanent annual award named after me, the *"Robert Louis Arnold Service Award"*, with my good friend and "voice" of The Vocal Majority, **Bob Jett**, being the award's initial recipient.

As if to introduce us to the Reunion Arena facility, The Vocal Majority was booked in January 1987 to sing there for the largest industry

217

convention in the world – the 60,000 members of the **National Home-builders Association**. Other notable activities leading up to that summer's *"We The People"* concert included:

- January paid booking for the **Society of Thoracic Surgeons** at the Loews Anatole Hotel;
- Chorus recording session in February for a new album titled *"For God, Country & You"*;
- VM and Stage Door Four March show at Lakeview Centennial High School for **Garland Evening Lions Club**;
- VM becomes the first outside group to perform for the **American Choral Directors Association** in San Antonio in March;
- The VM becomes the only entertainment act to perform *two years in a row* for the **National Association of Broadcasters** at the Dallas Convention Center, with the VM onstage with entertainers **Lee Greenwood** and **Ray Stevens**;
- An April trip to Washington, DC, to perform on the annual Spring Tonic with the **Alexandria Harmonizers Chorus** at Constitution Hall. (Our Nation's Capitol couldn't have been more beautiful with all the cherry blossoms in full bloom!)

All this activity happened during the first half of 1987, plus we received the announcement by the Barbershop Harmony Society that the Dallas Metropolitan Chapter had the honor in 1986 of donating the largest amount of money to the **Institute of Logistics** of *any* chapter in its history – over $9,000 for the year.

We also received the good news from **CBS Masterworks** that our *"Voices In Harmony"* joint album with the Tabernacle Choir would be released to the public in June – just in time for our huge event at Reunion Arena. Things seemed to be going well for the big show!

And we were very blessed with a new arrangement of the Bach/Gounod version of *"Ave Maria"* (in Latin), created by talented VM singer **Joe Spiecker**. It was expected to be ready to perform at the June Reunion Arena concerts.

To help promote the sale of public tickets to that event, we produced new VM bumper stickers, among other marketing tools, so members

could proudly drive around town advertising our logo. (Part of it looks familiar, doesn't it?) We were also informed that **WFAA-TV/Channel 8** would be video-taping both nights at Reunion Arena, and one of their popular news anchors, **John Criswell**, had agreed to be the narrator/announcer for both concert nights.

The Tabernacle Choir flew into Dallas International Airport on **Thursday**, June 18th, on two American Airlines jumbo jets (both staffed with Mormon pilots and crew who volunteered for the assignment), and we booked them into the **Loews Anatole Hotel** near downtown Dallas. That evening the choir, their entourage, and Vocal Majority singers and family members gathered at the Anatole for a gala reception, Tex-Mex buffet, and a shortened version of our Good Time Music Show.

On **Friday**, the choir and the VM got together in Stemmons Auditorium at the Anatole for a joint rehearsal. After dinner, the two groups moved to Reunion Arena for the Friday evening show.

That **Saturday**, the Tabernacle Choir hosted the VM and family members at **Southfork Ranch** for a Texas barbeque lunch. Then it was back to Dallas for that evening's show at Reunion Arena.

[**Author's Note**: Another chilling experience occurred that Saturday evening as The Vocal Majority sang *"Ave Maria"* in front of the Mormon Tabernacle Choir. As the chorus started the song, our record sales ladies had come into the arena and were startled to see a soft, white cross appear over the performers on stage. The cross image lasted until the end of the song and then disappeared. Was it a mirage? A trick that the lighting technicians snuck in? After the show, the lighting crew swore they had nothing to do with the image. However, several weeks after the event, I received a video tape of the concert from the Tabernacle Choir. *The image of that cross was clearly visible!*]

Sunday morning, the Tabernacle Choir did their regular CBS Radio broadcast from Reunion Arena, and by that evening they bid farewell to all of us as they winged their way back to Salt Lake City – probably tired but as excited as we were. *What a fantastic week it was!*

220

A commemorative booklet shown on the preceding page was pro-duced as a show program that included letters of congratulations from **President Ronald Reagan, Pope John Paul II**, the Mayor of Dallas, **Annette Strauss, Judge Warren Berger**, Chairman, Commission on the Bicentennial of The United States Constitution, a list of sponsors for the event, as well as biographies of both the Tabernacle Choir and The Vocal Majority.

Also printed inside the booklet was the entire text of the U.S. Con-stitution. And, since this was such a monumental undertaking, and this book is an historical record of that undertaking, I would like to beg your indulgence to re-write the impressive list of credits from inside that booklet – the individuals who put in an *enormous* amount of work to bring this event to fruition:

```
GENERAL CHAIRMAN – Frank Mahnich
EXECUTIVE PRODUCER/DIRECTOR – John Weekley
SOA Productions/Producer – Phil Anderson
        Production Staff – Nick Alexander
                          Lelon Furr
                          Steve Sem
                          Bill Smead
                          Joe Spiecker
SOUND/LIGHTING – Showco Productions
ART/GRAPHICS – C.L. West Designs/Cathie West
SPECIAL PRODUCTION ASSISTANCE – Ed Payne
                          Bonneville Media
SIGNING FOR HEARING-IMPAIRED – Cathy Huffington
ORCHESTRA – Anshel Brusilow
BUSINESS MANAGER – Tom Halverson
MARKETING – Bob Arnold
LEGAL ADVISORS – Jim Martin & Michael Bonesio
UNDERWRITING/DEVELOPMENT – Bob Clarke
HOSPITALITY – Chip French
SPECIAL EVENTS – Frank Harkness
TRAVEL ARRANGEMENTS – Dale Gaus
USHERS & ALBUM SALES – BYU Management Associates
```

WAS IT ALL WORTH IT?

From an artistic standpoint, it was one of the most awe-inspiring events I've ever been associated with. (Except for my marriage to my lovely wife of course!) Many of us are fortunate to have in our possession a video tape of that entire concert that is virtually flawless in its execution. Everything went off *musically* as well as anyone could have dreamed. Financially . . . not quite so much.

We had about 2,000 seats short of capacity for our audience Friday night, and had a 98% sellout Saturday night. The entire event lost several thousand dollars, and we spent the next year trying to make up those lost funds. I have to accept some of the responsibility for attendance not being up to expectations, since I was in charge of marketing the event. Unfortunately, the Dallas newspapers and other news media virtually ignored the importance of the event. You might also surmise that, still being in the strong "Bible Belt" during those mid-1980s, many in North Texas might not have felt very strongly about supporting such a heavily Mormon-led event. Who knows? The Vocal Majority regrouped and moved on from there, and it was part of my responsibility to replace those lost funds.

In the first *Vocalizer* written after the concert, I seemed to have a rather melancholy attitude about it: *"Both the Vocal Majority and the Mormon Tabernacle Choir made friendships – both collectively and individually – that somehow you believe will last for our lifetimes. Not only do we seem to have mutual respect and admiration for our individual styles of singing and our reputations, but an even deeper pride in the basic things each group stands for . . . devotion to a cause, and a commitment to excellence. A great bond has definitely been forged."*

One unforgettable "souvenir" of our collaboration with the Tabernacle Choir during 1986-87 was the release of our joint album on **CBS Masterworks**, *"Voices In Harmony"*. With the receipt of that recording, The Vocal Majority became the *first chapter* in the entire Barbershop Harmony Society to have a recording produced in a Compact Disk format. I doubt that that recording is available these days in *any* format, but it was a sweet reminder for those of us who had the opportunity to own one when it was first released.

The very next edition of the *Vocalizer* reminded me that August 1987 was the **15th Anniversary** of the chartering of the Dallas Metropolitan Chapter. It also reminded me that I have several more years to cover before I complete the memories I have about my tenure as *Vocalizer* editor and Marketing Director. *So, let's get on with it!*

Chapter 24
1988-89: HOW CAN WE TOP THAT?

If you were a singer or a family member associated with the VM in 1988, you might wonder how in the world we could ever top our experiences of the past fifteen years. That was the challenge our board of directors and music team faced, and we knew we'd better come up with some powerful "carrots" to keep the momentum going.

The first *Vocalizer* of 1988 advised chorus members to "bring your cassette recorders to rehearsals" (remember cassette recorders?) to capture two of our *four new contest songs*. Yes! FOUR contest songs instead of just two! The Barbershop Harmony Society judging system decided to throw us and our other competitors a curve by breaking the chorus contest into two parts. Each competing chorus was required to sing two songs on a Friday night, and two more songs on Saturday evening, with the combined scores of the two performances being the final score. It was the first (and only) time this contest format was required.

THE JUDGING SYSTEM CHALLENGES THE VM

The 1988 Convention was staged in **San Antonio,** and was the **50th Anniversary** of the founding of the Barbershop Society. Some of us

in the VM became a bit paranoid with a sneaking suspicion that the Society's judging committee was trying to make it more difficult for us to win another Gold Medal. The Society's judging committee changed the number of songs each competing chorus had to sing to FOUR rather than the traditional two. It certainly sounded like there would be much more work involved in learning and perfecting FOUR contest songs rather than just two. But we took the challenge with fire in our eyes. We were confident that our members were much better trained in the craft of singing than any of the other choruses competing against us, so we believed we could learn as many arrangements as was necessary to win any contest. And that first *Vocalizer* laid out a calendar of activities for 1988 that was meant to both challenge our singers and to give them the performing experience they needed to weather any storm:

- A big January paid performance for annual convention of the **Southern Industrial Distributors Association** at the Loews Anatole Hotel;
- February booking for executive meeting of **Wyatt's Cafeterias** at the Lincoln Hotel;
- March Good Time Music Show at Southfork Ranch paid for by the **Plano Rotary Club**;
- Paid performance to benefit the school music programs at Lake Highlands High School sponsored by the **Lake Highlands Exchange Club**;
- Large April performance fee to entertain the **Rubber Division of the American Chemical Society** at the Loews Anatole Hotel;
- April Friday/Saturday VM Annual Spring Shows at McFarlin Auditorium;
- Paid performance in June for the **Texas Hospital Association** at the Hyatt Regency Hotel;

The first January *Vocalizer* also recapped the previous year's record sales. With a 2-page ad in the *HARMONIZER,* and album/show flyers hitting 20,000 mail boxes from our mailing list, the VM record sales team received, processed, and mailed about 1,600 individual orders between Thanksgiving and Christmas. (Record Sales Managers *Dick and Dianne Couch handled all that work out of their garage!)* Orders came not only from the **United States**, but also from **Canada, Great Britain, Sweden, Holland, Germany, The Netherlands, and Singapore**. *We were becoming an international recording sensation!*

All the paid performances and recording sales helped to make it easier for VM singers and their families to travel to the San Antonio contest that summer, and upgrade our chorus outfits to enhance our Stage Presence scores. *It takes a few bucks to transport, house, clothe and feed 150 singers!*

Phil Anderson was named *Barbershopper of the Year* at the January Installation & Awards Banquet. **Nick Alexander** received the very first *"Bill Smead Memorial Production Award"*, and **Dianne and Dick Couch** received the *"Robert Louis Arnold Service Award"*. **Greg Elam**, the current Southwestern District President, installed our new chapter officers:

Larry Hearn – Immed. Past President
Joe Frazier – President
Joe Spiecker – Program V.P.
Bill Powers – Membership V.P.
Todd Wilson – Music V.P.
David Bowen – Corresp. Secretary
Rick Perkins – Record. Secretary
Rick Casey – Treasurer
Frank Eastman – Chorus Manager/At-Large Member
John Chandler – At-Large Member
Guy Nicosia – At-Large Member
Jim Martin – At-Large Member

[**Author's Note**: If you're wondering why you don't see my name in the list above, it was a part of my marketing contract with the chapter that I not be a voting member of the board.]

As proof that audiences who do NOT attend our regular shows can appreciate our brand of entertainment, the following is a thank-you letter from the General Manager of the **Southern Industrial Distributors Association** after our performance for their group in January: *"As you know, The Vocal Majority received two standing ovations, which I'm sure is proof positive as to how our convention attendees enjoyed your wonderful singers. The impact of The Vocal Majority's presentation was overwhelming – the sound, the costumes and not to mention the choreography. We thank you for the wonderful evening, which will long be remembered as one of SIDA's best closing programs."*

Under the heading of "Community Involvement", a February 1988 *Vocalizer* noted: *"In the Spring of 1982, **Jim Denton**, one of our charter members and the father of Chuck, passed away from a blood disease. Since that time, **Kay & Phil Anderson** have taken on the responsibility for conducting annual blood drives at VM rehearsals through the Wadley Bloodmobile. The VM was honored by the **Wadley Blood Center***

227

as one of 37 Dallas area organizations out of 1,300 with at least 50% of its membership donating blood during 1987."

A 5-YEAR LONG-RANGE PLAN

A long-range plan was formulated at a weekend retreat in the Fall of 1987 and developed by former chapter presidents **Bob Arnold, Bill Barstow, Tom Halverson, Frank Harkness, Ric Haythorn** and **Frank Mahnich**, along with 1987 president **Larry Hearn** and 1988 president **Joe Frazier**, with **Jim Clancy** also present. The following results were presented to the full chapter membership in the Spring of 1988:

> **MISSION STATEMENT**: *To be recognized as the best chorus performing in the world.*

> **OBJECTIVE AREAS OF FOCUS:**
> * The Barbershop Harmony Society
> * Academia
> * The Entertainment & Arts Community
> * The World Community
> * Corporate Operations

With some minor changes, those objectives have essentially been our focus each and every year since that date. Good long-range planning is essential for any organization – profit or nonprofit – to be successful and focus on their primary audiences, including their internal audience.

The VM signed a comprehensive agreement with **American Airlines** to be the "official airline" for our performance trips, with VM singer and travel coordinator **Dale Gaus** arranging for this perk. (Our marketing associates at Southwest Airlines had moved on, and we no longer had contacts with that airline with whom to negotiate.)

Chuck Mitchell and **Rosemary Calderon** led the chorus through an all-day Saturday choreography rehearsal in March that put the finishing touches on one of our contest up-tunes, *"Waitin' For The Roberty E. Lee"*. The other up-tune, *"Who's Gonna Love You/Honey Medley"*, featured choreography by **Chuck Mitchell** and **Nelson Coates**. The *Vocalizers* from this part of the VM history are the first to mention that practicing and

228

performing choreography for contests can inflict some *serious physical stress* on a singer's body. Consequently, we established a recommended exercise and diet regimen for all VM singers competing in the contest, and variations of the regimen have been instituted for each contest since. [**Author's Note**: We once estimated that individual VM singers put in around *1,000 hours of rehearsal time* during the six months prior to International contests. There is certainly work involved in being the best that you can be, but as founding VM member **Gary Parker** has been saying for almost five decades – *"Work is fun when progress is evident."*]

And, on June 18th, 1988, **Jim Clancy** married his Sweet Adeline Sweetheart, **Judy**, to the warm approval and raised voices of a great chorus of VM singers! And I think I can safely say *they lived happily ever after.*

Dallas Cowboys great **Roger Staubach** introduced The Vocal Majority as the featured entertainment at the Plaza of the Americas in April to kick off the membership campaign for the **Greater Dallas Chamber of Commerce**. One more example of the VM's efforts to become an involved community partner and expand its image as a viable arts organization. Also, the article featured below in *The Dallas Morning News* by staff writer **Harry Bowman** publicizes our Spring Shows and the occasion of the 50th Anniversary of the Barbershop Harmony Society, and is another example of the media exposure that was certainly easier to obtain during the 1980s than it is today. Area newspapers currently have so many community arts organizations to cover that the VM has a difficult time getting any press at all these days.

One of the top coaches in the Barbershop Society in the category of Sound and Interpretation – and former International President of the

Society, **Daryl Flinn** – visited us in May. Amid the flurry of well-paid bookings, and a two-night Spring Show and several Saturday rehearsals, the four songs we had prepared for the San Antonio competition were coming together quite nicely. And throughout all these preparations, **Jim Clancy** constantly reminded us of **Coach Vince Lombardy's** famous quote: *"Practice doesn't make perfect. Perfect practice makes perfect."* And we tried our best to live up to that motto!

Just prior to the San Antonio competition, our **Vocal Sorority** sponsored a *"Getting-To-Know-You"* informational luncheon for VM wives and sweethearts who would be traveling to the convention. The *Vocalizer* issue in June thanked **Susan Arnold, Dianne Couch, Evelyn Denton, Donna Wall, Elaine Belcher,** and **Barbara Haythorn** for coordinating the well-attended event. And by the way . . . This ladies luncheon was also done prior to the 1985 convention.

THE MAJORITY RULES AGAIN FOR GOLD V

The above headline at the top of the July 11, 1988, *Vocalizer* couldn't have been more emphatic. The VM scored a 90-point victory over the daunting **Louisville Thoroughbreds Chorus**, the only chorus to have ever beaten The Vocal Majority (twice) in International Chorus Competition. Quoting that *Vocalizer* edition: *"The Friday afternoon preliminary*

1988—The Vocal Majority became five-time international winners at the Society's 50th Anniversary convention in San Antonio. Jim Clancy again directed 145 Dallas Metro members to victory for the Southwestern District.

contest was a great first-place performance by the VM, but we were only ten points ahead of Louisville at that point. Saturday night for the Super Finals, the gloves came off and the VM showed no mercy. We received the only standing ovation of any of the final six competitors. Even though we were the first chorus on the Saturday program, the contest was OVER after our rousing "Robert E. Lee" arrangement quit ringing off the rafters of the San Antonio Convention Center Arena."

After a wild victory celebration at the **Dallas Elks Lodge** (courtesy of VM singer **Bob Nelson**), the VM looked forward to a more laid-back calendar for the rest of 1988:

- Paid performance for **BeautiControl Cosmetics** at the Grand Kempinski Hotel;
- Paid booking (with the **Stage Door Four**) at **Brookhaven College** for their *Community Concert Series*;
- Recording session for the new VM record album, *"For God, Country and You"*;
- VM performs for **Sweet Adelines International Convention** in Houston; [**Author's Note**: It is interesting to note looking back on that event that **Susan**, along with Record Product Manager **Dick Couch**, were the only VM representatives available to staff our record booth, and came away with $10,000 worth of recording sales.]
- Appearance at Southwestern District Convention in Dallas hosted by **Town North Chapter**;
- Paid performance in Waco for the **Airstream RV Association** in the Heart O' Texas Coliseum;
- An October Good Time Music Show at J.R. Ewing's **Southfork Ranch**;
- Annual VM Christmas Shows at the **Dallas Convention Center Arena**.

Shortly after we returned to Dallas from San Antonio, we received a very complimentary letter from the arranger of our contest up-tune and many other outstanding arrangements over many years, **David Wright**, who requested that his letter be sent to all VM members:

"I just have to tell you how very much I loved your singing and what a joy it was to have been a behind-the-scenes participant in such a quality effort. Also, I want you to know how strongly I feel about the musical organization you have built!

231

"Your contest performances were the most remarkable ones I have ever heard. I was proud to have my arrangements rendered so beautifully. You made me look good. The quality of these performances is a reflection of your hard work and dedication towards giving to the world such wonderful music. There isn't another musical ensemble on earth which puts forth the kind of sound you produce; it stirs the soul with its brilliance. I'm honored to be a part of it, and I've told Jim that I will be more than happy to do more work for the VM."

The calendar for the next year, 1989, was already shaping up with out-of-town performances in Florida, New Jersey and at Stephen F. Austin State University in Nacogdoches, Texas. *Why waste a talented and accomplished chorus and quartets on inactivity, right?*

To give you some idea of the financial burden the Dallas Metropolitan Chapter carried to compete in San Antonio, note what a July *Vocalizer* said: *"The VM treasury is understandably a bit low after paying out $200 per singer to go to San Antonio, plus buying YOU a travel shirt, plus transporting risers and costumes to San Antonio, plus renting expensive tuxedos for the Saturday night contest set, plus paying for all the extra expenses necessary to transport 145 singers to win a Gold Medal."*

We were also teased in an August *Vocalizer* with the prospect of receiving a new arrangement by **David Wright**, *"The Hallelujah Chorus"*. That arrangement has become a fixture on every VM Christmas show since that time. David arranged several of the songs we did in San Antonio, as well as contest and show tunes for many other Gold Medal choruses throughout the Barbershop Society.

It's always a special time when the VM releases a new record album. It had been a few years since we released *"The Secret of Christmas"*, so our fans and our singers were looking forward to digitally capturing some of our favorite songs from the past couple of years. *"For God, Country and YOU"* was released in December of 1988 in cassette, LP and CD formats to the general public with such song favorites as:

- God Bless The U.S.A.
- Waitin' For The Robert E. Lee
- Ave Maria
- Girl Of My Dreams
- Who's Gonna Love You/Who'll Take My Place Medley
- Mr. Leader Man/Strike Up The Band Medley
- Last Night Was The End Of The World
- Old Man River
- America The Beautiful
- Give Me Your Tired, Your Poor
- God Bless America

1989: "HOW DO YOU KEEP THE MUSIC PLAYING?"

That headline is actually the title of a song that dropped into the VM repertoire a decade or two later, and was a song composed by **Michel Legrand**, with lyrics by **Alan and Marilyn Bergman** for the 1982 film *"Best Friends"*. It pretty well sums up the question I think all VM singers had after the exhausting San Antonio competition. To lead us in answering some of those questions, on the following page is a list of **Directors and Staff** from the June 1989 *Vocalizer*:

President – KEN McKEE
Program VP – HANK PIVARNIK
Membership VP – RICK PERKINS
Music VP – PRENTICE BARNETT
Treasurer – DAN ABAR
Immed. Past Pres – JOE FRAZIER
Correspond. Sec. – DAVID BOWEN
Recording Sec. – DICK McCARTY
Board Members At-Large – FRANK
  EASTMAN, JIM MARTIN, MIKE
  JOHNSON, MIKE CHARLES
Musical Director – JIM CLANCY
Music Staff:
  GREG CLANCY, SONNY
  LIPFORD, GARY PARKER,
  TODD WILSON, JASON
  JANUARY, JEFF OXLEY,
  CHARLIE LYMAN, CONNIE
  KEIL, BOB & ROSEMARY
  CALDERON, DAVID WRIGHT
	Marketing Director – BOB ARNOLD
	Show Chmn – JIM PATTERSON
	Business Manager – TOM HALVERSON
	Travel Coordinator – DALE GAUS
	Costume Coord. – RANDY BURHAM
	Recording Mgr. – DICK COUCH
	Bulletin Editor – BOB ARNOLD
	Chorus Mgr. – MIKE JOHNSON
	Riser Travel – TOM MEEKER
	Choreography – CHUCK MITCHELL
	Rookie Choreo – JOHN CHANDLER
	Show Producer – JOE SPIECKER
	Show Announcers – BOB JETT & NICK
	  ALEXANDER
	Music Library – DON DEVENPORT
	Auditions – MIKE CHARLES
	Logopedics Chmn – JIM JENNEY
	Sunshine Chmn – BOB NELSON

The intensity of the 1989 first-half VM calendar was a bit more relaxed – *but not by much.*

- **FEBRUARY** – Good Time Music Show at South Fork Ranch, VM and Class of the 80s provide a full evening of entertainment for the **Tyler (Texas) Community Concert Association**, with the same two groups traveling to **Tampa, Florida**, to do two shows for the **Tampa Heralds of Harmony Chorus** at the Tampa Bay Performing Arts Center;
- **MARCH** –An evening of entertainment for the **Duncanville Regional Arts Association** at Duncanville High School;
- **APRIL** –Annual Spring Shows at McFarlin Auditorium, plus doing *"The National Anthem"* for the opening game of the **Texas Rangers** baseball game at Arlington Stadium;
- **JUNE** – VM, Class of the 80s, and Dealer's Choice travel to New Jersey to perform matinee and evening shows at Newark Symphony Hall for the **Montclair Barbershop Chapter**;

- **JULY** – Performance at the International Convention of the **Barbershop Harmony Society** in **Kansas City** and give away the Chorus Championship Trophy to the new winners.

Because the VM had the privilege of singing for **Vice President George H.W. Bush** twice during the preceding eight years, we sent the president-elect a congratulatory telegram after his recent November, 1988, election victory. In return, Mr. and Mrs. Bush sent the following response which we received early in 1989.

Since you may be unable to clearly read the note, here is what it said: *"The entire Bush family extends heartfelt thanks for your kind words. Though humbled by the awesome responsibilities before us, we look forward to the opportunity to work for a better America and for freedom throughout the world. That future can only be accomplished with the help and commitment of people like you."*

About the same time, we learned that the chapter had continued its record-setting donations to the **Institute of Logopedics** by kicking in over **$15,000** to the Society's charity during 1988, becoming the largest single donor chapter in history.

A surprise performance came our way in June by way of our friend, **Ron Chapman** of **KVIL Radio**. Ron was a one-of-a-kind showman who could successfully pull off just about any event through his station's promotion machine. He was intent on putting together a huge variety show to celebrate the 20th anniversary of KVIL. He invited The Vocal Majority to be a part of a two-city (Fort Worth and Dallas) extravaganza that also featured **Frankie Vali & The Four Seasons**, **The Bill Tillman Band**, *Saturday Night Live*'s **Dennis Miller**, and **The Gatlin Brothers**. *Ron sure knew how the throw a party!* What other Barbershop chorus could boast of that kind of company on the same stage?

Our 30-minute performance before 10,000 Barbershoppers and families that July at the Kansas City BHS convention went extremely well, with several standing ovations to reward our VERY hard work in preparing us to give away the chorus trophy and wish our new champions, the **Alexandria Harmonizers**, some well-earned congratulations. (It was listed in the *Vocalizer* that those Harmonizers had TWELVE REGISTERED QUARTETS in their chapter to balance a very well-run chorus program.)

The second-half calendar for 1989 took place at a more relaxing pace, since the VM was not yet eligible for District Competition that fall in New Orleans:

- A fun VM member golf tournament at River Chase Country Club;
- An outdoor paid chorus performance in the Dallas Arts District for the artfest known then as *"Montage"*, with VM family members receiving free tickets;
- A Good Time Music Show at Southfork Ranch;
- A recording session for a new VM album;
- Annual VM Christmas Shows at McFarlin Auditorium.

And so ended the very nice Vocal Majority year of 1989.

Chapter 25
1990-91: THE BETWEEN-CONTEST YEARS

The 1990 chapter year began with a lavish Installation & Awards banquet at the Loew's Anatole Hotel, and featured outgoing president **Ken McKee** getting inducted into the PAPAs – *Past Active Presidents Association*, and **Mike Johnson** getting the coveted *Barbershopper of the Year Award*. **Jim Martin** was installed as the president. **Randy Burham** received the *Robert Louis Arnold Service Award*, and **Joe Spiecker** captured the *Bill Smead Show Production Award*.

There's no better way to promote attendance at VM rehearsals than to spring new arrangements on the chorus. And no better way to improve your ear's "tuning ability" for harmony than arrangements like *"My Funny Valentine"* and *"I'll Be Seeing You"* (**Jim Clancy**), *"Stormy Weather"* (**David Wright**), and a custom **Gene Puerling** (honorary member of the Barbershop Harmony Society) arrangement of *"Stardust"* especially for The Vocal Majority. (Gene was a member of two close-harmony jazz groups, **The Hi-Lo's** and **The Singers Unlimited,** and a colleague of Jim Clancy.) *Talk about challenging!*

Performance activity slacked off slightly during 1990:

- Benefit show at Plano Campus of **Collin Community College** for their **Jazz Choir**;
- Annual VM Spring Shows at McFarlin Auditorium;
- Out-of-state performance at Kiel Opera House in **St. Louis** for **River Blenders Sweet Adelines**;
- Recording session in Dallas for portions of two new record albums;
- Out-of-state show for the **Maumee Valley Chapter** in Toledo, Ohio;
- A paid Dallas convention booking for **Zonta International** at Loews Anatole Hotel;
- VM performs with other a cappella groups at the Meyerson Symphony Center to benefit the **Children's Medical Center Foundation**;

237

- VM competes in the Southwestern District Convention in **New Orleans** to qualify for International Contest the following summer in Louisville.

It might be of interest here to note the chorus repertoire listed in the *Vocalizer* at the start of 1990 to see the variety of songs chorus members were required to have memorized and, in most cases, learned choreography and interpretations for. (Note: These arrangements did NOT include our Christmas repertoire.)

- On A Wonderful Day Like Today
- You Keep Coming Back Like A Song
- A Nightengale Sang In Berkeley Square
- The Texas Medley
- Patriotic Medley
- Danny Boy
- Who's Gonna Love You Medley
- Girl Of My Dreams
- Waitin' For The Robert E. Lee
- Star Spangled Banner
- God Bless America
- God Bless The U.S.A.
- Old Man River
- The Lord's Prayer
- Sweet Hour Of Prayer
- I'll Walk With God
- Ave Maria
- I Walked Today Where Jesus Walked
- Home On The Range
- I'm The Music Man
- Where Is Love
- Harmony
- Graduation Day/Blue World Medley
- One Voice
- My Funny Valentine
- Stormy Weather
- On the Atchison Topeka & The Santa Fe
- Stardust
- Deep Purple
- I'll Be Seeing You

We were notified by **Brookhaven College** that our arrangement with them for rehearsal space would end at the conclusion of the Spring Semester due to space limitation. Sooooo . . . we were once again in search of a place for the chorus to rehearse every Thursday night. The answer to our prayers came in the form of the **Sammons Center for the Arts**, a former Dallas Water Utilities pumphouse that the city had transformed into performance halls and offices for nonprofit arts groups like the **Dallas Shakespeare Festival, the Turtle Creek Chorale** and others. The facility had a large performance/rehearsal hall with great acoustics for a cappella singing, smaller rooms for section rehearsals, and office space for our administrative needs. It even had a board room for our regular Board of Director meetings. And it was affordable. The old adage we repeated to ourselves often had come true again: *"God loves The Vocal Majority!"*

What better place than the Sammons Center for the Arts to more firmly establish the VM as a full partner in the Dallas arts community. Even with a somewhat challenging parking situation, this venue became our rehearsal and administrative home for quite a few years.

Our *"Chapter of Champions"* reputation was enhanced even further in early 1990 when a reconstituted **Class of the 80s** took on a new

name – **Acoustix** – and swept past all quartets to win the International Pre-Lims Contest. The new foursome was made up of **Todd Wilson** on tenor, **Rick Middaugh** on lead, **Jason January** on Baritone, and **Jeff Oxley** on bass. Acoustix went on to WIN the International Quartet Gold Medal that summer in San Francisco, just six months after forming the group.

With a couple of personnel changes, Acoustix still performs at various venues today. I still remember tuning in to the **Dallas Mavericks** TV playoff game against the Miami Heat in 2011 and being surprised to see Acoustix introduced by the arena announcer to sing our *National Anthem* (**Jim Clancy**'s arrangement) – with **Jeff Oxley** singing lead and **Greg Clancy** on tenor.

For the first time, The Vocal Majority moved out of a church sanctuary or meeting hall into a professional recording studio to capture their

239

next album – **The Studios at Las Colinas** in Irving, Texas. The album was the 10th that we would release, and was titled, *"I'll Be Seeing You"*.

The recording facilities had a large room capable of mounting the entire chorus on risers, and a soundproof control room where our music staff could gather after laying down a music track and evaluate what we

just recorded. After we finished recording all the songs, our music team (**Jim & Greg Clancy** along with **Nick Alexander**) could then spend hours or days "sweetening" the chorus sound electronically with the recording engineer, and add whatever enhancements were necessary to produce the best product. Some of the most vivid memories of my time singing with the VM were those recording sessions, as we enjoyed the comradery and togetherness of listening to the sound of our own recorded voices, which were being captured for everyone to hear throughout the world for decades.

We weren't finished yet with our Good Time Music Shows; they were just too much fun to abandon. We held a fun show that September in the Crystal Ballroom of **The Grand Kempinski Hotel**. Besides the chorus, our featured entertainment was our own **Dixie Flyers Band** (fronted by **Red McDonald**), and our new International Quartet Champions, **Acoustix**.

Looming ahead of us in October was the Southwestern District Chorus & Quartet Contest in New Orleans, and a victory by the VM would cash our ticket to the next year's International Contest in Louisville.

HERE WE GO AGAIN!

That was the headline of the November 5, 1990, *Vocalizer*, signifying our ticket had been cashed at the Southwestern District Chorus Contest in New Orleans and we were on our way to Louisville in search of our sixth Gold Medal. That issue captured the impressive VM victory with these words: *"Not only did our chorus win by 108-points over an excellent* **Houston Tidelander** *chorus, but we cracked the 1,100 barrier for the first time in total points."*

As Christmas approached, the VM looked forward to having all

ten of our record albums for sale at the Annual Christmas Shows, including our new *"I'll Be Seeing You"* production. We produced a very attractive color brochure touting all our albums, along with tickets for our Christmas Shows titled, "Alleluia". That show title would become the name of our next album during the following year.

One of the goals of the chapter's long-range planning team was to apply for membership in the **National Association of Recording Arts & Sciences**, with the ultimate goal of being eligible for a **Grammy Award**. While we never did actually receive a Grammy, our membership in NA-RAS enabled us to have others nominate us for this prestigious award. Just another step in raising the level of professionalism within our organization in the minds of our singers and our fans.

We closed the year by nominating the following slate of officers for 1991:

President – JIM MARTIN
Immed. Past President – KEN McKEE
Membership VP – RIC HAYTHORN
Program VP – HANK PIVARNIK
Music VP – DENIS CONRADY
Secretary – DAVID BOWEN
Recording Secretary – MICKEY BONESIO
Treasurer – DAN ABAR
Members At-Large – VIC SASSONE
      RON NICHOLSON
      LYLE ROLOFSON
      MIKE JOHNSON

A December *Vocalizer* noted that 26,000 of those color brochures went out to VM fans throughout the world, and **Dick and Dianne Couch** reported they were processing about $1,000 of mail orders EACH DAY from our Post Office mailbox. The VM Christmas show ticket sales exceeded sales projections by 4%, making the three shows the most successful ever. Two of our chapter quartets, **Black Tie Affair** and a return of the **Dealer's Choice**, along with Todd Wilson's sister, **Wendy Wilson** (doing her Karen Carpenter imitation on *"Merry Christmas, Darling"*), all added to the variety and professionalism of those productions. (**Black Tie Affair** was an excellent quartet comprised of **Steve Brandt, Tom Knodell, Dave Evans** and **Nick Alexande**r. They were the runner-up in the Southwestern District quartet contest that year.) It was a fitting ending to a truly amazing 1990 year for the VM.

1991: MINING FOR GOLD IN LOUISVILLE AND AGAIN SINGING FOR PRESIDENT BUSH

It was with a certain amount of irony that The Vocal Majority would be traveling to Louisville in an attempt to capture a chorus Gold Medal. **The Louisville Thoroughbreds** were the only chorus to have bested the VM TWICE in International Competitions up to that point. However, they would *not* be competing in their home town that year because of the rigors of hosting the Barbershop Society convention. The Thoroughbreds had seven Gold Medals at that point, having won their last chorus title in 1984.

But we're getting ahead of ourselves. A lot of preparations and fund-raising had to be done between the January of 1991 and July when the competition would take place. The first rehearsals of the New Year featured hard work on the contest up-tune, *"Alexander's Ragtime Band"* (another spectacular **David Wright** arrangement), and the music staff was

working hard to find a comparable ballad to match the dynamics of that song.

The **Annual Vocal Majority Awards Banquet** featured the presentation of the ***Barbershopper of the Year*** *Award* to **Greg Clancy**. The January 28th *Vocalizer* explains why: *"From a cute, curly-headed 12-year old to semi-hippy to respected professional studio singer . . . many of us have known Greg through every stage of his life with the VM during the past fifteen years. His emergence as a section leader, music instructor, coach, and most recently as Assistant Music Director of the chorus, has been nothing short of phenomenal."* That newsletter also noted that **Dan Abar** was presented with the *"Robert*

Louis Arnold Service Award", and **Mike Johnson** was the recipient of the *"Bill Smead Show Production Award"*.

Other activities during those first six months of 1991 included:

- February benefit performance in Arlington for the **Kennedale High School Choir's** trip to perform at Carnegie Hall in New York City;
- March paid performance for the **DeSoto Arts Council** at DeSoto High School, also featuring Black Tie Affair;
- The VM performs with country music star **Lee Greenwood** at Texas Stadium in a tribute to U.S. military members, with The Vocal Majority backing up Greenwood singing his hit, *"God Bless The USA;*
- Annual Spring Shows at McFarlin Auditorium featuring the Dealer's Choice;
- April convention booking for the huge **American Automobile Association** at Loews Anatole Hotel;
- May convention gig for the national convention of the **Association of Professional Mortgage Women** at the Fairmont Hotel;
- June luncheon performance for the **Texas Society of Association Executives** at Dallas Convention Center;
- A new after-rehearsal *afterglow* location was established at **Pizzeria Uno** on McKinney Avenue. (After an evening of concentrated vocalizing, music education and strenuous choreography, socializing time with your "brothers in song" is a welcome reprieve.)

The Vocal Majority was booked by Dallas oilman **Ray Hunt** to entertain **President and Mrs. George H.W. Bush** at the Dallas Hyatt Regency Hotel (which is owned by Mr. Hunt); the photo on the next page shows (from the left) **Bob & Susan Arnold, President & Mrs. Bush, Judy Clancy's son K.C., Jim & Judy Clancy**. [**Author's Note**: True story – The first time we were invited by Mr. Hunt to sing for Mr. Bush, he was NOT the sitting president – only a candidate. So, I negotiated a substantial performance fee for that occasion. This *last* time, Mr. Bush WAS the president, so Mr. Hunt insisted we perform *gratis*. He was a deft negotiator, which is probably why he's a very successful businessman and I'm not. And because he had so many interactions with our chorus, I spied Mr. Hunt coming out of McFarlin Auditorium after one of our annual shows raving about the production. *He had paid his own money for the tickets – no comps involved!*]

244

To The Arnold Family With best wishes, Gy Bush

The March 3rd *"Spirit of America Rally"*, produced by area **Rotary Clubs** in North Texas and staged in the home of the **Dallas Cowboys**, Texas Stadium, was perhaps the highlight of our Spring 1991 calendar. It was one of the most awesome *"community involvement"* events in VM history. The stadium had about 75,000 seats, and virtually all of them were filled for this monumental tribute to those serving in our U. S. military.

[**Author's Historical Note**: **Dr. John Piercy** was known as *"Mr. Barbershopper"* in the Dallas area back in 1971 when we were considering the formation of The Vocal Majority. He was the baritone in the **Doo Dads**, one of the few area quartets to have competed in the International Quartet Contests finishing in 7th place in 1968, and they were the 1965 Southwestern District quartet champions. For many years, John was also the chorus director of the **Big D Chapter** in Dallas. John was my personal dentist back then, and he offered his dental office (after business hours) for a meeting of our fledgling formation group in the summer of 1971. **Bill Heard**, one of the members of that small group, came up with the name *"The Vocal Majority"* at that meeting. Twenty years later, John's son, **Kenny Piercy**, who was a very active member of the VM, invited his dad

245

to audition for the chorus. A *Vocalizer* "Hotline" from March 1991 con-gratulated Dr. John Piercy as *the newest auditioned singer in the VM.* I guess you could say, "What goes around comes around."]

A COMMITMENT TO EXCELLENCE WINS FOR A SIXTH TIME!

That headline pretty much said it all in a special edition of the *Vocalizer* in July 1991. *"Who'll Take My Place When I'm Gone"* was a ballad that made the audience in Louisville swoon after the last note was sung, and then rise up and cheer after *"Alexander's Ragtime Band"*. The judges gave the VM a 40-point victory over second place **Cincinnati Western Hills**.

A VM welcome home party at the Sammons Center for the Arts gave tribute to the many people who contributed to the Gold Medal win, including both the music team and chapter administrators who went beyond the call of duty to bring home this victory. Another important history-turning event took place in Louisville: **Nick Alexander** emerged as our new, *permanent* MC at our chorus performances. **Bob Jett** was having health problems at the time and had become inactive with the chorus, and Nick had filled in admirably over the past few years. But now HE was "The Voice" of The Vocal Majority, and he still is to this day.

Nick comes from a musical family. His father was Zeiman Broun-off, concertmaster with the Dallas Symphony Orchestra for 52 years – a record. His mother was a voice major at what today is the University of North Texas, and sang for many years in the chorus of the Starlight Oper-ettas, which later became known as the **Dallas Summer Musicals**.

246

Nick started piano lessons at age 6, and was already developing perfect pitch. Today, he can play just about any song he's ever heard on the piano, and is a great addition to VM parties and social events. Because of a splendid bass voice and great diction, Nick began working at Dallas-Fort Worth radio stations in his late teens, stopping for various lengths of time at **KNUS, KXOL, WFAA, KZEW** and finally **KVIL**, where he was operations manager. For the past 17 years, Nick has been running his own company, Nick Alexander Productions, which is an advertising agency, a production company, produces jingles, and his voice can still be heard on both radio and TV doing free-lance voice work. That's some great experience on the way to becoming "The Voice" of the VM today. And, finally, Nick was just elected to the *Texas Radio Hall of Fame* in November, 2017.

After the euphoria of our sixth Gold Medal had subsided, we focused on winding down the remainder of 1991 with a slightly reduced performance and rehearsal calendar:

- A paid August chorus performance before 30,000 people at the Cotton Bowl Coliseum as part of the *Pepsi Games of Texas*, sponsored by the **Dallas Parks & Recreation Department, The Dallas Morning News** and **Pepsi Cola**;
- A September evening show by the VM at **Brookhaven College** for their concert series, and included the **Dealer's Choice**;
- A paid performance at **Highland Park Presbyterian Church** for the church's *"Highlander Performance Series"*;
- An appearance as International Chorus Champions in Houston for the Southwestern District Convention & Contests, where **Jim Clancy** was officially inducted into the district's *"Hall of Fame"*;
- December Annual Christmas Shows at McFarlin Auditorium;

With 1991 closing and another Gold Medal in our collection, what could be waiting for us on the other side of the New Year?

Chapter 26
1992: OUR 20-YEAR REUNION & *TWO* NEW ALBUMS!

As 1992 dawned, we realized that it was twenty years since we had been chartered as a chapter of the Barbershop Harmony Society. So we began planning a *20ᵗʰ Anniversary Celebration*, and put long-time VM singer **Bob Cournoyer** in charge of contacting former VM members from throughout the world to come join us in August for the reunion.

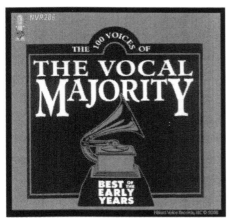

To commemorate the past two decades, the music team decided to do a "retrospective" album titled, *"The Vocal Majority: Best of the Early Years"*, and include our most popular songs from past albums. Some of our early records were not available in CD format, so it provided a good excuse to digitize some early numbers and offer them to members and fans who may not have heard them before.

The January Installation and Awards Banquet confirmed the following administrative and musical leaders for 1992:

President – PRENTICE BARNETT
Immed. Past President – JIM MARTIN
Membership VP – QUINN HUNTER
Program VP – VIC SASSONE
Music VP – DON KAHL
Performance VP – GUY NICOSIA
Chorus Manager VP – MARK LAMPE
Recording Secretary – MICKEY BONESIO
Corresponding Secretary – RUSS MAUCH
Treasurer – RON NICHOLSON
Members At-Large – JOE FRAZIER
MARTY TAYMAN

ROBERT J. KELLEY
RODNEY WHITE

The activity schedule for the first half of 1992 was full of variety and challenging opportunities for VM singers:

- A February performance for **Baptist Music Ministers** at Williams Square in Las Colinas;
- A Southwest Airlines flight to San Antonio to sing for the **Texas Music Educators Convention** at the Hilton Hotel, with the flight underwritten by the **Barbershop Harmony Society**;
- A March joint concert with the **Fort Worth Symphony Orchestra** in Tarrant County Convention Center;
- The VM leaves on the chartered Southwest Airlines plane bound for **Rexburg, Idaho**, for a full evening performance for **Ricks College**; (Ricks is the largest private junior college in the country with over 7,500 students, and is affiliated with the Mormon Church.); [**Author's Note**: The Ricks College performance stands out in my mind for several reasons. First of all, getting off the plane was an experience itself; being from the big city of Dallas you immediately notice the pristine, low humidity atmosphere. What a beautiful experience! The show that evening was another eye-opener. It was "Mother/Daughter" weekend at the college, and the theater audience was filled with enthusiastic female fans. In fact, Susan remembers hearing hysterical screaming coming from the auditorium as she and Dianne Couch were waiting for intermission. They opened the doors to the auditorium and witnessed a scene from the days when the Beatles first appeared in the U.S. Screaming women (young and old) rushed to the stage as my group, the **Folkel Minority**, were performing.]
- Huge paid convention show for the **Institute of Electrical and Electronics Engineers** at the Hyatt Regency Hotel;
- Benefit show in May at Meyerson Symphony Center for **City of Dallas Police Choir**;
- Large paid convention booking for **Educational Computer Conference** at Loews Anatole Hotel;
- Appearance in July in New Orleans at the **International Barbershop Society Convention** to appear as outgoing chorus

250

champions in front of 10,000 people inside the New Orleans Su-
perDome.

Never has the VM chorus members been asked to learn more music
faster than during the Spring of 1992. Besides a marathon recording session at the Las Colinas studios for part of our new Christmas album, *"Alleluia"*, and special joint numbers for the **Fort Worth Symphony Orchestra** concert – we also were gifted with a wonderful new **Joe Spiecker**
arrangement, *"Phantom of the Opera Medley"*, **David Wright**'s new
chart for *"Ode To New Orleans"*, and **Jim Clancy's** beautiful *"Tribute To
Nat King Cole"* (with instrumental backup).

A special edition of the *Vocalizer* came out during the summer of
1992 **"For Vocal Majority Singers, Friends & Patrons"**. The lead article in that issue dealt with the 20th year anniversary of the VM in the following article:

"It was a cold, blustery November evening in 1971 when 12 men gathered in a Dallas meeting room to test their voices in a new choral en-
 deavor. Several months later,
the group had a name, coined
by one of the new participants
who happened to be a former
singer with the New Christy
Minstrels, **Bill Heard**. He suggested "The Vocal Majority".
Not bad!

Twenty years later, after 6 International Chorus Gold Medals as "Best In
The World", along with 12
record albums and four videos, The Vocal Majority will
celebrate its 20th Anniversary Reunion with a gala
event the weekend of Au-
gust 28th and 29th in Dallas.
Invitations have been sent
out to over 130 former or inactive VM singers, as well as
current active singers, and

Dealer's Choice Reunion

responses are beginning to pour in from as far away as Saudi Arabia for the event. That evening, VM alumni, current members, wives and significant others will gather to reminisce, to socialize, and to be entertained by original members of VM quartets like the **Dealer's Choice,** the **Side Street Ramblers, Class of the 80s,** and (*horrors!*) the **Folkel Minority**!

A total of 92 former or inactive VM singers attended the Alumnae Reunion, coming from as far away as Massachusetts, Pennsylvania, New York, Florida, California, Missouri, Arizona, Virginia, Georgia, Saudi Arabia, and from throughout Texas.

The second half of 1992 was somewhat tame compared with the first half, as exemplified by the following calendar:

- A September joint concert with the **Dallas Jazz Orchestra** at the Village Country Club bringing back some great Four Freshmen arrangements for both the band and the VM;
- A paid performance to benefit a battered children's center funded by the **Lake Highlands Exchange Club** at Lake Highlands High School;
- The VM appears at the Saturday night show of the **Southwestern District Convention** at the Majestic Theater in Dallas;
- Paid performance for **Shepton High School Choral Music Department** at Plano Center in Plano;
- Paid performance for **West End Marketplace** Christmas Lighting in conjunction with **Children's Medical Center**;
- Booking for **Sewell Village Cadillac** employees' Christmas event at Loews Anatole Hotel;
- Three Annual VM Christmas Shows at McFarlin Auditorium, featuring Acoustix.

Most Barbershop chapters and other choral organizations rarely release even one record album. But in late 1992, the VM released TWO albums – *"Best Of The Early Years"* and *"Alleluia"*. The latter album was the second of several Christmas and inspirational albums the chorus has released over the years.

The name *"Alleluia"* was taken from one of the songs on the album, *"Randall Thompson's Alleluia"*, his most popular and recognizable choral work which was commissioned by Serge Koussevitzky for the opening of the Berkshire Music Center at Tanglewood.

One of the most popular cuts from that VM album is *"Little Drummer Boy"*, written by the American classical music composer and teacher Katherine Kennicott Davis in 1941. It was recorded in 1951 by the **Trapp Family Singers** and released on the choir's first LP *Christmas with the Trapp Family Singers* and released as a single (45rpm). The song was further popularized by a 1958 recording by the **Harry Simeone Chorale**. In my humble opinion, the version recorded by The Vocal Majority (arrangement by **David Wright**) is the most robust and inspirational version, and it is currently played on radio stations throughout the world during the Christmas holiday season.

In fact, we received a letter from a far-away radio station executive that was published in the *Vocalizer* that spoke to its universal appeal: *"During the month of December, we aired at least three weeks worth of music from your "Alleluia" CD, and received wide acclaim. The song "Little Drummer Boy", in particular, was very often the most requested, where not only listeners, but the announcers as well, received goose bumps with every playing. Many folks who didn't or don't appreciate Barbershop music have a new appreciation for the incredible talent that exists within The Vocal Majority."* It was signed, D. Neil Aitchison, General Sales Manager, CFCA-FM, Kitchener, Ontario, Canada.

Chapter 27
1993: PREPARING FOR THE NEXT
GOLDEN OPPORTUNITY

As copies of my past *Vocalizers* start to dwindle, and my time as bulletin editor for the Dallas Metropolitan Chapter wound down due to job pressures and teaching, I'll briefly skim through the final two years in this memoire with some highlights that meant a lot to me personally.

Throughout this journey during the first 20-years of VM history, I've tried to capture the names of the administrators who have been responsible for organizing and funding the exciting performances, recordings and out-of-town trips that made life as a VM singer so fulfilling. Personally attending meetings of the board of directors was not a particularly exciting thing for me to do, but it was a necessary part of helping to run an organization that I dearly loved. The board of officers and directors installed at the January 1993 Annual Banquet was a hard-working group that included:

President – HANK PIVARNIK
Program VP – MIKE JOHNSON
Membership VP – MARK LAMPE
Music VP – AL JOSEPHSON
Show VP – GUY NICOSIA
Chorus Manager VP – DON WILSON
Treasurer – BROOKS HARKEY
Immediate Past President – PRENTICE BARNETT
Corresponding Secretary – RUSS MAUCH
Recording Secretary – MICKEY BONESIO
Members At-Large – STEVE ZOGG
　　　　　　　　　JIM MARTIN
　　　　　　　　　DAVID DIFFEE
　　　　　　　　　JOHN RASCO

A new award was presented at that banquet that is still awarded today, the *"Jim Clancy Award for Outstanding Contributions To The Chorus"*. The first recipient was an emotional presentation to **Chuck Mitchell** by **Greg Clancy** for Chuck's brilliant coaching and inspiration for our visual performance efforts as our in-house choreography "guru".

The *"Bill Smead Memorial Award"* was presented to our wonderful team of lighting directors, **Sue Abar** and **Lil Eastman**. The *"Robert Louis Arnold Service Award"* was awarded to chorus manager **Don Wilson** for doing "just about every job that needed doing during the past year with undaunted professionalism". The top award of the evening, *"Barbershopper of the Year"*, went to **Ken Piercy**. Ken received his prestigious award that evening primarily because he had been expertly producing VM shows for the past several years.

The VM activity calendar for 1993 including the following events:

- January benefit performance for **Richardson School District choral music programs** at Berkner High School;
- February benefit show for **Denton High School Choir** at UNT in Denton;
- March paid performance for the **Duncanville Regional Arts Association** at Duncanville High School;
- Paid March performance for the **Dallas Military Ball** at Grand Kempinski Hotel, with 1,000 Metroplex military and retired military personnel, including U.S. Army Chief of Staff and many local VIPs;
- Three VM Annual Spring Shows in April at McFarlin Auditorium;
- Paid performance in May for 50th anniversary of **Jesuit College Preparatory School;**
- An appearance at **KAAM Radio**'s huge *"Growing Majority Expo"* at the Dallas Convention Center, with LOTS of on-air promotion by the radio station and 10,000 people expected to attend;
- Joint concert in June with the **Arlington Wind Symphony** at UTA;
- **Barbershop Harmony Society Convention** in Calgary, Canada (*VM not yet qualified to compete*);
- Paid July performance for **Soroptimist International** convention at the Loews Anatole Hotel;
- Paid performance in October for **First United Methodist Church of Fort Worth**;
- VM competes in **Southwestern District Convention & Contests** in October for the right to represent the district at International Barbershop Society Convention the following year in Pittsburgh;

- December benefit performance for **Shepton High School** choral music program in Plano;
- Excellent paid convention gig for the **North American Heating & Airconditioning Association** at Loews Anatole Hotel
- Annual 3-show VM Christmas productions at McFarlin Auditorium.

I always enjoyed re-printing letters we received from folks we performed for. One that was printed in a February *Vocalizer* really hit home: *"Words cannot express our gratitude for your participation in the 'Young Men In Harmony' concert on Thursday. The positive feedback from the students and community has been more than remarkable! We may never know how many young minds and lives were influenced and impressed by your performance, but I know about 60 little 'guys' in the Berkner High School area that will never forget their experience with you!"* The letter was signed, **Glenda Casey**, Choral Director, Berkner High School, Richardson ISD.

Early version of Vocal Majority record booth, with Bob & Susan in custom VM Western outfits. The VM investment in record booths over the years has resulted in several thousands of dollars' worth of additional proceeds at each show and convention. It also provides our show patrons with the opportunity to meet and greet our record sales personnel and learn more about the organization.

Our "staff arranger", **David Wright** from St. Joseph, MO, blessed us with another of his challenging-but-audience-pleasing arrangements, *"This Joint Is Jumpin'"* early in the year. That song was kind of the theme for our Spring Shows, as we constructed a "speakeasy" set with VM singers staged on several levels singing such prohibition-era songs as *"Waitin' For The Robert E. Lee"*, *"Slap That Bass"*, and *"Ode To New Orleans"*. The show's second half featured the

257

Dallas Jazz Orchestra joining with the chorus in some jazzed-up arrangements like *"Day By Day"*, *"Graduation Day/Blue World Medley"*, *"Route 66"*, and *"Mack The Knife"*. I remember that show being a real audience pleaser, and a strong indicator that future shows would be more like Broadway-style productions.

Right after our Spring shows, and eyeing the fall Southwestern District chorus contest in Houston in October, and the 1994 International Convention in Pittsburgh, we eagerly received **David Wright**'s latest contest up-tune arrangement – *"Runnin' Wild"*. *Boy, was it a wild audience-pleaser!*

Being a former radio disk jockey and program director, I was always interested in letters we received from radio stations about the albums I (as VM marketing director) would mail out when we'd produce a new album. One such letter that I re-printed in the *Vocalizer* just blew me away: *"I am a disk jockey on KMOX Radio here in St. Louis. I host a Saturday night program that covers jazz music in all its forms, and I recently borrowed a CD titled, "I'll Be Seeing You" from a friend who is a Barbershopper. I have played from this CD on several occasions, and the response has been overwhelming. You should know that our station is a 50,000 watt clear channel station reaching 48 states."* Signed, Don Wolff. About 150 radio stations in the U.S. and Canada received VM recordings at that time.

As the VM passed the 20-year mark in its history, one of the "Special Edition" *Vocalizers* listed some pretty impressive statistics: *"During the first six months of 1993 we recruited 33 new or re-auditioned singers. And our newest rookie crop had an average age in the early 30s. The youngest singer in that group was 14, and the oldest 60."* (I remember one year the chorus has *13 father/son combinations* competing in the contest, with the youngest son being 11 years old.)

As expected, the VM captured the 1993 **Southwestern District Chorus Championship** in Houston, and we were on our way to compete in **Pittsburgh** the following year. After that October contest and convention, we began pointing toward the busiest record sales season in the organization's history. A full-color brochure touting our video and audio albums, plus our Christmas shows, was sent to patrons on our 32,000+ mailing list, and a full-color ad was also placed in the Barbershop Society's *HARMONIZER* magazine. [**Author's Note**: Do you have any idea how much dedication it takes to input 32,000+ names into a computer database?

We all have **Susan** to thank for that laborious work to expand our mailing list.]

The Christmas shows, produced by **Joe Spiecker**, were deemed "the best ever". But most important . . . **Jim Clancy's mother** said: *"It was the best show I've ever seen".*

The exciting news announced on that show by MC **Nick Alexander** was that *The Lettermen*, one of America's most beloved singing groups, had been booked for our 1994 Spring shows. That marked the first of many internationally known performers to appear on future VM shows to expand the general audience appeal for our brand of entertainment. And, to end another fabulous year, it was announced that total membership in the Dallas Metropolitan Chapter had reached 202 singers.

Chapter 28
1994: WOULD PITTSBURGH BE THE LUCKY SEVEN?

The new year opened with lots of enthusiasm for VM singers. **The Lettermen** would prove to be a great incentive for members to sell lots of tickets to our Spring Shows. They had a 30-year reputation for selling out

shows and recording hit tunes like *"The Way You Look Tonight"*, *"Put Your Head On My Shoulder"*, *"Hurt So Bad"*, and their block-buster live album cut, *"Goin' Out of My Head/Can't Take My Eyes Off Of You"*. One additional reason this group made sense for our shows – other than the fact that they're an all-male vocal harmony group – is that our show's producer in 1994 was **Matt Tea**. Matt was a young member of the VM and a first-time show producer. He was also the *brother* of **Donovan**, the youngest member of the Lettermen trio. How neat was that! Plus, Matt wowed the audience (and his fellow VM singers) when he stepped in for his brother and sang one of the Lettermen songs on the show. Double neat! As a result of taking a chance on bringing in The Lettermen, our Spring Show ticket sales were *30% higher than any previous VM shows in our history.*

We knew we had made the right decision when we discovered that the Lettermen announcements during our Christmas shows resulted in our Spring Shows being *one-third sold out* to start the new year. A new focus

on the world-wide popularity of The Vocal Majority was illustrated by a new metallic gold, blue and white VM bumper sticker "available to fans throughout the world". Not only that, we had received in inquiry

261

from the **British Association of Barbershop Singers (BABS)** about being booked for their annual convention in Harrogate, England. The term *"international"* chorus champions now had a lot more meaning!

The New Year started out great from a media standpoint. **WFAA-TV Channel 8** did a 10-minute feature on the VM, produced by the station's **John Pronk** for a program called *"Prime Time Texas"*. That amount of prime-time coverage in the nation's 8th largest television market would have cost thousands of dollars.

Some other notable events occurred early on in 1984. **Jim Clancy**, who professionally not only sang lots of jingles for radio stations and commercial advertisers all over the world, also did voice-over announcing using his resonant bass voice. We learned that he was chosen by the national

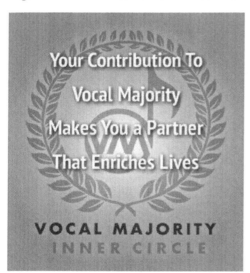

Whataburger chain of restaurants as their spokesperson. Our **Acoustix** quartet made their **Carnegie Hall** debut during a show sponsored by the **Big Apple Chorus** in New York City. And *"The Vocal Majority Inner Circle"* program helped expand the VM's annual income through charitable donations to our 501(c)(3) nonprofit organization (the Dallas Metropolitan Chapter of The Barbershop Harmony Society). This new program was headed up by marketing expert **Gary Hennerberg**, who continues in that capacity, as well as wonderfully handling internal and external marketing and communication efforts much like I did during the VM's first 25-years. As of 2017, there are almost 100 individual and corporate donors on the "Inner Circle" list.

The VM Board of Directors and Staff that would lead the organization's efforts during 1994 included the following:

President – HANK PIVARNIK
Program VP – MARK LAMPE
Membership VP – STEVE ZOGG
Music VP – GRAHAM SMITH
Show/Performance VP – GUY NICOSIA
Chorus Manager VP – DON WILSON
Treasurer – BROOKS HARKEY
Corresponding Secretary – RUSS MAUCH
Recording Secretary – MICKEY BONESIO
Immediate Past President – PRENTICE BARNETT
Board Members At-Large – TOM BERGMAN
                          JIM BURGESS
                          DAVID PRATT
                          MIKE SAUCEDO

The first half 1994 performance calendar was a little slim:

- February paid performance for **Shepton High School** in Plano;
- March joint performance with **Richardson Symphony Orchestra** at Richardson High School;
- Three April Spring Shows at McFarlin Auditorium with **The Lettermen**;
- Paid June performance at **Shreveport Summer Music Festival** in Shreveport, LA (*Jim Clancy's home town!*);
- Paid show in June at Botanical Gardens for **Fort Worth Symphony Orchestra Association**;
- July International Contest & Convention for the **Barbershop Harmony Society** in Pittsburgh.

However, our music team wasn't about the let us relax too much. Our contest up-tune for the Pittsburgh contest, *"Runnin' Wild"*, had some note *and* key changes to contend with, some moves were added to the "Texas Medley", and Greg Clancy was teasing us with a new *"Beatles Medley"* that was sure to be a favorite for *this* VM singer.

263

THE GOLD MEDAL STANDARD

THE MAJORITY RULES

Believe it or not, that was the headline in *The Dallas Morning News BEFORE* we won the Chorus Gold Medal in Pittsburgh, as the newspaper did a feature story about our *preparations* for the contest. But, that headline is VERY appropriate for what happened at the 56th annual convention of the Barbershop Harmony Society. The "Special Edition" *Vocalizer* published right after the contest put it this way: *"The Vocal Majority, with 148 hard-working, dedicated singers, won its seventh Gold Medal as 'Best Chorus In The World'. The VM won by only 20-points over the New Tradition Chorus from Northbrook, IL. We estimate that VM singers participated in more than 7,000 man-hours of rehearsals, shows and administrative tasks during the three months preceding the July 9 contest in Pittsburgh"*

That *Dallas Morning News* story about the VM resulted when **Dan Shine**, a reporter for the newspaper, did a photo story on our own **Mike Borts** who had a side gig doing the *"National Anthem"* at Dallas Stars hockey games. (Mike also sang *"Oh, Canada"* in French when a Canadian team played the Stars.) We also had some excellent coverage by local radio stations, including a half-hour interview by **KRLD Radio's Jody Dean** featuring the VM's **Jim Clancy, Bob Arnold**, and our **Dallas Knights** quartet. And our old friend **Ron Chapman on KVIL** did a 10-minute feature on our win in Pittsburgh during the week following our win – including playing a cut from one of our CDs.

[**Author's Note**: An interesting fact that many of our Vocal Majority members don't even realize today is that KVIL's **Ron Chapman** became fascinated with the chorus early on in our existence, and envisioned us eventually recording with a full symphony orchestra. We further peaked his interest when **Jim Clancy** received a full orchestral backup arrange-

ment from Salt Lake City musician **Bob Brunner** to accompany Jim's amazing vocal arrangement of *"No Arms Can Ever Hold You"*. That cut was included on our 2002 album, *"Love Songs By Request"*, and Ron went crazy for that arrangement.

He made a deal with the VM and Jim Clancy that he would underwrite an *entire album* if he and Clancy could agree on a selection of sentimental love songs adaptable to arrangements that would feature the full chorus sound and a large string orchestra backdrop. Ron fronted *$50,000 of his own money* to finance the production of our *"Vocal Majority With Strings"* album, which we reimbursed him from the sales of the recordings. He plugged that album on his KVIL Radio program and *sales hit the roof!!*

After the success of that album, **Jim** and our instrumental backup music arranger **Tom Merriman** collaborated on a second similar album called *"Vocal Majority With Strings Volume II"*. Another hit with the general public! So, now you know "the rest of the story" about our friend and angel, Ron Chapman.

Another interesting example of the curious popularity of The Vocal Majority was a Los Angeles-based film group that had been gathering miles of video during the preceding month in Dallas, Pittsburgh, and at the Barbershop Society's headquarters of Kenosha, WI. The project was to focus on our unique American music art form (Barbershop music) from the viewpoint of individual participants and their families. The film crew followed the VM around from rehearsals to shows to afterglows to contest sites in and around Pittsburgh. I'm not sure anything ever came of this

265

venture, or whether they simply couldn't find funding to complete it. But it was an indication of things to come in popularizing the Barbershop-style genre to a wider audience.

One special letter we received was from **Jerold Ottley**, Director of the **Mormon Tabernacle Choir**: *"Boy, you guys take no prisoners, do you? Congratulations on the achievement of your seventh gold medal. We've partied with you guys before, so we know that your victory celebration will be every-thing from exultation to exhaus-tion. Congratulations one and all! Greetings from all in the Salt Lake Mormon Tabernacle Choir."*

To finish out the last year that I will be covering in this memoir, let me make note of some things that were being discussed and some di-rections the chorus was planning to take that would see them through the next several decades.

First of all, **Judy Clancy** took a strong hold of our women's or-ganization and renamed it **VMW** (*Vocal Majority Women*), a play on the name of the famous automobile company, BMW. She has enlisted a *large* number of VM wives and significant others to support chorus activities at a level that has become simply awesome.

FIVE out-of-state performances were being planned for 1995, with a "swan song" performance in Miami at the Barbershop Society's convention, and including the impressive trip to England to entertain the **BABS** organization. Many more albums would be recorded, expanding the reach of our Dallas-based choral organization and exploring new and in-teresting musical genres.

And finally, Greg Clancy turned into his own man regarding how he handles the awesome responsibilities of being the man up front when the chorus performs. Although he's not his father, and doesn't have the arrangement skills that his father is so good at adapting to the strengths of our chorus year-in-and-year-out. But in some ways, he's just as creative

266

as Jim at exploring the "spiritual" relationship we have when we sing. As you'll recall from the first several chapters in this book, music can do unbelievable and powerful things to and for human beings. I'm pretty sure The Vocal Majority Chorus will continue to do that for many decades into the future – and inspire other choral organizations to reach for the same goals. *In fact, I'm counting on it!*

[**Author's Note:** 1996 would be my last year as Marketing Director and Vocalizer Editor due to the pressures of a heavier work schedule.

Chapter 29
MARKETING & BRANDING FOR COMMUNITY GROUPS

Throughout Part II of this book you've undoubtedly noticed the many activities, alliances and marketing successes that contributed to making The Vocal Majority one of the best-known and recorded choral ensembles in the world. As Marketing Director – a part-time paid position – during the group's first 25-years, I contributed many of the ideas for making this popularity possible. And please keep in mind that this was during an era when the Internet and social media were not yet major factors in the world of marketing and branding.

I remember being introduced to email in the early 90s when I first went to work for the Dallas County Community College District. And that was about the time that I bowed out of my marketing duties with the VM. So, the techniques we used to create brand awareness during those early VM years were more "hands-on" then electronic. Consequently, I'd like to talk about some very simple activities your community arts organization can do to get recognized in your community, and to grow your nonprofit group in both membership, staff and profitability.

Bob, did you say *profitability*? **Yes!** Just because your organization is a nonprofit doesn't mean it can't acquire considerable resources over and above its budgeted expenses. According to Wikipedia: "A nonprofit organization (also known as a non-business entity) is an organization that has been formed by a group of people in order "to pursue a common not-for-profit goal", that is, to pursue a stated goal without the intention of distributing excess revenue to members or leaders." There are several different nonprofit categories, but most arts/music organizations have a 501(c)(3) designation from the Internal Revenue Service that allows them to operate without paying taxes and many receive discounted postage rates from the U.S. Postal Service.

All that to say that all nonprofit arts groups can grow and prosper and benefit their artistic goals and community stature by simply following the IRS guidelines. The challenge is to find ways to *prosper financially* in a competitive environment that can help YOUR nonprofit group stand above and apart from others in your community and geographic area.

After the first few years, The Vocal Majority started to gain the attention of the local news media by providing a unique brand of entertainment that was different from anything else. We sang songs that people could relate to and everyone could appreciate the artistry that went into the performance packages we did. Granted, those 1970s and 1980s were days when there wasn't as much competition from locally-produced arts/music organizations as there is today. But we learned early on that positive press comes to those who go after it. We found that public relations was just creating a network of community contacts who could say nice things about you and promote your brand to others.

Today, that concept is exemplified by **LinkedIn** and **Facebook**, software applications that promote networking among business connections and friends of friends. But even with all the Internet and social networking tools that we have, good marketing and branding for nonprofits comes down to the basic hard work of going into your community and physically making connections with people who can spread the word about the good things your organization is doing.

Back in the 1980s and 1990s, when Barbershop and Sweet Adeline chapters throughout the country would bring me into their communities for weekend marketing workshops, they were desperate to learn the secrets of how the VM had so quickly developed their reputation for excellence and professionalism. These organizations – who sent their board of directors and chorus directors for the day-and-a-half session – were provided with the basics of marketing, public relations and branding. I called the workshop "Manufacturing Carrots" – a reference to the carrot-and-stick method of running a nonprofit organization. Essentially, the more "carrots" your group can manufacture, the more satisfied your employees/members will be and the more fondly your audiences will remember you.

Branding was not a term that was used back in those days, but today encompasses a wide range of practices. If you Google "branding", you come up with something like the following: "Branding is a way of identifying your business. It is how your customers recognize and experience your business. A strong brand is more than just a logo; it's reflected in everything from your customer service style, staff uniforms, business cards and corporate offices to your marketing materials and advertising."

Sprinkled throughout this book are references to activities and relationships the VM established to help us become famous – first in our own geographic region, and then at various locations throughout the world:

- Using our member connections to bring us in contact with radio, TV and newspaper reporters who could say nice things in their media about what we were doing;
- Joining community organizations like the Chamber of Commerce, the Visitors and Convention Bureau, the Press Club, the various arts councils in our area, and other organizations where we could make contacts and provide services to be noticed in the community;
- Taking advantage of our membership in the Barbershop Harmony Society by encouraging our various quartets to enthusiastically compete in Society-sponsored contests, as well as have an extremely competitive chorus that was quickly recognized by opinion leaders in the Society;
- Making connections in the area business community that ultimately led to invitations for the VM and our quartets to entertain at benefits and community events – and even opportunities to sing for two U.S. presidents four times – resulting in additional press and community exposure;
- Supporting high school music programs by performing free at fundraising performances, thus creating goodwill with area school choir directors, the boys in the choir programs (future recruiting), and the parents of those choir members (future show patrons);
- Producing quality record albums *as often as possible*, enabling us to expand our brand and sound to vast geographic areas in the U.S. and worldwide;
- Building a database of potential show patrons and buyers of recordings that expanded to over 32,000+ names and addresses, creating a consistent contact list for future shows, recordings and bookings; [**Author's Note:** Where did those 32,000+ names and addresses come from? At the start of our VM-produced shows, we printed up thousands of response cards that were stuffed inside each show program. Our show patrons dropped these cards into a box in the lobby of our show venues, and we inputted them into a computer database that just kept growing.]

271

- Through a database acquired through the Dallas Visitors and Convention Bureau, sending out brochures and recordings to the largest business meeting and convention groups that would be coming to the Dallas area and possibly needing entertainment for their attendees; [**Author's Note:** One year in the early-to-mid-90s, these efforts resulted in chapter income approaching $100,000.]
- Pursuing collaborations with companies (Southwest Airlines, American Airlines, Hunt Oil Company, IBM, Texas Instruments, etc.) to benefit the VM for travel needs and fund-raising opportunities;
- Finding local media outlets who were open to collaboration and co-sponsorships on shows and benefit concerts (KVIL Radio, WFAA-TV, Dallas Morning News and Dallas Times Herald entertainment writers, etc.)

If you're involved with a community arts/music group, a Barbershop, Sweet Adelines or Harmony, Inc. chapter, or maybe a high school or college music program, I hope the activities I have covered in this book can give you inspiration for making your program better known and respected in your area.

There are lots of research sources out there that show how music and the arts positively affects participants and the community in general. It's up to YOU to learn from the successes (and even the failures!) of groups like The Vocal Majority. Let me know if I've helped. Write me an email at barnold@tx.rr.com and let's talk about it.

E P I L O G

There is obviously much, much more to the ongoing history of The Vocal Majority Chorus. Since I ended my written history in 1994, the VM has captured several more Gold Medals in International Barbershop Society Chorus Competitions – a record total of 12 in all at this writing (**10 of which I have**). Who knows if or when it will all end?

As of the publishing date for this book, four VM singers have received ALL TWELVE Chorus Gold Medals – **Jim & Greg Clancy, Brian Belcher,** and **Mickey Bonesio**.

But the number of Gold Medals doesn't begin to define this singing organization. Over the past 45 years, the VM has truly exemplified *Camelot* among its members, their families, and their tens of thousands of fans throughout the world. Go to their web site (https://www.vocalmajority.com/) and check out their video, "Why We Compete" and other video testimonials from their own members of all ages to see why they have been so successful at keeping a "family atmosphere" and the spirit of Camelot alive, all the while staying very busy and musically competent.

Also, if you haven't done so already, slip on a pair of good headphones and play some of their recordings. You won't believe the quality of sounds you hear or the intricacy of the chords they sing. If you've never seen the VM perform, you'll get a thrill out of logging into *YouTube* and typing in "Vocal Majority"; all the videos you see online will thrill you! Better yet, go see them *in person* and let their sound and energy envelop you and blow you away.

Lots of people have asked, "What's the secret to the ongoing success of The Vocal Majority Chorus?" Maybe part of it can be answered by the following article taken from the *Northwest Soundwaves* bulletin of the **Seattle Barbershop Chapter** and reproduced in one of my *Vocalizers*:

"In my many conversations with a broad spectrum of our chapter membership, I am struck by the universal admiration of The Vocal Majority, and the desire to emulate their accomplishments. I am often asked, 'What is their secret? How did they become such a phenomenal success? How can we get from where we are to where they are in terms of musical quality and membership satisfaction?

"There are many elements that comprise the VM's success, but some of the key factors include:
- The willingness of every member to play an active role in the operation of the chapter, beyond just attending rehearsals and performing on the risers;
- Emphasis on drilling the musical fundamentals until every member sings every note and pronounces every vowel and consonant the same, thereby generating the awesome VM unit sound;
- Maintaining a quality image throughout its program, and spending the money and effort it takes to maintain that image;
- Selecting a musical repertoire that is highly entertaining to both Barbershop fans and non-Barbershop audiences alike;
- Using the talents of its musically skilled members to the utmost as coaches, section leaders and assistant directors;
- Communicating effectively to its members, patrons, and the general public through a well-organized public relations and marketing program;
- Having well-organized rehearsals and maintaining chorus discipline on the risers."

Uh oh . . . our secret is out! But one thing I'd like to add, and that's the ability of our musical and administrative leaders to help foster a "family atmosphere" in everything the chorus does. It's almost a *spiritual bonding* between members, and among actual family members who support our tireless efforts.

It was said so well recently by **Dr. Jim Henry** in his keynote address to Barbershoppers attending Harmony College: *"Barbershopping is not a hobby, it's a calling – a ministry."* Jim sang with the champion quartet, the **Gas House Gang**, for 18 years, and has long been a chorus director for the multi-gold medal chorus, the **Ambassadors of Harmony** from St. Joseph, MO. He went on to say, *"It isn't the gold medal that you need in your life, it's the gold medal moments, little gold medals you win every time you stand with your friends and master a new skill, or finally ring that bear of the chord, or rejoice at the birth of one of your chorus member's children, or weep at the death of their spouse or child.*

"But the great thing is that we not only receive these gold medals, we have the power and privilege of giving them away to the people we sing with and the people we sing for. How many lives have we changed, how many souls have we fed, how many troubled teenagers have been stirred to make a better future for themselves because of a song they heard us sing? How many men have been made vulnerable enough to call their wives and whisper to them, 'I love you'? We are making a positive difference – one life at a time, to a world that is in desperate need of it. Music does that. So now you have a viable reason to sing well. For, the better we perform, the more gold medals we give our audience members. And in turn, the more we receive ourselves.

"And what is particularly magical about singing in a good chorus or a good quartet is that there isn't a single one of you that, by yourself, impacts people as profoundly as all of you can together. You have been so blessed! You have been given the ability to sing at a very high level. Better than that, you've been given a spirit that drives you to improve on that

*ability. And better yet, you've been given musical and administrative lead-
ers who not only know how to make you and your soul mates better, but
dedicate themselves to it. You are so blessed."*

That's exactly how I feel after these past 45-years as the founder,
winner of 10 Gold Medals, 1 Silver, and 1 Bronze Medal, and a constant
music learner with The Vocal Majority Chorus. What would I *personally*
recommend to the Barbershop Harmony Society in general, and the Dallas
Metropolitan Chapter in particular, to expand their future popularity and
impact to all music lovers worldwide? Here are a few suggestions I hum-
bly offer:

- Make every attempt to attract *men of color* to our ranks. This goal
  was a big part of the Society's pitch to members at the most recent
  convention in Las Vegas, even featuring several young black men in
  video clips and on-stage appearances throughout the Saturday night
  spectacular. I've personally stressed the importance of this goal to
  my own chapter for many years, because we're essentially ignoring
  some great voices by not creatively promoting black and Hispanic
  singers to join us so we can represent the same racial image as our
  communities represent.

- Establish strong relationships with all types of arts organizations –
  not just music-oriented ones – in our communities so that we are per-
  ceived as a valued arts contributor. Dallas has worked very hard to
  establish an "Arts District" to enhance the city's image as an all-
  American metro area. The VM needs to re-visit that effort and partner with other musical groups in joint concert ventures.

- A cappella singing has been bursting on to the pop music scene over
  the past decade as a "cool" genre. Take advantage of this new popularity by emulating some of the styles and arranging some of the
  songs of the most popular a cappella groups.

- I remember actually being verbally abused by some members of the
  Barbershop Society staff when I was teaching at COT Schools back
  in the early VM years for promoting "non-Barbershop" songs and
  harmony in our repertoire. But we (the VM) stuck to our strategy of
  expanding our repertoire to appeal to a wider audience, and I think

the Barbershop Society has learned from our continuing experimentation. I can see that effort in the wider variety of songs performed by our top BHS quartets and choruses, and the changes in the Society's judging system that now allow for more latitude.

- Be more aggressive in our relationships with the news media to feature more publicity about our activities and accomplishments. Granted, back in the early days of the VM – during the 1970s and 80s, there was *less competition* from other arts organizations in our geographic area. Today, almost every municipality has at least one community chorus and numerous theater groups – all vying for media attention. We simply have to find ways to tell our story better and make media contacts realize how important our art form is and how REALLY GOOD we are!

- Find ways to involve older members and chorus drop-outs in our organization's activities. Barbershop chorus singing is not so much a young man's game as it is a HEALTHY man's avocation. It takes a healthy body and lots of stamina to perform some of the stuff we do. The VM has had an "Emeritus" designation for non-chorus members for several decades, but that organization has fallen into disrepair due to neglect and a lack of creative ways to keep older and inactive members satisfied, motivated, and involved.

I can't conclude this book without recognizing one VM member who meant so much to all of us through many decades – **Jim Tuggey**. Jim had a very distinguished military career prior to his retirement, and continued his involvement with military aircraft by spending his last working years as a worldwide helicopter sales manager for a private company. He also became the unofficial Vocal Majority photographer, spending thousands of dollars out of his own pocket for professional photography equipment and editing software whenever photos were needed of VM shows and special events. He also personally underwrote the formation of the VM's "Emeritus" program for members who were retired from the chorus but who still wanted to participate in show attendance, recording purchases and pre-show dinner gatherings. Jim now resides in a senior living facility, but his contributions to our organization will never be forgotten.

I relinquished my VM marketing title in August of 1996, and my last appearance on stage with the Vocal Majority chorus was in 2006 during our annual Christmas shows due to mobility issues. But because of the relationships Susan and I have established throughout these past years, I intend to be an *Emeritus* member for the rest of my life, and to continue to enjoy those wonderful chords sung by ever renewing generations of singers who become VM members and ask themselves, *"How come I didn't know about all this before?"*

Now, if you'll excuse me, I'll slip on my set of headphones and turn up *my* favorite VM cut from **The Music Never Ends** album – *"A Beatles Celebration"* – YAH! YAH! YAH! *Some of those songs that daddy used to sing!*

IN SHORT, THERE'S SIMPLY NOT
A MORE CONVENIENT SPOT
FOR HAPPY EVER-AFTERING
THAN HERE IN CAMELOT

ACKNOWLEDGEMENTS

This book was a lot more difficult than I expected. I've been a writer all my life, but writing a *book* is a lot different than writing radio and TV advertising copy, brochures, record album liner notes, and show programs. When I say that the book was 25 years in the making, it's literally true that I've been reading books about famous musicians, movie and TV stars, and the psychology and physiology of how music and the arts affect all of us for *at least* the past 25 years. It was about time to put down my thoughts and research into a cohesive collection of short articles that could help readers truly appreciate the power of music and the legacy of the choral music organization I helped to start in 1971.

It was the "cohesive" part that was the challenge. I even read books and articles about book writing, including an excellent non-fiction book by novelist Stephen King. Once, in the middle of the summer, I thought I was finished with the manuscript. But Susan encouraged me to pursue several *more* years of Vocal Majority research, and write until there were no more *Vocalizers* left. I gritted my teeth and continued to the end – *and I'm so glad I did.*

After Jim and Greg Clancy read an initial draft of the manuscript and helped me to correct some factual errors, Susan spent *many* weeks going over the semi-finished manuscript to add her memories of the events and dates where I was a little foggy, and to make sure the language and grammar were correct.

I can't imagine writing a book like this without the Internet. There were so many facts, names, images and dates that I discovered on *Wikipedia* and *Google* that I lost count. I'd also like to acknowledge the databases of information provided on the web pages of the Barbershop Harmony Society – especially their online catalog of old *Harmonizer Magazines* that were a joy to re-discover. I never realized that I wrote so many articles in that publication over the years. I'd also like to thank the webmasters from the Southwestern District of the Society for historical web pages that enabled me rediscover facts about our chapter quartets and the chorus.

I'd also like to thank *YOU* for the courtesy of reading my words in this book, and hope you've learned some things from the experiences

I've had while living through the years of Camelot. I sincerely hope your ensemble or organization can profit from our successes and mistakes, and know that *being the best in the world at something is indeed possible!*

Printed in Great Britain
by Amazon